W9-AGC-001

Dear Mrs. Roosevelt

Dear

Letters from Children of the Great Depression

Mrs. Roosevelt

Edited by ROBERT COHEN

THE UNIVERSITY OF NORTH CAROLINA PRESS   Chapel Hill & London

© 2002

The University of North Carolina Press

All rights reserved

Designed by Richard Hendel

Set in Quadraat and Emma Script

by Tseng Information Systems, Inc.

Manufactured in the United States of America

The paper in this book meets the guidelines for

permanence and durability of the Committee on

Production Guidelines for Book Longevity of the

Council on Library Resources.

Library of Congress

Cataloging-in-Publication Data

Dear Mrs. Roosevelt: letters from children of the Great

Depression / edited by Robert Cohen.

p. cm.

Includes bibliographical references and index.

ISBN 0-8078-2747-9 (alk. paper)—

ISBN 0-8078-5413-1 (pbk.: alk. paper)

1. Roosevelt, Eleanor, 1884–1962—Correspondence.

2. Presidents' spouses—United States—

Correspondence.   3. Children—United States—

Correspondence.   4. Poor children—United

States—Correspondence.   5. United States—

History—1933–1945—Sources.   6. Depressions—

1929—United States—Personal narratives.   7. United

States—Politics and government—1933–1945—

Sources.   8. United States—Social conditions—1933–

1945—Sources.   9. Children—United States—Social

conditions—20th century—Sources.   10. Children's

writings, American.   I. Cohen, Robert (Robby)

II. Roosevelt, Eleanor, 1884–1962.

E807.1.R48 D43   2002

973.917'092—dc21   2002006409

cloth   06 05 04 03 02   5 4 3 2 1

paper   06 05 04 03 02   5 4 3 2 1

For Becky and Daniel

Contents

Illustrations

Acknowledgments

The historical sensibility that shaped this book is not mine alone. My interest in American social history was sparked by Jesse Lemisch and Leon Litwack, inspiring teachers whose pioneering scholarship on the history of workers and African Americans taught me and generations of historians the enduring value of "history from the bottom up." I also owe an intellectual debt to Robert S. McElvaine, a historian whom I met on only one occasion, but whose classic book on the letters of Depression Americans, *Down and Out in the Great Depression*, opened a new window onto the lives of the poor and influenced my own work. Closer to home were my father's Depression stories about his childhood days in a Brooklyn ghetto, instilling in me a deep interest in the history of youth, poverty, and the New Deal era.

This book also grew out of my work with history and social studies teachers in Georgia and New York. These teachers helped awaken me to the value of youth sources in teaching history to students young and old. My thanks to all the teachers in my history and social studies classes in the schools of education at the University of Georgia and New York University for their insights and encouragement in this letters project. I am grateful to the McPhaul Center preschool at the University of Georgia, the Children's Workshop, my colleagues Maris Krasnow and Suzanne Carothers at New York University, Mary Mason in the Gwinnett County public schools, and my graduate students at NYU for helping me see how these letters could be used in classrooms with high school, middle school, elementary, and even preschool students. My thanks to Bryant Simon of the University of Georgia history department—with whom I taught a seminar on the 1930s—for giving me my first opportunity to share these sources with undergraduates. I am especially grateful to the public school students who read the youth letters to Eleanor Roosevelt so carefully and compassionately and who welcomed me into their classrooms.

The initial work on these youth letters came while researching my article on Eleanor Roosevelt and youth for a special New Deal issue of *Social Education*. My thanks to John Sears of the Franklin and Eleanor Roosevelt Institute—who edited that special issue—and to the editor of *Social Education*,

Michael Simpson, for inviting me to write that article. I also owe a debt to Thomas Thurston of the New Deal network for making some of my favorite youth letters to Eleanor Roosevelt available on-line at the New Deal website that he administers for the Franklin and Eleanor Roosevelt Institute. The enthusiastic response to our posting of these letters helped to convince me that my idea for this book of letters really did make sense.

John Inscoe of the University of Georgia's history department organized lively and stimulating panels for teachers on the history of youth at the Organization of American Historians and American Historical Association conventions, which enabled me to share my research on the youth letters with both teachers and fellow historians. The AHA panelists Grace Palladino, Susan Cahn, and Inscoe offered valuable criticism and advice, as did my colleagues at NYU, Diana Turk and Jon Zimmerman.

To compile a collection of letters on this scale requires extensive time and work in the archives. Fortunately, the archive in which I needed to concentrate my research, the FDR Library in Hyde Park, New York, is staffed by skillful archivists whose assistance made this work much easier. I owe a large debt to the FDR Library archivists Karen Anson, Robert Clark, Virginia Lewick, Robert Parks, Mark Renovitch, Raymond Teichman, and Alycia Vivona. Nancy Velez at the Library of Congress and Karen Anson of the FDR Library provided crucial help with the book's illustrations.

Grants from the Franklin and Eleanor Roosevelt Institute, the University of Georgia, and New York University enabled me to make the many trips to Hyde Park that were necessary for the completion of this project. Among the best days that I spent up in Hyde Park were those that overlapped with Lawrence and Cornelia Levine's research trips there for their book on FDR's fireside chats, and I thank them for both their comradery and advice—as we came to the same surprising revelation that editing a book of this sort is in many ways more difficult than writing a monograph.

My colleagues at New York University facilitated the completion of this project in ways too numerous to list. My thanks to Joel Westheimer, Kendall King, Charles Sprague, and Chelsea Bailey of NYU's education school and to Molly Nolan of NYU's history department. My graduate assistant, Emily Klein, provided much needed help in the final stages of this project.

One of the joys of working on a book connected to the life of Eleanor Roosevelt is that it draws you into the circle of dedicated and talented biographers and historians who study her. From their ranks I am especially grateful to Allida Black and Maurine Beasley for encouraging me in this project.

David Perry at the University of North Carolina Press made this book possible through his consistent support and his sage advice. His enthusiasm for this book helped me press on with the work at a time when the tragic events near my home in lower Manhattan made it difficult to complete even this labor of love. My thanks to Mark Simpson-Vos and Pamela Upton at UNC Press for all their assistance and to Fred Kameny for his superb copyediting.

This book is about youth, life, and love, all of which I have enjoyed in great abundance thanks to my wife, Becky, and my son, Daniel, and it is to them that this book is dedicated.

Dear Mrs. Roosevelt

I read in the paper of your kindness that what a kind Santa Claus
you were towards your poor people. . . . I know that your heart is kind
to wards the poor. You did a lot for our country too. We will always
remember you like we remember George Washington.
—I. L., a ten-year-old girl from Pennsylvania,
writing to Eleanor Roosevelt, asking her for funds to pay
for a bus to carry poor children to school in the winter,
December 29, 1933

*Sketch of Eleanor Roosevelt that a sixteen-year-old boy from Missouri drew and sent to the
First Lady in 1935. (From the collection of the Franklin D. Roosevelt Library, Hyde Park, N.Y.)*

Introduction

Ernestine Guerrero, the daughter of an unemployed carpenter, came of age in San Antonio, Texas, during the Great Depression. She was not one of the movers and shakers of American history, but merely one of millions of youths who grew up poor during the nation's worst economic crisis. It is not surprising, then, that Guerrero's name fails to appear in history books on the Great Depression, the New Deal, and Franklin and Eleanor Roosevelt. Although historians have taken no notice of Guerrero, a piece of her historical experience has been preserved by the Franklin D. Roosevelt Library and Museum in Hyde Park, New York. On display is Guerrero's large wooden sculpture of a clock case, "The Chimes of Normandy," and the letter she sent along with it to President Roosevelt in 1937. The sculpture, which Guerrero began working upon during her late teens, consists of 156 pieces and reflects long and skillful wood-carving work. Guerrero's letter to the president explained that it took her a year of working with a coping saw to develop her carving skills sufficiently to begin shaping the clock case and another year to complete this fretwork sculpture. But it is less the craftsmanship of the sculpture than Guerrero's circumstances, materials, and motivations that make so memorable her decision to work on it and send it to the president. She offered this gift to FDR in gratitude for the assistance that New Deal dollars had provided to her impoverished family. Guerrero had gathered the materials for her sculpture from the wooden boxes in which her family's food relief had come during the hardest times of the Depression. She wrote to FDR that her sculpture was the outcome of her desire to show her appreciation by creating "something pretty" to give him "out of those boxes" of federal food aid, which had meant so much to her and her family. "This is the best I have ever done in my life," Guerrero wrote. "I know that you have many pretty things, but please accept and keep this piece of work from a poor girl that doesn't have anything, also to show you how much we admire you . . . as a man of great ideals and a big heart toward humanity."[1]

Ernestine Guerrero with the sculpture she sent to President Roosevelt in 1937.
(Photo courtesy of Franklin D. Roosevelt Library, Hyde Park, N.Y.)

"The Chimes of Normandy" and Guerrero's letter to the president attest that impoverished young people in Depression America could be eloquent and even artistic in expressing their response to the crisis of their times. They suggest that youth was no barrier to serious concern and thought about the economic crisis, poverty, and the New Deal's expansion of federal aid to the needy—and that one might learn much about the meaning of the Depression by listening to the voices of its young victims.[2] The problem, of course, is how to get at those voices which have now faded in the more than half a century that has passed since the Great Depression ended. Is it still possible at this late date to be instructed by the youth of Depression America as to what it was like to be young and poor during the worst economic crisis in our nation's history?

The answer is a resounding yes. And the sources enabling us to hear from these impoverished youths are housed, appropriately enough, in the same building that displays Ernestine Guerrero's sculpture and letter. The archives of the FDR Library contain many letters from poor Depression-era teenagers and children. Much of this correspondence is in the "Material Assistance Requested" files of the Eleanor Roosevelt papers, which include thousands of letters from Depression Americans of all ages who wrote to Mrs. Roosevelt between 1933 and 1940 asking for direct financial and material aid.[3]

Both Eleanor Roosevelt and her husband received unprecedented amounts of mail from Americans. The public sent FDR more than three times the mail of any previous president. In her first year in the White House, Mrs. Roosevelt received more than 300,000 pieces of mail, far more than any previous First Lady. And it was not merely the number of letters that was unique, but also their origins and character. Unlike in prior administrations, the majority of letter writers were from the working class and wrote to seek aid rather than merely voice an opinion. According to Leila Sussmann's study of those who wrote to FDR during the 1930s, "18.3% requested immediate relief; 15.1% requested employment; 11.3% requested loans for homes; 7.2% requested loans to save their farms." The First Lady in particular attracted letters from the poor because both in print and on the radio she repeatedly indicated her interest in hearing from ordinary Americans about their problems—and discussed their correspondence sympathetically in the national media.[4]

The First Lady's staff did not segregate the teens' and children's letters; they included youth letters in the same alphabetical and chronological files as the correspondence from adults. But by gathering and analyzing separately the requests for material assistance that young Americans between the ages of five and nineteen sent to the First Lady, it becomes possible to understand the concerns and problems, the idealism, desires, and despair which linked needy youths in Depression America. The youth letters came from the children (mostly daughters) of the working poor, of one-horse (or two-horse) farmers and tenant farmers, of the unemployed, and of newly penurious members of the declining middle class.[5]

Needy youths had special problems and concerns, but their history cannot be understood if it is read in isolation from the larger Depression experience that transcended generational lines — affecting young, old, and the middle-aged alike. When President Roosevelt took office in 1933 unemployment had hit a record high of 25 percent, and despite the New Deal it remained in the double digits for the rest of the decade.[6] This was an economic catastrophe for millions of parents and children as unemployment, in the words of President Roosevelt, left "one third of a nation ill-housed, ill-clad, ill-nourished."[7] When one gazes at Dorothea Lange's classic Depression photograph of that impoverished migrant mother, one also sees her ragged children clutching this worried and weary farm worker, symbolizing the hurt felt by millions of poverty-stricken mothers and children in the 1930s. And the mountains of mail that needy Americans wrote to Mrs. Roosevelt and the president are a diverse lot: there are letters from desperate mothers and fathers concerned about the future of their impoverished children and letters shakily handwritten by worried senior citizens who agonize over the prospect of becoming a burden to their children, as well as the letters from the needy young people who are the subject of this book.

The economic crisis that sparked this letter writing provoked pain in more than just the young, but it hit the young with special force. Children and teens were among the most economically, educationally, and psychologically vulnerable to the ravages of the Depression. Relative to the rest of society they had less education, less vocational training, and less job experience. This meant that those who hit the constricted job market of the 1930s in their teens and early twenties would be less attractive hires than slightly older Americans who had obtained more experience and training before the Depression. Consequently, youth unemployment rates soared above the national average. Surveys in 1934–35 show unemployment rates among sixteen- to twenty-four-year-olds at 45 percent in Pennsylvania and Michigan, 40 percent in Dayton, 42 percent in Boston, 44 percent in Indianapolis, 47 percent in Detroit, 53 percent in Denver, and 57 percent in Newark. The picture was even worse among sixteen- and seventeen-year-olds: their unemployment rate in the mid-1930s was 56 percent in Bridgeport, Connecticut, 60 percent in nonagricultural areas of Pennsylvania, 63 percent in Springfield, Ohio, and 69 percent in Massachusetts. The Welfare Council of New York City reported in 1935 that nearly 80 percent of sixteen-year-olds who were out of school and looking for work in the city could not find jobs.[8]

Depression America's young were disproportionately represented below the poverty line. The Relief Census of 1933 found that 42 percent of all relief recipients were under sixteen years of age, though this age group constituted only 31 percent of the U.S. population. Children below working age were utterly dependent on their parents, and when their parents lost their jobs, as was so common in the Depression decade, hunger often resulted. Surveys revealed that a fifth of all children in New York suffered from malnutrition at the height of the Depression. In the impoverished coal regions of Illinois, Ohio, Pennsylvania, and West Virginia the malnutrition rates for children may have exceeded 90 percent. Low incomes could also lead to other health problems, since the unemployed and working poor lacked funds to obtain medical care when they needed it. According to a study of Depression-era Pittsburgh, it was partly because of this lack of medical attention that poor families suffered through 40 percent more illnesses than middle-class families. The situation was nearly identical with regard to dental care.[9]

The onset of the Depression further hurt the young by throwing many schools and colleges into crisis. Declining tax revenues led to severe educational retrenchment and school closings. Rural school systems, always the most poorly funded, were particularly hard hit. By 1934 some 20,000 rural schools had closed, disrupting the education of about a million students. Southern states often solved their revenue crises by cutting back their school terms.[10] Poverty forced about 80,000 college students to drop out of school during the 1932–33 academic year, making this the first peacetime year in the twentieth century when college enrollments declined.[11]

These and other difficulties faced by low-income youth led government officials, the press, and educators to speak of an American "youth crisis" in the 1930s. Adults in Depression America aired intense anxiety about the Depression's impact upon the young. When they spoke of the youth crisis, adults expressed fears about the lasting damage that the Depression could do to the young, and how that negative impact might threaten America's future.[12] They worried that the Depression was denying the essential education and training, the job experience, and the confidence that the younger generation would need if it was to lead America in the future. Such fears were evident from the very titles of contemporary studies of the youth crisis, such as *The Lost Generation* (1936) by Maxine Davis and *Youth—Millions Too Many?* (1940) by Bruce Melvin; they were also reflected in the reams of bleak statistical reports on the status of youth issued throughout the Depression by the American Youth Commission.[13] Even Hollywood tapped into adult

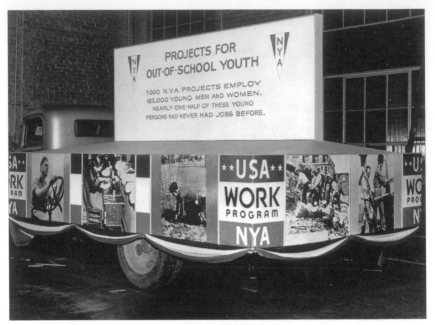

A float in the 1937 inaugural parade pays tribute to the aid that
the National Youth Administration provided to needy young Americans.
(Photo courtesy of Franklin D. Roosevelt Library, Hyde Park, N.Y.)

America's guilt over this failure to provide jobs, education, and hope for the
coming generation. Hollywood's top box-office star in the mid-1930s was
a child, Shirley Temple, whose movies often featured her as an orphaned
girl overcoming poverty, hardship, and abandonment. Such films reassured
Americans that though the Depression had left them unable to provide for
the young, all would turn out well anyway.[14]

Through federal work-relief, student aid, and job training programs for
sixteen- to twenty-four-year-year-olds, and by allocating funds to assist
poor and disabled children, the New Deal sought to solve or at least alleviate
the youth crisis, and perhaps also to ease the adult world's guilt about that
crisis. Needy Depression teens were assisted most by the National Youth
Administration (NYA) and the Civilian Conservation Corps (CCC). Between
1936 and 1943 more than two million low-income students were able to
continue their education through NYA work-study jobs, and by the end of
the Depression 10 percent of all American college students were being supported with NYA funds. The NYA employed another 2.6 million youths in
its out-of-school relief projects. The CCC employed 2.6 million teens and
young men in its reforestation camps. Millions of dollars in the Social Secu-

rity program aided poor children. Low-income children and their parents were also assisted by the Works Progress Administration, which for the first time made free nursery schools (more than 2,000 of them) widely available. The Federal Emergency Relief Administration prevented some 4,000 school closings by funding teacher salaries ($14 million worth) in America's poorest states. New Deal dollars also funded free school lunch programs and 70 percent of all new school construction between 1933 and 1939.[15]

This is an impressive record of youth relief, especially when compared to that of President Roosevelt's predecessor. The Hoover administration had, for example, responded to the job crisis of college youth not with positive steps anticipating the NYA, but only with a narrow-minded and totally ineffective ban on the employment of foreign college students. Ambitious as it seems when compared to Hooverism, however, the New Deal's youth program—as President Roosevelt himself admitted—assisted only a minority of the nation's needy youths. Even during the NYA's peak years budget constraints kept it from employing more than one-sixth of America's jobless youth.[16] Thus the New Deal addressed but did not solve the youth problem; it helped millions of needy youths while also neglecting millions of needy youths. As one southern farm boy put it in a letter to Mrs. Roosevelt: "We want to thank your husband Mr. Roosevelt for his good plan he has planned for us poor people. We know it is for the poor people good. But it seems it hasn't reached us yet much."[17]

This ambiguous legacy is evident in the letters that needy youth sent to Mrs. Roosevelt. In one sense, the letters can be seen as a testament to the failure of the New Deal's youth program. Had the program been a total success, these thousands of needy teens and children would not have continued to write to the First Lady in despair because lack of clothing, transportation, or tuition had forced them to drop out of school.[18] But on the other hand, the letters themselves are a testament to the way in which the New Deal made ordinary young Americans feel connected to their government in Washington. These poor people's letters are a paper trail that no scroogelike government could have generated. In their hour of need, poor youths felt they could turn to the First Lady for help. To grasp the significance of this, just compare it to the present age of antigovernment cynicism, during which—at least before the events of September 11, 2001— even members of Congress regularly bashed Washington and claimed that the federal government was not the solution to problems but the cause of them.

The needy youths who wrote to Mrs. Roosevelt often displayed a striking degree of trust in the First Lady and the president, and of love for them. Many of the letters were more than cries for help; they were highly personal statements, autobiographical accounts, in which the youths explained their material and social deprivation with the kind of candor one usually reserves for close friends or family members. Often the teens confided to Mrs. Roosevelt about feelings of deprivation that they were keeping from their parents (so as not to make their mothers and fathers feel guilty about being unable to provide for them). Despite their youth these letter writers were keenly aware of just how personal and sensitive was the information they were sharing with the First Lady—a fact demonstrated by the frequent requests that the authors made to keep the content of their letters confidential and out of the hands of reporters.[19]

Poor teens and children opened up to Mrs. Roosevelt (and through her the president) in this way because most felt that she was on their side— that she cared deeply and personally about their plight. "I've often heard how good and kind you were to poor folks, especially children," wrote a fourteen-year-old girl from Virginia in her letter to Mrs. Roosevelt.[20] Such phrases found their way into thousands of the First Lady's letters from needy youths; they were in part a reflection of lower-class gratitude for the extensive work relief programs that the New Deal provided to the poor, and the close identification of the president and Mrs. Roosevelt with those relief efforts. "We remember back when President Roosevelt said he would help the forgotten man and he has certainly done so," a teenage girl from Illinois explained.[21] A teenage boy from Pittsburgh hired by the NYA wrote: "Words cannot express my gratitude to our President, who has made this [employment] possible for me and thousands of others."[22]

Some of the young letter writers picked up positive attitudes toward Mr. and Mrs. Roosevelt and the New Deal from their parents. "Mother votes for Mr. Roosevelt all the time," wrote an eleven-year-old girl from Ohio. "We have his picture right by the sewing machine and mother thinks God sent him to lead us out like he did Mose[s] with the children of Isreal." Another eleven-year-old midwestern girl explained that she was "writing this letter for mother said Mrs. Roosevelt is just a God mother to the world . . . Mother said you was an angle [angel] for doing so much for the poor." "Mrs. Roosevelt," wrote a sixteen-year-old boy from Little Rock, "we are all so thankful for what you have done for the suffering and depressed and mother and dad prays every night for our Dear President and wife."[23]

That phrase "dear president and wife," as well as the content of many other letters to Mrs. Roosevelt, indicate that the letter writers saw the

Roosevelts as a team. Some wrote to the First Lady, in fact, because they thought that she offered the best prospect of reaching FDR. The writers assumed that the president was far too busy to give to his correspondence the same personal attention that the First Lady could to hers (not realizing just how hectic her schedule was).[24]

Rarely in the letters, however, was Mrs. Roosevelt seen solely as a surrogate for the president. Most of the teens and children who wrote to her were also responding to her as an individual who had made a strong impression in her own right. Their fondness for Mrs. Roosevelt was an outgrowth of the way that she was redefining the role of First Lady through her unprecedented social activism. Transcending the old image of the First Lady as a social hostess for the elite, she embraced a new liberal activism on behalf of those at the bottom of society.[25] She traveled far more than any previous First Lady had done, visiting impoverished areas to spotlight social problems, keep her husband informed, and assess the progress of New Deal relief programs. A famous cartoon in the *New Yorker* captured both this activism and how unprecedented, even astonishing it seemed to Depression Americans: two miners, black with coal dust, look up from their mine, and one says to the other, "For gosh sakes, here comes Mrs. Roosevelt!" Another memorable cartoon had one hobo telling another, "pull up your socks and straighten your tie," because "You never can tell when you'll run into Mrs. Roosevelt."[26]

Nor was it simply Mrs. Roosevelt's travels that conveyed her concern for the poor. The First Lady was so outspoken that Depression Americans heard from her almost daily. Mrs. Roosevelt had a radio show each week in which she spoke to a national audience. She also published a daily column, "My Day," which appeared in seventy-five newspapers and reached four million people across the country. A typical "My Day" column found the First Lady commenting on some aspect of American poverty and promoting federal aid programs for the poor—accompanied by firsthand observations on New Deal work relief projects that she had visited.[27] All of this contact with Mrs. Roosevelt and her liberal conscience made millions of Americans, including her young letter writers, feel a sense of personal closeness to the First Lady. A fifteen-year-old girl from Maryland, writing in 1935, began by articulating this sense of proximity: "I have read so many editorials and articles you have written . . . that I feel I almost know you through the feeling you put in your writing." "I hear you on the radio," wrote a young girl from Ohio, "and you sound so kind and nice." And a teen in Alabama informed the First Lady that although with a stranger she

"For gosh sakes, here comes Mrs. Roosevelt!"

Eleanor Roosevelt's travels and activism in behalf of the poor and
working class were so unprecedented for a First Lady that they drew the attention
of the press, including cartoonists. This cartoon reflected an actual event,
as Mrs. Roosevelt did go down into a coal mine with some miners.
(© The New Yorker Collection, Robert Day, 1933. From cartoonbank.com.
All Rights Reserved.)

would feel reluctant to request assistance, "I have read your columns in the
paper and enjoyed it so much until I feel like you're a friend of mine and
not a stranger." [28]

Beyond her advocacy for the poor, Mrs. Roosevelt's connection with
youth work gave the young an additional reason for seeing her as a friend.
The First Lady was a former schoolteacher and settlement house worker
who was especially familiar with and outspoken on youth problems.[29] No
resident of the White House has ever approached the level of concern, activism, and empathy that Eleanor Roosevelt displayed for American youth.
She played a prominent role in founding the NYA and ardently defended
its work in providing emergency employment to students and aiding out-

of-school youth. The First Lady sat on the NYA's advisory board and was its most prominent and persistent supporter, using her columns, travels, and radio broadcasts to praise NYA programs and urge that these be expanded.[30]

Eleanor Roosevelt conveyed a strong sense of urgency about addressing the problems of the young. "I have moments of real terror," she explained in 1934, "when I think we may be losing this generation. We have got to bring these young people into the active life of the community." From start to finish in the Depression decade she insisted that a society which neglected the young was turning its back on its own future—killing "the goose that lays the golden eggs . . . It has been said in this country we should deal with first things first, and in my estimation . . . the first question before us is action on the problems of youth."[31]

Mrs. Roosevelt's interest in the problems of the young and her passionate commitment to federal aid to needy youth generated additional headlines because it led her into an alliance with the American student movement of the 1930s. This alliance proved controversial with many adults in the second half of the Depression decade, because the student movement's major organizations, such as the American Youth Congress (which the First Lady praised and for which she raised funds repeatedly), had a leftist tinge —since both communists and socialists figured prominently among its leaders.[32] But almost none of the needy youths who wrote to Mrs. Roosevelt showed any concern about this controversy. Instead they were inspired that she cared about their problems and took youth seriously enough to address audiences and organizations of young Americans. "I have," wrote the disabled son of a tenant farmer in Texas, "heard you talk to the youths of our great United States of which I am one—I have been uplifted by your talks and that of your husband . . . and I am not going to give up." An eighteen-year-old Philadelphian, forced to drop out of school at fourteen because of her poverty, told Mrs. Roosevelt that she knew the First Lady would be sympathetic to her plight because "I know from reading the papers that you are interested in young folks."[33]

Eleanor Roosevelt expressed her interest "in young folks" through charitable as well as governmental work. She annually donated tens of thousands of dollars that she earned from her radio broadcasts into nongovernmental programs and personal assistance efforts in behalf of needy youth. Her biggest gifts, channeled through the American Friends Service Committee, were to the school for underprivileged children in Arthurdale, West Virginia—where her donations, along with those of her friend Bernard M.

Baruch, kept the school afloat through the bleakest Depression years. Mrs. Roosevelt also personally subsidized scholarships for needy students, aided disabled children, and engaged in a host of other charitable activities for impoverished youngsters. It was typical of her that after winning $1,000 as the Woman of the Year in 1934 she donated the prize money to a truck driver's eight-year-old son, who suffered from infantile paralysis—the same disease that had struck FDR. She would pay for this bedridden boy to spend six months at the Warm Springs treatment center for infantile paralysis that her husband had founded.[34]

These efforts, and particularly the ways in which her earnings from radio and news columns were used, attracted considerable press attention. And so children and teens who wrote to Mrs. Roosevelt were sometimes as attracted to her because of her personal acts for poor youth as they were by her political activism.[35] This was on the mind of a thirteen-year-old girl from Minnesota who wrote: "I have been very interested in you because I read in the papers how much you were doing for the poor children and crippled children. I want to thank you for doing so much good for the little children cause I know how tough it is now." Similarly, an unemployed black teen from Buffalo hoped that Mrs. Roosevelt would help her, because she had read that the First Lady used some of the money she made "from writing to help some boys and girls go to school" through her scholarship fund.[36]

Although most of the young letter writers adored Eleanor Roosevelt and all her work—public and personal—on behalf of the young and poor, admiration was not the only sentiment that the First Lady aroused. The hardships wrought by the Depression had heightened certain forms of class consciousness in American society, as the economic crisis dramatized the gap between the haves and the have-nots. And some of that consciousness manifested itself in a significant minority of the letters that poor Depression teens and children wrote to the First Lady. These letter writers, despite their limited age and experience, were aware and resentful of the tremendous economic divide separating them from Mrs. Roosevelt; they responded to her less as a liberal activist than as a rich woman, resenting her as one might resent an affluent aunt who—though kindly—had yet to share her riches with all of her poor relations.

It was in this resentful spirit that a fourteen-year-old girl from Texas complained to Mrs. Roosevelt about her poverty, her difficulty in traveling miles to school on horseback, and her taxing physical workload: "I have done a boy's work ever since I was five years old. This week I have been breaking land with a sulky plow and three mules." She dramatized this complaint by contrasting her poverty and hard labor with Mrs. Roosevelt's affluence and easy workload: "When I read how you get $3,000 for each radio broadcast, I can't help but think how unjust the world is." The same kind of unflattering comparison appeared in the letter of a twelve-year-old from Michigan: "I have heard that you get lots of money and that you have life easy. Our way is quite different." A poor teen from Connecticut, after writing admiringly of the First Lady's "trip out west to visit those miners," her work to clothe poor children, and her "kind face," blurted out, "Mrs. Roosevelt you have too much money, why won't you please help me" with funds to buy Christmas gifts.[37]

Other young letter writers wondered whether the First Lady, even with her benevolence toward the poor, could actually understand the humiliations they suffered. Thus a youth in Kentucky, despondent that poverty kept her from dressing up so that she could attend her graduation, noted bitterly: "you all of high class could finance yours [graduation] and look forward to a happy graduation day while I am of poor class . . . [with] no means to finance my graduation. It is a pleasure to graduate but it gives me more heartache than pleasure." "I ask for your simpathy," wrote a poor Minnesota girl, "tho' I little expect it, because you have never been deprived of the finer things of life by a stubborn depression that is taking its own sweet time about saying adios."[38]

Such negativity was really not a commentary upon Mrs. Roosevelt herself. Few of those voicing resentment implied that she flaunted her wealth or used it selfishly. Instead they displayed a vaguely anticapitalist sensibility. Though the young letter writers who expressed class resentment toward the First Lady were too unread politically to articulate a complete political ideology, they were implicitly criticizing Depression America's inequitable class structure and implying that it was immoral for a society to divide itself into rich and poor. A thirteen-year-old girl from Michigan, for example, noting that she had spent four years waiting in vain to receive a bicycle, complained that with "8 in the family $44 a month is not enough to live on. Do you think it's fair? Well I sure think it's terrible . . . I wish you would do something about it. I think there is some crooked work, don't you think we should get more than $44?" A similar note of disdain for social inequity echoed through the letter of a girl from Illinois frustrated in her attempt to secure funding for nursing school: "Millionaires do not think anything of giving thousands of dollars for expeditions and a lot of different things, but when one asks for a small sum that would be sufficient to help a person get a life job, they will not do it."[39]

In a sense it is remarkable that the youths expressed any resentment, since there would have been a natural tendency to hide any sentiment that might offend the woman they were asking to come to their aid. The class resentments must have been strong indeed for them to overpower this inclination to be deferential to the First Lady. One can only speculate, but it seems likely that other young writers also felt such resentment and repressed it out of deference to Mrs. Roosevelt.

This resentful minority together with the adoring majority compose the whole political spectrum of needy youth who wrote to Mrs. Roosevelt. The striking thing about this political spectrum is that it does not have a right wing. Virtually none of the poor children and teens who wrote to Mrs. Roosevelt took a conservative position on the role of the federal government or of the First Lady in American life. All at least implicitly welcomed the increasing involvement of New Deal Washington in public efforts to relieve the poor.[40] And the same is true of their attitude toward Eleanor Roosevelt's work in converting the First Ladyship into a bully pulpit for fighting poverty. What complaints there were came, as suggested above, from a sense that more such activism was needed and that not enough was being done yet to aid those at the bottom of Depression America's social order.

This does not mean that the youths were entirely free of the older individualistic ideal of self-help associated with American social conservatism. Many were conflicted about that ideal. Even as they asked for governmental aid or personal assistance from the First Lady, these young people would note proudly that their families were not on government relief rolls. As one teen from North Carolina explained, "Though we are poor, we try to hold off embarrassment, for you know it is 'hard to be broke, and harder to admit it.' "[41] There was a strong sense that it would be shameful to "go on the dole." In a similar spirit, Eleanor Roosevelt's young correspondents insisted that they would repay her for her assistance, and that they and their parents wanted to work. They showed a reverence for the work ethic and a sense that only the most dire emergency had led them to appeal for governmental aid.

. . . .

It would be a mistake, however, to focus too much on these letters as political documents. The letters are often only implicitly political. Most of the writers were too young to vote, and electoral politics was the least of their concerns. Although they offered a few phrases (usually positive) about the New Deal, the president, or the First Lady, most of the letters concern not politics but social and economic life, the history of adolescence, childhood, education, work, and the family.[42] They tell us more about how Depression America's needy young people lived than about their political ideology.

The letters illuminate the lives of their young authors because of the way the letters are structured. To understand that structure it is helpful to put oneself in the shoes of a needy youth. She feels a desperate need for something important to her young life—for example, a winter coat or money to pay for her schoolbooks—but neither she, her family, nor her friends can raise the money she needs. So she decides to write to the First Lady requesting help. The first thing she would probably do in the letter (after getting past an awkward greeting to so important a person) would be to explain who she is, what she needs, and why she and her family are unable to afford it. In the course of explaining herself and her needs to the First Lady, she almost has to write at some length about her economic, social, and educational history. She is, in effect, offering a condensed autobiography. And it is the autobiographical segments of the letters that open a window into the lives of Depression youths.

As historical sources, all forms of autobiography have their problems. Memoirs written in old age may, for example, suffer from anachronism and the dimming or selective memories of their authors. But since the letters from these children and teens were written when the crisis of the Depression was a live issue rather than a fading memory, they are more immediate and probably more accurate. There are of course limitations as well, for the letters offer only their authors' perspective on events, and only a snapshot of their young lives: they cannot tell us how the lives end up or how the adults in the authors' families might have interpreted events differently. But given that historians and most writers of memoirs are adults, the youthful bias of these letters is an asset, since it restores a measure of generational balance to our collective memory of the Great Depression.

There remains one other problem with the youth letters, one shared with virtually all autobiography: they are exercises in self-justification. Adult memoirs are often written as much to justify and defend as to explain or faithfully recount the author's life. The youth letters share this self-justifying character, but the motivation behind them is different. Whereas the authors of published memoirs seek to ingratiate themselves with the public for the sake of posterity (or for the sake of selling books), the youths whose letters appear in this book are writing to Mrs. Roosevelt to justify themselves and their cries for help. So unlike the self-serving distortions of the published memoir, which may stem from vanity, here the distortions were probably made to build a better case for the material requests that the authors presented to the First Lady. Nevertheless, only a very few of the letters seem distorted at all. The point is that we must read the letters critically, taking into account that veracity may at times have been sacrificed for the sake of winning Mrs. Roosevelt's heart.[43]

Being critical of these letters as historical sources does not mean that we should be dismissive of them. Even taking into account the youth and self-interest of their authors, the letters offer powerful testimony that calls into question some of the scholarly world's assumptions about American lower-class family life during the Great Depression. For instance, social scientists and historians have argued that the Depression had a traumatic impact on the American family. By throwing men out of work the economic crisis was, according to these scholars, disorienting and disorganizing for many families; it undermined the authority of fathers, since they could no longer perform their customary role as the family breadwinner. Wives and children lost respect for the father, the father himself lost his self-respect, and tensions swirled in a family world turned upside down by economic catastrophe.[44] This portrait of collapsing paternal authority in the Depression family is not, however, supported by most of the letters that needy teens and children wrote to Eleanor Roosevelt. In most cases the children and teens who commented upon their fathers (or mothers) did so in terms that were either not judgmental or quite positive. Most seemed to understand that the economic crisis rather than some failing on the part of their father (or mother) was responsible for their poverty. The letter writers often stressed that their fathers were hard working and that their long periods of unemployment or very low-paying jobs came despite diligent efforts to find better economic opportunities. Many of the writers depicted their fathers and mothers as unselfish—recalling how generous their parents were until the Depression struck.[45]

These young daughters and sons were well aware that their fathers could no longer play their traditional role as breadwinner. In fact, some knew precisely how long their dads had been out of work or how little they made each month in the temporary work relief jobs provided by New Deal agencies. But rather than direct their anger at their fathers, the writers express a tender mixture of sadness and compassion. Some of the most moving letters are from children and teens who could see how heartbroken their parents were at being unable to provide for their families. Thus a fifteen-year-old from Cleveland, after noting his parents' anxieties about being unable to pay the grocer and the landlord, wrote: "I just can't stand anymore to look at the crying and thinking my parents do. . . . My heart just seems ready to burst." On the verge of getting evicted, a girl from Brooklyn confided to the First Lady: "My father tries to be gay about it saying as lightly as possible 'Who cares. Who Wants to live here anyway.' But under all his jokes I can see he is suffering terrible my pop is very sensitive."[46]

Of course it is possible to read these letters more skeptically, and to privilege "damaged family" scholarship over first-person "undamaged family" testimony. Some might even be tempted to write off the testimony altogether. One could argue that the children and teens were weaving a kind of fairy tale for Mrs. Roosevelt: that to prove themselves worthy of her help, the young letter writers had to establish that they and all their relations were virtuous—and that all that was needed to make the world right for them was material aid.

Suspicions of this type ought to be raised, and the letters need to be read carefully if they are to be contextualized and rendered useful as historical sources. But in this case the skepticism is not justified. Indeed, with regard to the letters and paternal authority during the Depression one finds the exceptions proving the rule. Only a relative handful of youths writing to Mrs. Roosevelt for aid made bitter complaints about their fathers. These complaints in no way lessened the power of their appeals for aid but if anything heightened it, because the letter writers seemed to be struggling against both a merciless Depression and a bad parent. Demonizing one's father, in other words, could have been a good strategy for an appeal to Mrs. Roosevelt to play the role of surrogate parent (at least financially). Thus it is striking that so few of the letter writers employed the strategy and scorned their parents. That most instead depicted their parents glowingly suggests that it is the "damaged family" scholarship rather than the letters that needs to be viewed with some skepticism. Moreover, even the few writers who criticized their fathers depicted them not as weakened by the economic crisis but rather as having too much authority, which they exploited to abuse their sons and daughters physically or psychologically.[47]

Perhaps scholars have reached conclusions about Depression families so much at odds with the evidence of the letters because the scholars have been focused so narrowly on adults.[48] By contrast, in most of the youth letters parental authority was just not discussed. Most children and teens seem to have moved beyond the issues of hierarchy and authority within the family; they had a realistic sense of how the economic crisis disempowered all members of lower—class families, that it was not just fathers and mothers but youths too—sisters and brothers—who were unable to find jobs or sufficient income. Their letters constitute a recognition that only by reaching beyond their class for aid from Mrs. Roosevelt and New Deal Washington could they help pull themselves and their families out of economic trouble.[49]

The family egalitarianism of the youths not only limited any tendency to blame parents for their troubles, but also gave the letters a somber tone. This was a generation of needy young people that did not privilege youth over adulthood, did not see childhood and adolescence as periods of innocence and play in which the young merited special protection. There was an almost adult sensibility to the letters, in that most youths felt that they had to ask Mrs. Roosevelt for necessities rather than more frivolous items (as if play were decadent or inappropriate at a time of crisis). Even when requesting items that we might think of as recreational, the pressure of poverty often prompted the writers to describe them in adult terms. Thus requests for bicycles were repeatedly made in terms of their use for basic transportation and work rather than as playthings. For example, a young girl from Massachusetts wrote in 1935:

> The school which I attend is very far and as I am not very healthy I often get pains in my sides. My father only works for two days a week and there are six in my family, it is impossible in almost every way that I get a bicycle! I am in eighth grade and am very fond of school. Sometimes I have to miss school on account of the walk [is] so far. . . . I assure you that the bicycle [needed for transportation to school] shall not be used as a pleasure but as a necessity.

Similarly, a fourteen-year-old girl from Missouri asked the First Lady for a bicycle so that she could better assist her stepmother:

> My step-mother is very good to me. . . . She takes in washings and I have to walk for six or eight blocks and then carry the washings home . . . before school and it has been very cold here. If you could send me a bicycle to ride when I go after washings for her I would appreciate it.[50]

Here the young seemed adultlike in their distance from the play and frivolity that we associate with youth, suggesting that economic necessity and the extreme work ethic born of the Great Depression had stolen their childhood. A teen from Chicago had this in mind when she complained that she "had been denied the good times" of a protected childhood. "When I reached the age of ten I was told that my playing days were over and they were."[51]

There was little childlike innocence in the letters regarding the psychological burdens created by the Depression. Parents, and particularly fathers, obviously carried the heaviest burden, since they shouldered strong feelings of guilt over their failure to fulfill their traditional role of providing financial support for the family. But young people did experience adultlike anxieties about their own powerlessness with regard to their family's economic plight. Some felt genuine regret at being unable to find work so that they might help their families out. As a nine-year-old from Boston wrote, "My mother cryes because maybe we'll lose the store. I always sorry because I'm still very young and can't help much."[52]

Others felt badly about being another mouth to feed or having unmet economic needs that left their parents feeling glum. In some cases this led the children to express an almost parental solicitousness toward their own parents. This was true, for instance, of a sixteen-year-old girl from Virginia. Though her lack of Easter clothes "brought tears" to her eyes, she wrote: "I am trying to be a heroine by not let[t]ing my mother and father know that I am worr[y]ing."[53]

Notwithstanding these examples of adultlike behavior, it would be an exaggeration to say that teens and children of the Depression era were simply miniature adults, oriented toward the older generation rather than their own. Actually, the peer society of youth was of great importance to many of the letter writers. The letters suggest that if the Depression fueled a crisis in personal relationships, that crisis centered on youth's interactions with their peers rather than with their parents. Most of the anger and shame in the letters focused not on fathers or mothers but on the ways in which low or declining income jeopardized their relationships with friends in their youth peer groups. For the young, the world outside the home was where the future rested: where friends were made, education or job training obtained, careers secured, and romance pursued. Children did not want to have their poverty render them outsiders in their peers' world of school and play, and teens feared similar material embarrassments coming at crucial moments when milestones were supposed to be reached in their social and educational lives.[54]

Youth peer culture itself promoted such anxieties among needy children and teens by requiring at least a modicum of material attainments. Thus when two girls from Lackawanna, New York, wrote to request bicycles they stressed, "in our city mostly all the girls and boys of the younger generation enjoy the privilege of having a bicycle and we feel very out of place. For this reason we are mocked and scorned and left out of many social activities." When a fourteen-year-old girl from Iowa wrote in to request clothes she explained, "the kids at school make fun of you if you can't dress fine." A teen from Michigan wrote that she would feel humiliated if she ended up as the only girl in her class who could not dress properly for graduation: "I hate to go on the stage with the other girls in my shabby dress."[55]

It may seem odd that during the Great Depression the peer culture of youth could remain so materialistic. But the social class complexion of the youth peer culture needs to be borne in mind. Public schools were often sites for interaction between several socioeconomic classes: middle class, lower middle class, working class, working poor, and unemployed. However, the letters suggest that this interaction was unequal. The middle class tended to drive youth culture, leaving those in the lower classes to respond to its challenging material demands.[56] Impoverished students felt a mixture of shame, envy, and anger about their inability to dress as the more fortunate youths in their schools did. School authorities seemed to have reinforced this tendency by refusing to acknowledge that the norms of school dress and social organization needed to be modified to take into account the problems of destitute students.[57]

The anxieties that the young expressed about losing face in their peer culture can be read in two ways, which have contrary ideological implications. Consider the girl who feels herself an outcast because she lacks the material possessions of her schoolmates. Her feelings could have anticapitalist implications, as the student may sense that society is unjust if it allows for some to own such things while others must do without. But on the other hand the feelings may reflect youthful adherence to a central value of the capitalist marketplace: acquisitive individualism, according to which people define themselves and derive their own sense of self-worth (and gauge the worth of others) by assessing how well they have succeeded in the competitive drive to accumulate material possessions.[58]

There is not one answer as to which of these readings applies to Depression youth, since both tendencies are visible. Yet it is impossible not to be impressed with the grip that acquisitive individualism and the ethos of the consumer society held over even many needy youths during the worst depression in American history. Despite the Depression the values of the marketplace were continually directed at the young through newspaper, magazine, and radio advertising. The influence of these values seems quite strong, as is clear from the newspaper advertisements that some youths sent to the First Lady to show her what they wanted.[59] Poor youths knew what they were missing. "I see so many girls of my own age wearing pretty clothes, it just makes my heart ache to know that I can't afford even to dress decent," wrote a self-described "poverty stricken girl" from North Carolina." Even the poorest tenant farmer's child, as the novelist Harry Crews recalled of his impoverished rural southern roots, could get his hands on the Sears Catalogue and dream about getting what other children had. Crews used to refer to that catalogue as his "Wish book."[60]

Nor did the disparities between classes affect only the poor. Some of the most anguished letters in the First Lady's files came from youths who might not have qualified as poor but had recently fallen out of the middle class. Listen, for instance, to the complaint to Mrs. Roosevelt of a girl from New Jersey about her need for an Easter outfit:

> Do you realize that "Easter" is at hand? Do you realize how many hearts are broken on this account? Do you realize how difficult it is going to be for most people? I am a young girl of fifteen [15] and I need a coat. I have no money, nor any means of getting any. My father has been out of work for two years . . . We were once the richest people in our town but now, we are the lowest, considered the worst people of Port Morris. For Easter some friends of mine are thinking of getting new out-fits and I just have to listen to them. How I wish I could have at least a coat.[61]

Although acquisitive individualism was strong, it was not the only influence on the way that youth reacted to hard times. As the resentful letters to Mrs. Roosevelt suggest, a significant minority of the young saw the injustice of a marketplace that awarded luxuries to the few and not even bare necessities to many.[62] The peer culture's pressure was a force to be reckoned with, but so was survival, and for some of the letter writers the primary concern was something as basic as keeping warm in the winter. Many of the children and teens who wrote to Mrs. Roosevelt for clothes, for example, were not out to look stylish in front of their friends; they were hoping to get anything at all—and often asked for used clothes—to help them and their family get through the winter. Moreover, especially with regard to educational opportunity, there were youths who displayed no concern or even awareness of their status in the peer culture. These letters show an egalitarian sensibility, a view that education ought to be a right rather than a privilege—that a just society would not permit poverty to force bright students to drop out of school.[63]

This diversity of responses to hard times partly reflects the differences in status between letter writers. In general those who were the poorest, the most desperate economically, and the most isolated from the peer society of youth at school tended to be the least affected by acquisitive individualism—while those most strongly connected to peer society tended to be the most acquisitive and market-oriented. But this is more of a general tendency than an absolute division. What must be recalled is that people have the capacity to hold ideas that are inconsistent or even contradictory—and this is especially true of youths who often have had too little time, experience, or education to develop an ideologically coherent response to their economic problems. It was quite possible to be simultaneously pulled in both directions, to desire possessions that could impress one's friends (to want to do better in the capitalist race to possess), while also expressing at least implicitly a loathing for the class system that left others so much better off. One does find instances of this contradiction in the letters, as in that of a girl from Tennessee who in 1934 asked Mrs. Roosevelt for a loan to help her stay in school so that she could pursue her "one ambition . . . to be a writer." She displayed a strong sense of class and a recognition of the unfair burdens that poverty placed upon her, but she was also determined to avoid humiliating herself within the peer culture of youth, whose members could afford to continue their schooling:

> I know the road to authorship is a hard one. With an education it would be hard for a poor country girl like me but without even a high school education it means 'you're just a flop.' My English teacher said that I had talent and if I would keep on I could reach success but how can I 'keep on keeping on' with no backing? I hope you understand, I hope you help me, yet do you understand, how could you? You've never been a farm girl like me. Can you imagine getting up before "Sun-up" and going to work in the tobacco patch and all the time be thinking of school days coming when there'll be no school for you, thinking of the hundreds of memories and things that happen in school life . . . thinking of the gossips that will wag their tongues when you drop from the school gang and thinking last, *What will I ever amount to?* No you can't imagine it, who could unless they've had experience as I have.[64]

Letters such as these call into question one of the more popular historical assumptions about the Depression's impact on American youth: that the emotional strain on the young was limited since poverty was so widespread. Baby boomers like me grew up hearing our parents insist that as Depression kids they did not know how poor they were, since everyone they knew was poor—and so there was little shame associated with indigence. This view has been reinforced by influential oral histories, such as Studs Terkel's Hard Times.[65] The letters to Eleanor Roosevelt make it evident that many children and teens did know how poor they were, felt shame about it, and realized all too well that neither all Americans nor even all their friends had been as badly hurt by the Depression as their own families had been. This recognition that not all were in the same boat economically was one of the leading motivators of youths who wrote to Mrs. Roosevelt for help— as the young sought to redress the inequity which had left them so much more needy than those around them.[66]

Far from being unaware of differences in social class, Depression youths proved extremely sensitive to symbols of those differences. Dress patterns, for example, were among the central ways in which status and its unequal distribution was recognized by the young. The most poignant memories of the poet Philip Levine of his school days in Depression-era Detroit concerned such marks of class differentiation. Even as an elementary school student, Levine, the son of a working stenographer, noted at least three different class groupings in his school: the small affluent group, the employed working class (which included his family), and the desperately poor:

Entering the second grade, I began to notice for the first time how differently we students dressed, and at the same time how many of us wore the same clothes. There were four boys in my class aside from me who wore sweaters which bore the figure of a stag knitted in white against a maroon background. It too had been on sale at Hudson's, the maroon a dollar cheaper than the navy blue. There was one boy who wore far more elegant sweaters in subtle hues of brown and fawn; even his checked socks were in matching colors. . . . I noticed too that my teacher seemed to defer to him, to call on him only when he raised his hand and clearly knew the answers to his questions, whereas she was continually trying to make fools of the rest of us. This boy, Milton Journey, was always driven to school in a long white La Salle convertible. . . . On winter days, after school, Milton would wait in his long blue overcoat inside the main doors until his mother stopped and honked from her sedan. Milton would toss back his straight blond hair, shrug, and go out into the weather to accept his privileges. Another boy, Fred Batten, disgusted me . . . He wore no socks, and often that winter the skin of his ankles were raw and swollen. One day he caught me looking at his ankles, and he turned away from me in silence. I began to notice several other boys and girls who bore these same "wounds," and I did my best not to stare at them. Winters in Michigan were fierce, but I never left for school without a warm jacket, socks, a cap that covered my ears . . . gloves, and a scarf. Not once did I go off without a sacked lunch, nor were lice ever found in my hair, though weekly I had to bow for the health officer's inspection. Many of my classmates were not so fortunate and were taken off for their "treatment" and returned, heads bent and reeking of kerosene. Lunchtimes grew particularly difficult, for many students had nothing to eat except the free carton of milk that was provided by the school. By the age of ten I'd decided that it was easier to walk the mile back to our apartment and eat my lunch in privacy than to bear the envious glances of many of my schoolmates.[67]

Discomfort over class divisions could be more painful than even Levine's words suggest. While Levine, a sensitive young boy, felt awkward over having more than his classmates, poorer children—as their letters to Mrs. Roosevelt attest—experienced shame, anger, and humiliation over the outward signs of their deprivation. For children on relief and their parents this issue of dress, of looking indigent, was a sore point. Eleanor Roosevelt's close friend Lorena Hickok found this out for herself in 1934 and reported on it (from Texas) in one of the most memorable letters that she sent from the field as an investigator for the Federal Emergency Relief Administration. Hickok noted that a mother of two on relief had asked her, "[Why doesn't the government] give us materials and let us make our children's clothes ourselves instead of making us take them from the sewing rooms [funded by the New Deal]? You've no idea how children hate wearing 'relief clothes.' " Another impoverished woman told Hickok how

> her little boy suffered Hell wearing to school trousers she got from the sewing room. 'He says every kid in town whose family is on relief wears those pants,' she said. 'That's how you know they're on relief.' The material was striped, quite conspicuous, she said, and evidently they got a few bolts of it and made up several hundred pairs for boys whose families were on relief. God, I don't blame the kids! Those stripes suggest a Georgia prison camp.[68]

The letters to Eleanor Roosevelt are in essence about how the young thought of and dealt with material inequalities (both necessities and status symbols) and constricted social and educational opportunities in a time of widespread economic distress. Almost all the letter writers had been hurt by the Depression. The level of hurt varied. Some of the writers had lost their homes, dropped out of school, gone hungry, suffered without medical attention. Others had been dealt what for adults might seem lesser blows — such as being unable to dress up for parties and graduations. But for youths new to social life, adolescence, and want, these hurt too, enough to reduce some to tears.[69] In that all were hurt, one could say that all were victims of the Depression. The term "victim," however, implies passivity and powerlessness. Although it is true that the youths felt powerless because they could not fund their needs, they were not passive. The act of letter writing was a testament to their refusal to be passive in the face of hard times. Children or teens who put pen to paper and wrote to the First Lady complaining about their suffering and requesting assistance were asserting themselves and demonstrating a level of historical agency. Some wrote more than once, expressing disappointment at their unmet needs and insisting that the First Lady hasten to relieve their suffering.[70] However small a step the writing of a letter may seem to us in retrospect, especially compared to the protest marches and strikes that usually command the attention of historians of the Great Depression, in their own way the letters are an impressive form of protest: protest without a protest movement, a quasi-political act by Americans too young to participate in the political process, a refusal to accept hard times and suffering silently, a populistic insistence that those at the top of the political system must know how those at the bottom were hurting and be forced to do something about it.

There was a distinctive gender dynamic to this form of protest. Most youths who sent material assistance requests to Mrs. Roosevelt were female.[71] This is obviously because Roosevelt was a mother and grandmother who had often used women's magazines and similar forums to reach the American public: before entering the White House she had edited a magazine for mothers, *Babies—Just Babies*, and soon after becoming First Lady she published *It's Up to the Women* (1933), an advice book designed to assist women in holding their families together through hard times.[72]

If such maternalistic activity made Mrs. Roosevelt a magnet for young female letter writers, this attraction was intensified because of the special interest that the First Lady had taken in the plight of needy *girls* and young *women*. She had been the most influential public figure advocating that New Deal youth relief efforts benefit females as well as males. Thus when the CCC restricted its work projects to males Mrs. Roosevelt led the drive for parity by providing federal educational camps for jobless females (popularly known as the "she she she" camps). She prodded the Civil Works Administration in this direction too, and by fall 1933 she was credited in the press with helping to create 100,000 female work relief jobs. Mrs. Roosevelt was also instrumental in a high-profile effort in New York to establish canteens where female job seekers could rest and take solace as they looked for work.[73] This sort of activity added to the feeling among female teens and children that Mrs. Roosevelt was especially sympathetic to their problems.

The predominance of females among the young letter writers to Mrs. Roosevelt may, however, have had as much to do with the gender politics of Depression America — in both the larger polity and the American family — as it did with the First Lady herself. In an age when politics was dominated by men, letter writing constituted one of the few avenues that young girls had for airing their economic grievances.[74] And since girls traditionally were not weighed down by the role of family breadwinner, or at least not socialized into it, they could open up to an outsider such as Mrs. Roosevelt about their family hardships without feeling that they were revealing some personal failure. Freed from some of the guilt and shame that oppressed boys, they could ask for help more easily. The collection of letters in this book is further weighted toward female writers because for whatever reason females were more expressive in discussing their lives, needs, hopes, and fears, and their letters were simply more illuminating and better suited to publication.

Readers of this collection of letters will quickly notice that the cries for help from Depression youth make for painful reading. It is true that not every letter is depressing. A few even border on the humorous, such as one from the child in Texas who thought that the First Lady had at her disposal "a big machine to make money," or the one from the miner's daughter who had heard that the White House attic was stuffed with used clothing, or the young boy in Missouri who asked Mrs. Roosevelt not to jail him for writing to her.[75] But in general the letters are sad, oppressively so. At times they may well seem redundant, since many strike the same note of deprivation and of a desperate longing for relief. Yet that very redundancy, that very oppressiveness, may be the only thing enabling us today to grasp what it meant to be needy and young in Depression America.

To enter the Depression decade through these letters is to encounter a very different world from the one evoked by all the famous New Deal narratives, Roosevelt biographies, and history textbooks. In these letters the glory and drama of great unfolding national events are largely absent, and chronology barely matters. Aside from the references to one New Deal program or another little distinguishes the letters that poor youths wrote in the twilight of the New Deal era from those written by their predecessors at its dawn. It is the static quality of the letters, the continuous, pressing, wearying, and unmet hunger for things that are frustratingly out of reach that conveys the oppression felt by these young letter writers. They leave the readers suspended in a story with no end, and with only the slimmest hope of a happy ending.

The pain might be easier to bear if the book allowed readers to avert their gaze—if, for example, they could be diverted with stories of the more affluent youths of America in the 1930s, such as those depicted in *Parents Magazine*, *Boy's Life*, *College Humor*, or any of dozens of magazines devoted to the young and to child-rearing. The story of how the sons and daughters of "the better half" lived in the 1930s is well worth telling, and indeed must be told if the decade's social history is to be understood fully.[76] But those were not the youths whose lives were seared by the Great Depression or whose fate stirred the conscience of Eleanor Roosevelt and her generation of liberal reformers. As painful as it may be, if we are to obtain an interior view of the youth crisis of the 1930s, we must listen to the voices of the needy young girls and boys caught up in that crisis. They are representative not of their entire generation, but of those who constituted the bottom economic tiers of the Depression generation—those whom the New Deal was supposed to assist.

Beyond conveying the realities of the Depression, these letters may serve an additional purpose of value to Americans in the twenty-first century. The American electorate, and particularly its politicians, often debate about the poor and pontificate about the character and shortcomings of needy youth. We talk at and talk about the poor. But we rarely listen to them. Even those who study poverty often put their own spin on things, as they depict the poor in ways that serve their own ideological agendas. Given all this, it seems an almost novel idea to allow poor youths to tell us in their own words about their plight and their hopes, their loves and fears, their values and character. If we can learn to listen to these needy young people from the distant past, perhaps we can begin to do the same for their youthful counterparts in the urban ghettos and rural trailer-parks of America today.

In this spirit of listening to the young I have let the topics of their letters shape much of the organization of this book. The chapters are centered around the kinds of material requests that the letter writers sent to Mrs.

Roosevelt. The opening chapter provides the background for understanding the social conditions of low-income youth in the Depression decade; it is arranged into sections devoted to clothing, debts, evictions, hunger, health and medical care, household conveniences, and death and burials. Chapter 2 brings together letters devoted to many different levels and areas of education, with sections devoted to primary and secondary school, vocational school, the arts, and higher education. The chapter also covers those special milestones and celebrations in the school world, graduations and proms. Chapter 3, on social life, consists of letters on marriage, recreation, and holidays, revealing the ways in which youths struggled to keep the economic crisis from taking the joy out of their interactions with family and friends.

Sizable minorities in Depression America had to contend not only with the new problems wrought by the decade's economic crisis but also with America's old prejudices. Chapter 4, on minorities, covers groups that fit into this category, including African Americans, immigrants, feminists, and the disabled. Note, however, that letters from these groups are also found in other chapters of the book, since I wanted to highlight the minority experience without isolating or ghettoizing minority letter writers. Thus if an immigrant letter seemed to speak more to a general concern, say education, and offered little commentary on the immigrant milieu, that letter is likely to appear in the chapter on education rather than that on minorities.

The book closes with a brief epilogue outlining the ways that Mrs. Roosevelt and her staff reacted to these requests for aid by needy youngsters. The limits of liberal humanitarianism come into view here, as the demands of poor youths proved far too great even for the generous and caring First Lady. The record of Mrs. Roosevelt's material request files suggests that despite the innovative New Deal youth programs that she championed, and her considerable private gifts to the poor, all too many of the cries for help from Depression youth were cries in the wilderness—answered only with form letters.

. . . .

The privacy of the letter writers has been preserved by identifying them only with their initials and hometowns. I have, however, removed even the initials of those who specifically requested in their letters that Mrs. Roosevelt not make their correspondence public. This seemed to me a fair compromise, enabling us to hear the voices of the writers and learn the historical lessons that they teach without placing their names in public view.

There is some overlapping in the topics covered in the letters, since many of the writers expressed multiple requests in their correspondence with Mrs. Roosevelt. It is a function of how disruptive the Depression was, and how needy these youths were, that their letters cannot be fit into one neat historical package.

Out of respect for the authors of the letters and in the interest of preserving the historical authenticity of the sources that they created, I have resisted both the temptation to correct grammatical or spelling errors and the condescending use of [sic]. I trust that readers can discern for themselves where such errors occur. But a word of advice may help the reader navigate through letters employing very unconventional spelling. Phonetic spelling is used frequently: "mabe" for "maybe," "thot" for "thought," "effert" for "afford," "no" for "know," "to" for "too," and sometimes "ar" for "or." There is also a tendency to abbreviate and just leave out letters: "ans" for "answer," "por" for "poor," "appreiate" for "appreciate." The letters' authors were often aware that their limited education left them unable to write standard English, and many apologized for this in their correspondence. If an apology is necessary, however, it should be from the social and educational system of 1930s America, which left many youths too little schooled to spell or communicate well enough to work in white-collar jobs. In this sense too the errors in the letters—all of which are published verbatim—are themselves valuable as markers of class and social inequity in Depression America.

We are way far back in rent. . . . Every week we go to bed one
or two days without anything to eat. My brother and I go down to the
railroad track to pick up coal to keep warm. If only the railroad
pension go through daddy will have steady work on the railroad.
We hardly get enough to wear. . . . I hope mother or dad wont find
out I am writing to you because they don't want to let anyone know
how hard-up we are.

—A. M., an eighth-grade student from Colorado,
asking Mrs. Roosevelt to send her some clothes, May 7, 1935

Children at play in a depressed neighborhood in Pittsburgh, 1933.
(U.S. Housing Authority photo courtesy of Franklin D. Roosevelt Library, Hyde Park, N.Y.)

chapter 1

Ill-Clothed, Ill-Housed, Ill-Fed

When it came to discussing the scope and depth of poverty in Depression America, President Roosevelt did not mince words. In his second inaugural address, on January 20, 1937, FDR had spoken of "millions of families trying to live on incomes so meager that the pall of family disaster hangs over them day by day. . . . I see one third of a nation ill-housed, ill-clad, ill-nourished." The president pledged to eliminate this spreading scourge of poverty, and insisted that "the test of our progress is not whether we add more to the abundance of those who have much; it is whether we provide enough for those who have little." Three years later, speaking before the White House Conference on Children in a Democracy, FDR proved equally candid in assessing the Depression's impoverishment of young Americans:

> I have been called to task, as you all know, because I have reiterated many times something about one-third of America—the ill-clothed, ill-housed, ill-fed—on the ground that I was saying something derogatory. I have been telling the truth, and you good people have sustained me by your statement that more than half of the children of America are in families that do not have enough money to provide fully adequate shelter, food, clothing, medical care, and educational opportunity. Why should we not admit it? By admitting it we are saying we are going to improve things.[1]

This chapter takes its title from FDR's speech. The youth letters published here deal primarily with the lack of basic necessities, including those the president so aptly described in referring to youths who were "ill-clothed, ill-housed, ill-fed."

The White House Conference on Children, which FDR addressed, brought together experts on youth, poverty, and social work in the final year of the Great Depression; it aired a wealth of information that is worth considering as background to the youth letters in this chapter. The proceedings of the conference's session on the economic resources of families and communities enable us to see how Depression America's experts on social policy defined poverty. The first line was drawn at $903 a year, considered adequate to sustain a family of four on an "emergency budget." The biggest expenses were $340 for total food costs ("less than a dollar a day for four people, all of them active"), $168 for housing, $128 for clothing, clothing upkeep, and personal care, and at least $128 for household operation—which included "fuel, light, etc."[2]

Slightly above this emergency level was the "maintenance level" of income, set at $1,261, which included a bit more for each of the essentials, and most notably provided for a family convenience unavailable in the emergency budget, "an indoor bathroom and toilet for [the family's] exclusive use." Neither the emergency nor the maintenance budget was adequate for medical care for a family of four and neither allowed for an automobile. According to the conference's data, over a third of American families "did not have in 1935–1936 incomes that would have purchased the 'emergency' level budget," and over half of American families had incomes below the "maintenance" level budget.[3]

These figures must be borne in mind when one reads the many letters to Mrs. Roosevelt from children and teens who mentioned monthly family incomes of under $100, as they suggest just how deprived these youths were of the necessities of life. The White House conference's findings connect with the poor children's and teens' letters to Mrs. Roosevelt in other ways too: both make clear that youth poverty was especially severe in rural areas, which had proportionately more children than cities did. Rural adults were ill equipped to shoulder their heavier burden since "50% of non-relief farmers received an annual income of $965 or less."[4] Rural poverty was reflected in the letters to Mrs. Roosevelt, as many of the youths making material requests to her came from farms and villages—and about the only advantage that farm families had over their urban counterparts was that some could grow their own food.

Urban poverty was widespread too. About 57.1 percent of urban wage earners had annual incomes ranging from $500 to $1,500. The White House conference estimated that at least half "of the city children in America are in homes where income is too low to purchase for the whole family the items of the 'maintenance' budget."[5] With good reason, then, urban youths were well represented in the requests for material assistance to the First Lady, asking for necessities that they could not afford.

The conference and the letters also show that large family size contributed to distress, as a combination of low income and the high cost of meeting the needs of numerous children often proved economically devastating. According to the final report of the White House conference, "per capita income decreases sharply as the family increases in size."[6] An impressive number of the youth letters to the First Lady came from members of large, needy families. And as the conference pointed out, perhaps harshly, children made demands on a parent's time, and the parent who had to stay home with the children could not be out generating income. The connection between children and poverty could also be seen in the national relief statistics. At the height of the Depression 21 percent of all families with children were on relief, compared with 13.3 percent of families without children.[7]

The data presented at the White House Conference on Children in a Democracy, as well as those from the census taken that same year, make it possible to see precisely the hardships of daily life for those near the bottom of Depression America's social order. At the conference, for instance, a Farm-Housing survey from 1934 was cited revealing that less than 12 percent of farm dwellings had bathtubs and only 8 percent had central heating, 18 percent a home plant or power-line furnishing electricity, and 17 percent running water in the house. The census found that though these conditions were more widespread in rural areas they also occurred in urban areas, where 12 percent of dwellings lacked refrigeration, 23 percent lacked a private bath, and 42 percent had no central heating.[8] Viewing the nation as a whole "the 1940 census included information on 35 million dwelling units: 31 percent lacked running water, 32 percent used an outside toilet or privy, 39 percent did not have a bathtub or shower (even one shared with other tenants), 27 percent lacked any refrigeration equipment."[9]

The meaning of such statistics, as the historian Richard Polenberg notes, was that in Depression America "social status . . . determined not only whether one could enjoy luxuries, but whether one could take a bath, preserve food, or stay warm."[10] This was a world which could generate letters such as that from the twenty-three-year-old daughter of a WPA worker, who wrote in 1938 to express her longing to fulfill the great dream of her teenage years: to own a bathtub. She begged the First Lady to help her realize this dream, since her own poverty had left her discouraged: "I just can't make it come true. . . . It seems that as soon as I have even a little bank-account someone either gets ill or an urgent bill comes up that must be paid."[11] Letters such as this, along with the White House conference and census data on youth and poverty, offer powerful evidence of how profoundly different Depression America was from the more affluent America of today. In our own era, when the young demand computer games, designer clothes, and other luxuries, it is difficult to envision a time in twentieth-century America when youths would dream of owning a bathtub. Clearly it will take an act of historical imagination to understand the stark, crude deprivation of the 1930s, and the ways it shaped the dreams, desires, and fears of Depression youth.

. . . .

The first group of letters in this chapter consists of requests for clothing. This is also the largest group in the chapter, as clothing was by far the item that children and teens requested most often of Mrs. Roosevelt. Clothing was requested so frequently because it figured prominently in the lives of lower-class youths, not only because of its basic function but because it was the most tangible sign of class, one that created great anxiety about status among low-income youths

It is almost impossible today to capture how large clothing loomed to poor Depression youths in their struggle for personal comfort and respectability. When they looked at their world—friends, schoolmates, pictures in newspapers and magazines—they saw person after person clothed better than they were. This constant reminder that they were doing so poorly relative to most of America was as oppressive to them psychologically as the discomfort caused by inadequate clothing was physically.

It is worth noting the very different manner in which middle-class historians today and low-income youth in the Depression era viewed Mrs. Roosevelt. Historians see in Eleanor Roosevelt a liberal political figure, a feminist icon, a mother, wife, grandmother, and humanitarian. When Depression youths looked at Mrs. Roosevelt they saw much of this too, but they—and especially female teens—also literally *saw* the First Lady, saw her clothing and really thought about it. They wrote to her about the "lovely clothes" she wore. They noticed how many outfits she had, and after thinking about this, felt it safe to ask her for her used clothing, since they assumed that she (and her friends) had, as one needy North Carolina teen put it, "so many clothes" that she did "not know what to do with them" all. When they looked at Mrs. Roosevelt's pictures in the press at least some poor teenage girls during the Depression looked the First Lady over for her clothing size.

When photographs of an elegantly attired Eleanor Roosevelt—shown here in the Monroe room of the White House in 1933—appeared in the press, they prompted letters from needy girls who guessed the First Lady's dress size and asked for her old clothes. (Photo Harris & Ewing, Stock Montage, Inc.)

Thus one Massachusetts teen who asked Mrs. Roosevelt to send her some used dresses for her mother noted: "I know anything you may have will fit her because I've seen your picture and she's just like you."[12]

. . . .

Among the images that evoke the Depression experience none do so more powerfully than those dealing with hunger. The photographs of long queues of desperate men waiting on breadlines have become an emblem of Depression America's poverty. This is why in the recently opened FDR memorial in Washington, the sculptor George Segal chose a breadline as the subject for his depiction of Depression-era urban indigence. Hunger was also the specter behind the most haunting Depression image of rural poverty: Dorothea Lange's photograph in 1936 of a migrant mother and her two children at a pea picker's camp in Nipomo, California. As Lange explained: "I saw and approached the hungry and desperate mother, as if drawn by a magnet . . . She said that they had been living on frozen vegetables from the surrounding fields, and birds that the children killed. She had just sold the tires from her car to buy food. There she sat in that lean-to with her children huddled around her."[13]

The hunger of Depression America's young also received its share of documentary attention from writers, such as Louis Adamic. His panoramic work *My America, 1928–1938* included a chapter titled "The Doorbell Rang: 1932." In it, Adamic told of a cold winter morning in New York City, when after hearing the bell he raced out to the front of his house to meet the postman, only to find two children:

> a girl, as we learned afterward, of ten and a boy of eight. Not very adequate for the season and weather, their clothing was patched but clean. They carried school books. "Excuse me, Mister," said the girl in a voice that sounded older than she looked. "but we have no eats in our house and my mother said I should take my brother before we go to school and ring a doorbell in some house"—she swallowed heavily and took a deep breath—"and ask you for something to eat."

Adamic had heard rumors of hungry "children ringing doorbells" to ask for food "in the Bronx, in Harlem, and in Brooklyn, but had scarcely believed it." After inviting his hungry visitors in, Adamic fed them and learned that these children of an unemployed house painter often rang doorbells in pursuit of food when, as the young girl put it, they had "no eats at home."[14]

Such anecdotal evidence of malnutrition among the young has been reinforced by the data gathered by public health officials during the 1930s, especially the early Depression years. In New York City, the Health Department reported in 1932 that 20.5 percent of the schoolchildren it examined were undernourished. The following year, a study in Boston found 17.79 percent of high school students at least 10 percent underweight, and a study in Pennsylvania of more than 500 children found that 23 percent had lost weight over the past six months. By the fall of 1933 Secretary of Labor Frances Perkins was stating publicly that "somewhere in the neighborhood of one fifth of all preschool and school children are showing signs of poor nutrition. . . . No amount of statistics can take the place of a lamb chop and a glass of milk at the right moment."[15]

Perkins's words echoed those of FDR about one-third of the nation's children being ill fed. Some letters that poor youths sent to Mrs. Roosevelt, including those in this chapter's second section, demonstrate that hunger was a real threat. But on the other hand, it is striking how rare it was for young letter writers to appeal to the First Lady for either food or money for food. There is no way to say with confidence why such appeals were so rare.

Possible explanations may be gleaned from the scholarship on the social history of eating in America and on Depression-era poverty and relief. Harvey Levenstein, the leading historian of the American diet of the Depression decade, has argued that FDR, Perkins, and public health officials vastly overstated the extent of malnutrition during the 1930s. He attributes this tendency toward overstatement to the relatively undeveloped state of nutritional science in Depression America, which left public officials with only crude and inaccurate means of measuring malnutrition. For example, the widely used method of estimating malnutrition rates based on whether students were below the average weight for their height and age "ignored hereditary and ethnic variations" and thus tended to inflate malnutrition estimates. Levenstein also pointed to a drop in deaths from vitamin deficiency diseases during the Depression decade and hospital reports indicating that by the mid-1930s there were no signs of widespread malnutrition.[16] If we are to believe Levenstein, relatively few letters came to Mrs. Roosevelt from hungry children because there were not nearly so many of these unfortunate youths as FDR himself had thought. The paucity of such letters might also be seen as a sign of the New Deal's success in administering relief to the poor. James T. Patterson, a historian of poverty, has argued that New Deal relief dollars helped stave off "widespread malnutrition and unrest." He points out that by February 1934 New Deal relief agencies were supporting 28 million Americans, some 22 percent of the population, insuring that many poor people at least had enough to eat.[17]

Before embracing such optimistic conclusions about the New Deal and the containment of hunger, however, it might be wise to consider the nature of the letter-writing process itself, and how it might have led to an under-representation of those without sufficient food. To write to Mrs. Roosevelt one needed to be literate and to afford pen, paper, envelope, and stamps. If requesting and expecting to be sent material aid by return mail, one also needed to have some kind of home or return address. Such requirements might well have excluded those who were out of range of much of the New Deal relief network, the poorest of the poor, migrant workers and the homeless. Writing letters also required a degree of hopefulness that may have deterred those who had been desperately poor even before the Depression. And it was these groups that even Levenstein agrees were more likely than the rest of the population to be suffering from malnutrition.[18] In any case, the letters from hungry youths in this chapter, though representing only a small minority of the correspondence sent to Mrs. Roosevelt, are a reminder that those at the bottom of Depression America's social order were in some cases making do without enough to eat.

Although malnutrition came up infrequently in the youth letters to Mrs. Roosevelt, other health problems appeared often. It was common for letter writers to mention that their poverty had been brought on by the illness of a parent, which burdened families with doctor's and hospital bills, while disrupting or ending the earning power of the disabled adults. This connection between poor health and poverty was reflected in the relief statistics: one out of 20 families on relief but only one out of every 250 middle-class families were headed by disabled adults unable to work. A Milbank study in 1933 found that the illness rate was 60 percent higher "among persons whose economic status had dropped from that of reasonably comfortable circumstances in 1929 to poverty in 1932 than that of their more fortunate neighbors who suffered no such decline." This same study found that the sickness rate was 40 percent higher in families of the unemployed than in families with full-time wage earners. Although such studies indicate that the poor needed health care more than the rest of the population, this care was often inaccessible to them. While the average family in Depression America spent $59 annually on medical care, the poor spent less than half this amount.[19] The letters in the health section of this chapter are a reminder that it was not only physicians but dentists and optometrists whose services were out of reach of poor children and teens.

The chapter's letters about evictions, debts, and household conveniences voice the concerns of youths from the "ill-housed" sector of America, of whom FDR had said, without exaggerating, that "the pall of family disaster hangs over them day by day." The imminent loss of the family home caused anguish which crossed generational lines, as did other unmanageable debts, yielding letters which speak of shame and tears in both parents and children. The letters about household conveniences, much like those about clothing, find the young keenly aware of the contrast between their own poverty and the more comfortable home lives of others, who had the furniture and other amenities about which the poor could only dream.

In his second inaugural address and his speech to the White House Conference on Children in a Democracy, FDR focused quite understandably on what Americans needed to live with dignity. But as suggested by this chapter's section on burials, poverty literally followed families to the grave—so much so that even the young had to concern themselves with their family's inability to afford proper burial. One finds teenagers, then, asking Mrs. Roosevelt not for items for their own lives, but for aid in attending to the deaths of their parents.

CLOTHING

. . . .

■ February 26, 1934
Petroleum, West Virginia
Dear Mrs. Roosevelt,

I just wondered If you ever received a letter from a little girl like me. I am eleven years old the 24 of March. This is my fifth year in school. I think I will soon be ready for sixth Grade. I have got five perfect certificates and one gold star of honor. I have . . . a hard way of getting what edication I have. But I expect to keep on trying. I have to walk two mile and a half to school through the mud. My Father is almost blind. We have no income of any form. Father has never recieved one cent of the money that the unemployed is supposed to get. We sure could use it. We have been told by many people that you was very kind to the poor and neady. So I thought I would ask you if you would or could send me a few things to wear. I wear size 12 year old dresses and a 14 year old coat. I am four feet and six inches tall and weigh 80 pounds. I also would like to have a pair of shoes size 3½ wide weidth. I would be the happiest person in the world. If I would recieve a package from you for my birthday. You would never miss this small amount

A teen from Ohio included these sketches, advertisements, and specifications with her letter to Mrs. Roosevelt in 1936, to show the First Lady the clothes that she hoped to receive from her. (From the collection of the Franklin D. Roosevelt Library, Hyde Park, N.Y.)

I have asked for. My relation helped to put President Roosevelt where he is. I dont ask for anything fine just serviceable. I do hope you will fix me up a little package and mail to me at once. My friends will be surprised.

Mrs Roosevelt please dont have this printed or broadcasted, as some of my people have radios and all take papers and I dont want any of them to know I asked you to send me the things. But God knows I will remember you. And you surely will be rewarded. I send you my love and best wishes.

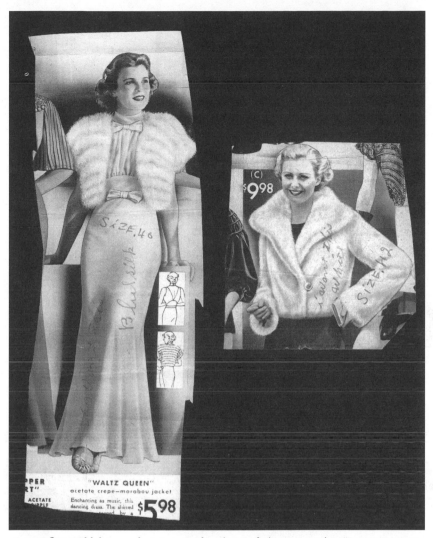

A teen from Oklahoma who wrote to the First Lady in 1937, saying "I want to go to School and hadn't no dresses to ware to School," included these advertisements with her letter, her clothing size penciled into the ads. (From the collection of the Franklin D. Roosevelt Library, Hyde Park, N.Y.)

[Clairton, Pennsylvania
Acknowledged Mar. 1, 1934]
Dear Mrs. Roosevelt,

I'm sorry this had to be written on funny paper. But honest its very funny to live I wished sometimes that I were dead. It was Sunday when I wrote this letter to you. I had just come up stairs to sleep I have been crying, so please excuse my writing. On Sunday, I sit around and cry myself to sleep, I'm not aloud out never. I'm always in the house, no body comes to our house, because its so old fashioned and not a place for fun. I'm not aloud to buy books like True Stories or any other kind. I'm sick I hate life. I go with my girl friends to school sometimes But they don't appreciate me because I'm poor and haven't got clothes like they do I wished and wish for clothes I hope that some day I will enter a contest and win some money . . . I hate every thing now because life seems blind I love my mother dearly my dad works 3 dys a wk he gets $40 a mth. But he has lot of old bills to pay from before when he did not work I wish I had work I would help my dad although he is mean to me As old as I am I still get beaten Well you would say (Why) because sometimes he gets drunk and starts to Beat us for silly things I'm sick And tired Dad buys me some things once in a great while. But how long I only have 3 dresses for school. One of my girl friends gives me shoes But O God Bless her. Please help me, Id like to get some nice clothes and some furniture for our house I want to brace up I want to go with my friends and show them kindness. I want to cooperate well with others . . . I want to be loved . . . Please Ans to M. S. . . . because I have a cousin that has the same name & she might get the Answer

Please Answer Soon.

Im 15 year old In 8th grade

Don't show this letter to *nobody* Please

Won't you help me dear Please send me some money so I can do something I want you to write to me as a friend Please write/Answer I would like to have an answer. Thank You.

I'll be

Your Friend forever

Excuse my errors

■ Dows, Iowa

March 24, 1934

Dear Mis. Roosevelt

I am a girl 14 yrs. old I am asking a favor of you & a big one to. Will you please send me some cloths or some money for some If you can. My girl friend wrote to. we both don't have any cloths. The kids at school all make fun of you if you can't dress just so please let me here from you & please dont publish this letter or us girls shall get a terriable beaten.

May god bless you

■ Brownsville, Penn.

May 25, 1934

Honorable Mrs. Roosevelt,

My uncle has been telling me of the help you have been giving to the miners and their family's and I am an miners daughter. Age 18. I never finished school Because I was ill. My heart was bad. It has been well for the past two years. But I cant afford to go to school as my father is unable to work But draws a government pension which is enough to support us but as we have a large family it is not enough to dress us. I have earned my tuition for Business College working for a lady in our town. I visited a girls club in California and one of the Subjects was the Description of the White House and it was said the attic of the White House was over flowing with discarded clothing if this is true and you would send me some I am rather . . . clever with a needle and I would be forever grateful

A. E.

■ Barboursville, W. Va.

August, 23, [1934]

Dear President & Wife;

This is the first time I or Any of my people wrote Any president. And I am here to ask you for $8.00 to get me a winter coat. This may seem very strange for a girl 12 years old to do but my father is a poor honest working Laundry man and he works on a percentage a week we have 10 in our family and my father does not have enough money to get him a bottle of Beer. He is a democrat and did all he could to have you voted. The N.R.A. [National Recovery Administration] is coming alone fine. As little as I am I know just as much about depression as a grown person. I'm 12 years old and am in the 8th grade curly hair Brunette & brown eyes & fair complexion & weigh 76 lbs. Hoping to hear from you soon I remain your true Democrat

J. A. G.

P.S. We would have loved if Mrs. Roosevelt when she was visiting Logan to come around to our small town she was only about 60 miles from here.

■ Union City Pa

Sept 5, 1934

Dear Mrs Roosevelt

How are you? I am just fine. I am just asking you to send me a dress my father can't effert to even get me a pair of stockings My dad only works

1 day my brother don't work can't find a job I don't have no shoes to wear to school I am thirteen yrs old get size for a dress 14 and shoes 5½ my father can't hardly effort to buy us children food to eat. There is 10 of us children I don't have one pair of stockings to wear Well my dear Mrs Roosevelt I hope you send them stuff for I'll be waiting for the package. I never had a nickle in my life for my self my dears Mrs Roosevelt will you please I always have to cry for clothes I'am ragged going to church and School I'am waiting for the package.

Good Bye Mrs Roosevelt

J. T.

Royse, City, Texas

Sept. 6, 1934

Dear Friend:

Well I don't suppose you know who I am. But I'm a 16 year old mother-less girl that has to work hard for all she gets. I have a brother & a sister & daddy We are working at day labor for a living and don't get much of that to do. In the winter I could piece quilts if I had any scraps. We are trying to keep off the relief this winter so we are keeping every penny we can to buy groceries this winter, Whether we have sufficient clothes or not. We haven't even enough furniture. We haven't any bedsteads, a stove, or cabinet. some of our Neighbors are letting us use their stove, cabinet, & one bedstead. I thought you might have some old clothes, coats, and shoes. or any kind of clothing you could send to us. I have read so much about your kindness I know if you have any you will send them. I would send some money for postage but haven't any. Address to your loving friend Miss D. H.

Alliance, Ohio

December 5, 1934

My dear Mrs. Roosevelt:

. . . I go to the Alliance High School. I am eighteen years old and a senior.

We live on a small farm near Freeburgh Ohio. My father has been out of work for five years. A girl can't get many small necessities in life when there is no income. At noon I walk down town and see the pretty clothes but can not get them.

The main reason for my writing this letter is to ask you what you do with your old clothes. My mother makes over what few I get but that isn't many. There is three from our family in High School so there isn't much chance for me or sisters & Brother getting any. I wonder if you would send me your old ones so mother could make me a couple of dresses for School or anything. They would be greatly appreciated I am sure.

I am five feet six, wear 5½ shoes, dark brown eyes and hair medium complexion and skinny. I weigh only 100 pounds.

I am writing this letter in school and have one eye on the teacher so I am not Writing as nice as I can. . . .

P.S. You may wonder why the fancy stationery but it was given to me for my birthday. I hope you can send me a few that aren't needed by you.

(Please do not Publish this)

■ Double Springs, Ala.
Dec 27, 1934
Dear Mrs. Roosevelt,

I know you get letters like this almost every day. But here is one I hope and pray will be answer. I live in Ala. on a farm, and it seem mighty hard for us. we have so much sickness in our home We have a farm. But it seems if there isn't something done we will lose it. We owe lots of Hospital Bills. Wasnt for that we would Be in a better shape. My father and one of my sister had a operation the same year. My mother and father is in very bad Health. I am the oldest child at home and I am only 16. Mrs. Roosevelt if you please will send us a few dollars not to pay our debts But to get us a few clothes to wear. if you can't send us none, please answer my letter and tell me why you can't. if you possible can just send us a little bit. don't never think it will be wasted for it won't. I am sure it would be put to good use. we want to thank your Husband Mr. Roosevelt for his good plan he has planned for us poor people. We know it is for the poor people good. But it seems it hasn't reached us yet much. Mrs. Roosevelt this is my first time to write any one for any money. or any of the familie. But I know you are very very rich. And we have to work hard. I don't dread working if we could only get one thing much for what we raise. Now if you please will send us a few dollars and it will gratley Be appirshed. And we never can and never will thank you enough for it. Please answer my letter.

Your friend that lives in Ala.
E. B.

■ Park Rapids, Minn.

January 6, 1935

My dear Mrs. Roosevelt,

My first thot was to write to the President, himself, for I know him to be a very kind man, but, unfortunately a very busy man too. So now I am writing to you instead in the hope that you will once more show your kindness in making me happy.

Understand please, that I am not accustomed to ask for or take charity, but so long my desire to have the nice things most other girls enjoy has gone unfulfilled that I now ask you, whom I like many others consider a literal fairy-godmother, if it would be an atrocity for me to ask you for a snow suit?

I have a pair of second hand skiis and something that answers the purpose of a sled, but I am actually ashamed to appear before my friends—join their fun and sliding parties in my tattered overalls and old coat, both of which I have sadly outgrown. I ask for your simpathy tho' I little expect it, because you have never been deprived of the nice things of life by a stubborn depression that is taking its own sweet time about saying adios. Perhaps you think it an extravagent thing to ask for? Not a real necessity? But I have been forced to be satisfied with bare necessities for so long that I often revolt and indulge in a usually useless longing for—a snow suit. And of course many other things but a snow suit especially—of any kind and description but preferably "different"—if I may be choosy.

I am sixteen years old, five feet four inches tall, and a senior in High School. Just between you and me, in my next letter I hope to inclose a clipping from our county paper announcing the High School honors. My honors??

Sincerely,

C. B.

P.S. If you cannot send me a full suit, maybe I can do without the jacket—fix up something here maybe. But please. Oh please.

■ Scotts bluff Nbr.

Feb. 10, 1935

Dear Mrs. Roosevelt

I am sending you this few lines to tell you to do me a favor. But please do not tell no body nor put it on the paper. please. Well I am a girl of 15 years old. I go to school. But wish for two things my father work on the relief and what he gets for the food and we can't get no clothing and you kown when you go to school. like to have something fair to ward. the other girl are all dressed good and Gee! they have so good and pratty permannet and good dresses that they have. Gee! If I had some where to work to get me a permemat I would go. just to get me one. But I can't get no work. Well. Mrs Roosevelt could you do me a favor I know you have some old dresses that you don't want no more would mind giving them to me please for me and my sisther and If you have an old coat you don't used no more I have one but it is no good no more. and If you give one you don't want no more I'll do a little praying to God up in heavents. so that he bless you for your kind heart and our good Prisd Mr. Roosevelt. and yous more for your are doing for us that are poor. Now mrs. Roosevelt I must close with love and honor to our president and mrs. Roosevelt from a franid Now don't for get my need please & don't put it in the aid of papers. please thin all about me asking so plase do that. my sisther is 17 years old.

Your truly

■ [Rushsylvania, Ohio]
March 29, 1935
Dear Mrs Roosevelt.

I am writing you a little letter this morning. Are you glad it spring I am. For so manny poor people can raise some more to eat. You no what I am writing this letter for Mother said Mrs Roosevelt is just a God mother to the world And I though ma be you had some old cloths you no Mother is a good sewer and all the little girls are getting Easter dresses And I though that you had some you no papa could wear Mr Roosevelt shirt and cloth I no. My papa like Mr Roosevelt And Mother said Mr Roosevelt carry his worries with a smile You no he is always happy. You no we are not living on the relief we live on a little farm. Papa did have a job and got laid on 5 yr ago so we save and got two horses and 2 cows and hogs so we can all the food stuff we can ever thing to eat some time we don't have ever thing but we live. But you no it so hard to get cloth. So I though mabe you had some. You no what you though was no good Mother can make over for me I am 11 yr old I have 2 brother and a sister 14 yr old. I wish I could see you I no I would like you both. And shoes mother wears 6 or 6½ and papa wear 9. We have no car or no phone or Radio papa he would like to have a radio but he said there is other thing he need more. Papa is worried about his seed oats. And one horse is not very good. But ever one has't to worie. I am send this letter with the pennie I get to take to Sunday school mother give me one so it took 3 week Cause mother would think I better not ask for things from the first Lady. But Mother said you was an angle for doing so much for the poor. And I though that would be all rite this is some paper my teacher gave for X-mas. My add is C. V. . . .

■ Buffalo, N.Y.
   Jan. 6, 1936
   Dear Mrs. Roosevelt,
   I heard that you have been very good to the poor, and I am writing this letter to see if you can help me. I had to leave school because I didn't have any clothes to wear. I will be very thankfull to you if you can gather some clothes sizes 18 or 20.
   I am 17 years of age and was in my 3rd year of high school when I have to leave. My height is 5 ft. 4½ in. and weigh 135½ lbs.
   My father is working and making a little money but we are barely living. He has 3 children besides myself to support. I've looked for work every day but I don't seem to have any luck. I am still wearing my summer coat and have a very bad cold.
   All I am asking for is a few dresses and a winter coat.
   Thanking you for any thing you can do
   P.S. Please do not have this letter published in any way, as I am writing this unknown to my parents.

■ High Point, N.C.
   [received Jan. 22, 1937]
   Dear Mrs. Roosevelt,
   If it does not bore you too much to get letters from poor people, please read this. I am a very poor girl, 17 years of age. Dady works in a veneer plant. He makes very little and there are six of us for him to provide for. You can imagin how hard it is for us, wiht house rent, grocery bills, water bills and then have to clothe us on what is left of his wages. I never have any spending money, as other girls do. We use kerosene lamp, because we are not able to use Electric lights, we sometimes burn candles. I am sure you have never known the heart of a poverty stricken girl. I see so many girls of my own age wearing pretty cloths, it just makes my heart ache to know that I can't afford to even dress decent. I only have 3 dresses that are fit to wear in public. One of these was given to me by a friend. I made one of them myself. I get the cloth off of a remnant table at Penney's store here at High Point. I paid $1.98 for the other one last winter. I wore these dresses

all last winter and this winter. Just wearing the same dresses over and over, while my friend's get new ones real often.

Please pardon me for being so awkward in writing to you, as you can very readily see that I dont have much education. You must also forgive me for being so personal, but I am so worried about my present condition that I felt like I would not dare to ask you for a new dress, no that would be entirely too much. I treasure very highly even a $1.98 dress. I know you could send me one of yours and never miss it. You always have such lovely clothes. I have always wished I could have just one dress as pretty as some that you wear. I am really in need. I just wish there was some way I could work for you to prove to you my appresheation. You are so sweet and kind I know you won't dissapoint me.

I am sure that you have friends there, who perhaps have so many clothes that they don't know what to do with them. Tell them about me and please try to get me some dresses that have been already worn, I will be so proud of them, I could never express my appresheation to you. Send me anything that can still be worn. I can were a size 16 dress.

I would like to hear from you at once.

Thank you very much.

If you are not able to help me at present, please write to me.

You may rest assured that I have told you the truth, because I am a Christian. I believe you will trust me. If there is a doubt in your mind about this write to Revern C. K. G. . . . for further information.

My name is A. S. . . . I just put the word Important on the envelope so you would be sure to read this letter.

Miss A. S.

P.S. Please mail me the dresses, if you can get up any for me.

Please let me hear from you at once. I trust that you won't take this letter as an insult.

◾ Wallins, Kentucky
[acknowledged Jan. 28, 1937]
Mrs. Roosevelt

I am a boy of 15 and am a sophomore in Wallins Hi school.

I want to borrow $30 from you at 6% interest to be payed back within two years. I want the money to buy me a suit as I am tired to being a wallflower and not being invited to parties.

You may think I am very egotisical (pardon spelling) but my mother gets a check of $30 every mo. from the government and this buys our groceries and there is very little left for clothes.

You think back to when you were in high school, and you'll see what it is not to have any clothes.

I solemnly pledge to pay you back within 2 yrs.

Yours,

C. H.

P.S. I am 5 ft 6 in, tall

chest 36"

pants size 30–32

Springfield, Mo.

December 5, 1937

Dear Mrs. Roosevelt:

I suppose you will think it quiet funny, to receive a letter from a little down-hearted girl in Springfield.

Well, as I was laying here in bed, only able to lay on my back, I thought of you, who might be one who could help me. I have tried, but in vain. I am trying to go to school, but as I have had a very bad attack of appendisidis I have been out of school amost two weeks. Seeing the Dr. takes every little bit of money, we managed to bring in, and that isn't much. If I was even able to attend school, I rather believe I couldn't as my clothes wouldnt suit. I attend the big High School here in town, and there are around 3,000 students attending.

I am 16 years of age, have gray eyes, blonde hair, fair complexion, and am 5 ft 5 in tall and weigh 120 lbs. All my friends like me but, Dear Mrs. President, Could you imagine the feelings, of a lonely child, who is sure she could look as neat and pretty as the others who take part in everything, if only she had barely a few of the necessities of life during these school days. As it is, I see them all, dress in their beautiful party dresses, go to parties and enjoy themselves, and the fact remains, that I hurry home and then cry myself to sleep, on being so down-hearted and blue. They invite me to their parties, yet I can not go. Then they Know the reason. And as I lay here in bed tired and weary, praying that Dear God will look down and help me, my thoughts come to you and God alone, at these moments. Here I think of my Dear Daddy who tries, but in vain, and my blessed Mother, who does every thing in the world for me, and would give her life, but neither can she provide me with the necessities of life in my school days. I do not expect to do as some of them do, but if I could only have *some* decent clothes, and other necessities and enjoy a few pleasures, that only come once in life.

Only those that have had experience, know of the pains and sufferings I have to bear, as I lay for hours and hours on my back in my bed begging God to help, and now it seems as if God has told me that you might be one who could, and would help me.

Dear Mrs. Roosevelt, please do not accept me as a beggar, because I'm not, but as I write this I say, "Oh Lord, Let me not be dissapointed again." Yet I'm willing to give or take what the Lord would have me too, and still live in hopes.

Dear friend, if you can, and if you want to make a child the happiest one in the world, please help me, and let me hear from you soon. You don't know, you don't see, or wouldn't realize how happy I could be, if only I could have a friend come to my house, as others do, and enjoy a few of the many pleasures offered in this world. You don't know how I would appreciate Your help, and Your reward in the future as Dear God can give You, and as I Keep striving, and going on to school, I hope, and truely believe that someday, success will be mine, and those who have helped may be rewarded. I have some dear little sisters and a sweet mother & Father, who would also be happy. No one Knows I am writing You, but my only self, and I'm living in hopes with God, that You will answer personally to me and help me.

A Blessed Friend

Miss M. M.

■ Westminster, S.C.

Feb. 21, 1938

My Dear Mrs. Roosevelt,

I guess you are surprised to hear from a South Carolina girl, but hear I am writing to "The First Lady" it must be wonderful to be so glorious and famous as you are I see your picture often in papers and magazines, and you look so kind and pleasing. I read the story "This is my life" that you wrote, it was just grand.

I am a poor girl, my birthday is Wednesday Feb. 23 I will be 17 years old. I never get any nice clothes like other girls, I don't get to go to parties, dances, movies, or have boy friends my parents wont let me. Dozens of boys call for me to go out but Daddy meets them at the door with no, no, not braging or anything, but I am nice looking if I had some pretty clothes to dress up in. I have blonde hair large round blue eyes, fair complection, am about 5 ft. tall wiegh 120 lb. wear a 6 slipper. I wonder if you would be so kind as to help me get some spring clothes I need so much. Only a few dollars will help me so much.

I was in the 10th grade at school and had to stop and go to work in a cotton mill and don't make enough to Buy my self clothes So please, please, Dear Mrs. "First Lady" won't you help me since you have so much I wish you could see how the poor people around here have to live. Will you help me please let me know by return mail I will be ever so greatful

Please don't let this letter get in the paper.

Sincerely,

Please, I hope I can depend on you to help me. I know you will you are so kind.

■ Birmingham, Ala.

July 27, 1938

Dear Mrs. Roosevelt.

I'm writing you in regard of this W.P.A. work which my Father works on. He did make $36 per month but I think he will get a raise of $4.80 on the month But he has five to support Three children and I'm the oldest one fifteen years of age but to young to hold a job. I can't go to Church or Sunday school any more for the need of clothes.

Mother and daddy dont go either because their clothes are to bad.

If you have any clothes that you dont want mother can make them fit us. Please Mrs Roosevelt dont mention this over the radio or in the papers. my school mates would nag me to death. but if you think its false call or write. Relief Headquarters Birmingham.

Thanking you I am

■ Rogersville, Mo.

Jan. 16, 1939

Dear Mrs Rosevelt:

I am a girl 19 years old and love pretty cloths but never could have them we are poor people and I am writing to you to see if you would send me some of your cast off clothing please do Mrs Rosevelt. We live in what I would call a high headed community and the girls all have nice cloths and make fun of me because I don't have if they knew I wrote this letter to you they would laugh sure enough. I can't even go to Sunday school on Sunday on account of cloths and I havn't got decent shoes or dresses to wear to look for a job. so if you will send me some of your dresses, slips, brassieres, panties and a coat because I do not have a coat at all, and if you have any shoes, Mrs Rosevelt I am telling the truth before the Lord. thats its pitiful the way I'm looked down on. You may think I'm stretching things but I'm not. and maybe I can pay you back the money it took to bring them some time so please do mrs. Rosevelt, please do. I would sure write you a big letter of thanks Mrs. Rosevelt you may have recieved other letters like this one. You may think I'm putting up a big fish story but I sure telling the truth and my dady & step mother would appreciate any thing you & Mr. Rosevelt might send them. so please send us some things if you will we will be three smiling people and Mrs Rosevelt please send them as soon as possible and write me a card a day or two before so I can be at the mail box to get it. so I will close with a million thanks and with lots of love

M. K.

I have your picture in the paper me & you are about the same size I can wear your cloths O.K.

■ Poplar Bluff, Missouri
March 8, 1939
Dear Mrs. Roosevelt,

I don't know how to begin, but this is my last hope is through you. And I do know your rich, and I'm poor. I'm a girl of 14 yrs and don't want my parents to know I'm writing this letter to you. They would never quit Punishing me for it, so before I start If you don't care to do this, Please destroy this letter and don't let my parents know, I'll begin, I never had a spring coat and Mother said she couldn't buy one for me this spring, Most of the other girls in school has one or going to get one. And oh, I wish for one so bad Would you please send me/ And when I get to work I'll pay you for it, I just won't get one any other way. I wear size 12 in Junior. Please don't Publish my letter My parents would hurt me so

Waiting
Your friend

■ Mena, Arkansas
June 3, 1939
Dear Mrs Roosevelt

I certainly am ashamed to sink so low as to have to write this. Please don't say any thing about this to any one, please.

Mrs Roosevelt, I have written to you for help if you will help me. My father has a job in the little plainer here and the largest check he has ever drawn was fifteen dollars. There is four in our family. I am seventeen years old and my brother will be eleven tomorrow. We use three or four dollars for groceries and Dad spends the rest at the pool hall. I have been trying to get work for about three months and I can't find a thing. Maybe it is because I look so shaby. I like pretty clothes as much or more than most girls but what few I do get are on credit.

Mrs. Roosevelt, why I have written is, I plead that if you will, would you send me ten dollars for a few cloths. please would you. If you would I will tell God how good you were. please believe this for it is the truth. Honest it is.

Sometimes Dad works at a cafae for a dollar, but he eats it up.

Please *never* say a word about this to *any one. please.* If my parents find out about this they would kill me.

If you intend to answer please do so immediately for I will be in suspence. I am still trying for a job and if you help me and I *ever* get work I will try to pay it back.

Respectively yours,

■ Epps, La.

Nov. 18, 1939

Dear Mrs. Roosevelt,

As I have heard some information on you buying up sweaters and coats for the people who haven't any coats or sweaters to wear this winter, I would like to know if it is true or not. If it is I wish you would remember me and my little sisters and brothers when you start sending them out to others. I go to the Epps High School of West Carroll Parrish in Louisiana. I have three (3) brothers and two (2) sisters. All going to school except one smaller brother. We need these sweaters to wear to school. I don't have a coat for the winter so I would like very much to get a package containing one for me and sweaters for my buds and sisters. This would be a good Thanksgiving present for us youngsters. I am a senior at Epps, La. school. Sweaters to fit 18, 16, 14, 12, 7, and 5 years will be sent by you, I am hoping. If you will send these all in my name. We are just like orphans as our dad is sick all time and mother can't work and earn living for eight people. Although we farm we didn't make much cotton due to land acreage cut short. If this is not true about this matter on the sweaters and coats, maybe you can just send me one. You can spare a little money for a coat for a poor girl who wants to finish school and look decent as the other girls. Maybe you have an old coat you could send me or some old clothes. Please try to please me by sending a package by Thanksgiving addressed to the following address. If you send me this you will be doing your deed for one time, I know. This is all I know, I am one of your friends at sixteen years of age. Weight 130 pounds.

Your truly,

(Miss) M. C.

■ New Bedford, Mass.

[Acknowledged Mar. 12, 1940]

My dear Mrs. President Roosevelt

Please forgive me for writing and asking you this big favor from the bottom of my heart. Please don't tell anybody I wrote you this so nobody can make fun of me. My mother is not working for a long long time, she has had 7 operations and we have living on welfare getting $4.00 a week for me & my mother. She has tried so hard to get work but its hard she's tried to get on W.P.A. but its hard. We pay 3.50 rent every week because rents are awful high now. Now the favor I'd like to ask you is please if you have any clothes you don't want if you could please send to my mother & me. I don't care so much for me because my mother needs it most she's been wearing a thin thin coat with 2 sweaters all torn and she has made over for me most all her things. I know anything you may have will fit her because I've seen your picture & she's just like you. I am 14 yrs. old & have left school to help my mother at home. My mother & I live alone as father went away with another woman & are divorced. So please I pray Mrs President if you have any thing we would be so thankful for & please for the love of God keep this plea a secret between us two. I have prayed for a job but N.Y.A. is only for girls 16 over. Please don't be mad at me but people make fun of mommy the way she dresses but we haven't got it. I hope to hear from you soon. May God Bless you & our President & the little old Mother we see in pictures. I love her too.

Forever Your True friend

X X X X X X X X X X X X

God Bless You and all your Family

[The writer draws three X's enclosed in circles, marking them "One for Pres., one for you, one for Mother."]

. . . .

■ Gettysburg, S.Dak.

Jan 8, 193[4]

Dear Mrs Roosevelt:

A young girl from a God forlorn country is writing you. I will be 16 years old Jan 16. We are so poor we haven't hardly enough to eat. I have 2 sisters and 1 brother and father. Mother is dead over 5 years. She was killed in a railroad collision. I have to keep house. We haven't had a crop for 8 years. We get about ¼ can of cream in two weeks and that is only 10 cents so we can't buy anything. Eggs we haven't any. Would you be so very kind and send us a little money to buy a few neccarry things. I suppose you get many letters like this but if you can please send a little I would thank you from the bottom of my heart.

As ever your Friend.

A. N.

■ Daleville, Ala.

Feb 12. 1934

Dear Mrs Roosevelt,

I want to write you and ask a favor of you for mother said you would help us. She said she thanked God for such people as you and our president. I am a little 13 year old boy the only boy in our family of seven four of us have been in school. I have just finished the sixth grade and a sister of mine have finished the ninth and dady just can't get us books for we have not been able to farm now in two years and havent got anything except dady gets two days a week on the road the CWA [Civil Works Administration] work. I dont want to be a beger. I just want to ask you to please loan me fifty dollars to buy a mule with so we can raise us something to eat at home. seven of us have to live and pay house rent out of just four and a half a week and you know we live hard and don't get scarcely any clothes at all if you will lend it to me we will do our dead level best to pay it back this fall please reply by return mail.

Well good by

from your friend

C. D.

■ Salida Colo.

May 7—1935

Dear Mrs Rooselvelt,

I was just wondering, if you could do something, so I can graduate from the Eight grade, It will take about $10.00 and then I got to make my confirmation and there is three of my other brothers, too, and one sister, beside me. The work relief don't do right here, they give those girls in the relief office $20 a week, and they only support theirself and they give a man with, a family of seven, $48.00 a month, last month they gave us $46.00, when he should get $58 at the least. How much do you think a family of seven should get? Mother hadn't no light, now because we didn't have enough money to paid for them . . . and we are way far back in rent. Some men here get $6.00 a day, and they only got two or three in a family, because they are the boss or timekeeper. I think if Mr. Rooselvelt get the old-age Pension [i.e. Social Security] in it will be a lot better than the relief work. Every week we go to bed one or two days without anything to eat. My brother and I go down to the railroad track to pick up coal to keep warm. If only the Railroad Pension go through daddy will have steady work on the railroad. We hardly got enough to wear, we have to wash out our clothes and put them back on. Gosh! Mother can't get a haircut, her hair looked terrible.

If the Old Age Pension go in these girls got to go out and do something else, beside working on the relief. Gosh! I used to be able to take care of baby but now the big girls get the job, we used to only get .10 cent, to take care of a little girl, but the girls, that take care her, now get .50 a day and .50 cents a night. I read a lot a about you in the papers we get from the neighbors. My mother and Dad don't know I am writing to you. Please answer as soon as possible. Gosh! May 15th we have to try to make our confirmation if we can get some clothes and a dollar each too. I hope mother or dad wont find out I writing to you, because they don't want to let anyone, know how hard-up we are.

Please Please write immediately. I heard you help the poor peoples. I wish God blessed you, and lct you luck. Please answer as soon as you received this letter.

Your's Very Truly,

Miss A. M.

■ Wellesley Hills, Massachusetts
  May 18, 1938
  Dear Mrs. Roosevelt,

Perhaps you may not be able to help me but nevertheless I am appealing to you. My daddy is out of work and our home is gone. I mean daddy is in New Hampshire trying to earn a little money, Buddy, my brother, is living with my grandmother and I am with a friend of my mother's in Wellesley. I want a home. We need money! Can't you help us? Last night when I went to see daddy, he hadn't had a decent meal. I don't want him to go hungry. And Buddy won't get half a chance where he is living. I am only sixteen and there is nothing much that I can do. With a little money my father could get back on his feet and maybe start a new rink somewhere. You see he runs a rollar skating rink. Bud and I are whizzes at it—almost.

Do you know that when Buddy was four he was paralized from the hips down and he couldn't see or talk and now he is the fastest rollar skater in Nashua. He had infintile paralysis once. But you can't keep a good man down. You should see him now. But I can't make a man of him if we are separated all the time. Please, you wouldn't miss a little money would you? I hate to ask for money because it sounds so much like begging. Maybe it would be better if I said borrow.

You seem so nice and understanding that's why I have turned to you. Please keep this confidential, won't you? Nobody knows I am doing this and I don't care to have anyone know. You understand just how I feel, don't you. I hope I am not imposing too much upon your kindness but we need your help.

Sincerely,

■ Chicago Illinois
  March 30, 1939
  To Mrs Roosevelt.

This letter may not be plesant but I am writting to you not because I want to but I've got to. My father lost his job a few months ago with the W.P.A. Why. because he is not a citizen. We are seven in the family. I am the oldest 16 years old. The smallest is 5 years old. My father when working use to get 85.00 dollars a month with the W.P.A. Now that he lost his job he hasn't even seven cents to his name. Not even enough to take a street car if he wanted to go and see at some other work. (Let me tell you some thing. On Thanksgiving Day my mother was crying and couldn't get up from bed because she couldn't see us like the way we were. We on that day had to eat (Neck bones) while others had (fried chicken) like you did. Then came Christmas we had a few lbs of chicken (yes, because my mother didn't want to see us like the same way we were on Thanksgiving. Yes my mother had to mark it down at the bucher. That is what my family is up against. My brother and I some times even went to bed with out supper because we understand that the others need it more that we do. . . . I happen to be an ambitous person. I wrote in my spare time two storys which I think is going to do my family a great deal good. But in order to sell it I need money for train fare. There it is again money. I need your help as soon as possible.

Thank You

D. D.

Ill be glad to pay you back If everything turns out all-right.

HEALTH

. . . .

■ Vinemont, Ala.

March 12th, 1935

Dear Mrs Roosevelt,

I am a sick girl 13 years of age. My name is M. N. B. I have been sick three (3) years. Was operated on last February for abseses in kidney, and my left kidney removed. Dr. L. T. of Birmingham performed the operation. I still have pus in my bladder real bad and am not able to work, my Parents have paid out every thing they have made for (3) three years on me. We still owe this Dr. in B'ham ($69) sixty nine Dollars. We farm and it is very hard on us. I just wonder if you would help me just a little, my Parents have a (35) thirty five acre farm here but owe (6) Six hundred Dollars on it, and just have so much sickness and cant get any Price for what they raise. See, if you could pay this Dr. for me, then I could buy me more nourishing food. I go to school and am in 7th grade.

Please, Mrs. Roosevelt, dont try to put us on relief for we dont like that, I hope to get an answer from you real soon.

Your little Friend in need,

(Miss) M. N. B.

■ Milltown, N.J.

March 25, 1935

My dearest President and Mrs Roosevelt;

Just a few lines to let you know, I am in good health, whishing this letter will fined your all well.

Mrs & Pres. Roosevelt, in the first place I must tell you my name, O. C. — 14 years old.

I am writing to you Pres. & Mrs Roosevelt, to ask if I may ask one question, but I must first tell you my story.

Well you see Pres. & Mrs Roosevelt, I was doctering, for a while, with out my mother and Dad knowing it, in fact they don't know it yet, & I owe Dr. F., $7.50 I haven't any idea how to earn this amount, I was doctering for an infected arm. Every time I went the Dr. charged me $1.50, & I went 5 times.

Could you kindly please help me Pres. & Mrs Roosevelt. Plese don't write to my prents about me owing ths money. But if you will kindly help me I will greatly, & certinally appreciate it. If you help me Pres. & Mrs Roosevelt, send my note or your letter, to this address:

O. C.
Milltown Public School
Milltown, N. J.

I will certinally appreate your help.

Let me tell you one more thing, Pres. & Mrs Rosevelt, this summer aunt Joan, is going to take me on a vacation down at West Virginia, & while were going, I'll stop in & visit you, & then you can see who I am. Hows that?

Pres. & Mrs Roosevelt, could you send this amount by April 5. I'd like to pay this out, before my parents receive a bill from the Doctors office. O.K. Please.

Sincerely, yours,

O. C.

■ Milltown. N.J.

April, 2, 1935

My Dearest Mrs & Pres. Roosevelt; —

I have received your loving note, which was singed by Mrs. Roosevelt's sect'y. I was very worried to see you were unable to help me out. Please Mrs. Roosevelt, please help me out, I owe Dr. F., $10.00 now. & I am not able to earn it, I only have five cents saved, please, please do, something,

& I'll tell no one you send me some money. Some day I will help you. Right this minute I crying because I can't earn it. I don't want my parents to find, please send me something before April 15. Please. Help me.

Sincerely,

O. C.

■ Port Angeles, Wash.

May 5, 1935

My dear President and Wife:

Guess you will be surprised to get a letter from me, but you have made so many sick boy and girls happy that I wonder if you might help me.

My mother was a Republican all her life but this time voted for you. Some people tell me you are not for the poor people but I do think you are and so to day way out here in the Big West I have decided to write and ask you for money to learn to talk plain.

Dear Folks, I can't ask the govement for I realize they have lots of children like me in the U.S. I am a christian and I know you are I hear you had millions of dollars even before you become our president and now you get so much money every month and I just have learned to love you well enough, hearing so much about you that I feel you love me too and if you knew you would send me a little money to help me.

Fourteen years ago, I born with a cleft lip and palates cleft also.

Before Daddy left us five years ago, mother and him were going in to Bible College but these hard times come and my Daddy gave up God and all of us and told Mother to see what God would do for us now. Daddy is not well and I hear from him once in a while my mother is a photographer (good one too) . . . My sister had to work Relief for us all. Mother and her both went through major operations last summer. Mother cries and prays so much. Her work is so scarce she will have to ask for more food tomorrow.

How I'd like to see you Dear President. Your picture is on my wall.

Many tell us you turned over to Old Wall Street and forgot us But I just know you haven't and I pray to God to bless you both safe every day.

I have had thirteen operation but I will have to be given special lessons if I ever talk right.

Dear folks, please help me so I can be worth something to my country some day.

Should you want to know more about me, write Rev. E.H., Port Angeles, Wash . . .

Please forgive and write a letter in your hand writting even if you would think I am asking to much when I ask you for money.

Thank you,

Your friend

E. J.

▪ Statesville, N.C

July 9, 1935

Dear Mrs. Roosevelt,

I guess you have received a lot of letters like this but I have come to the place where I dont know what to do. I am only 16 years old and the only help my Daddy has and he was sick most all winter and Spring and I am just out of the Hospital (still wearing a bandage) and a big bill to pay and we are going to lose our home if there isn't something done at once. Daddy's health is bad he is just about to lose his mind worring over it we have made it very well all through the depression untill we got sick and then got be-hind some. We have never ask any-one for any help no way and if we can only get through this we can get on our feet again.

Five hundred dollars will pay off the dept for our home if we can get it by the 20th of July and they say they will sell it if we cannot come with the money and we just cant the bad luck we have had the last six months. We have worked hard and put every thing in our home. We havent run a car since we have been trying to pay for our home. It sure dose hurt us now to have to loose it all and I have read in the papers about you being so sweet to help other poor people to have a place to stay. Our little home is all that we have and if it is sold from us on the account of sickness we will be in a fix so if you will please help me to help my daddy I will do anything in my power any way I can to pay it back, to help you or any one else out any way I can. That is how hard up against it we are. $500.00 would pay the debt off on our home but we will be glad to get any a.mount. I know there is money for Charitable purposes but I want you to please not say anything about this what ever. We are willing to work and pay every penny back If you will send it to me and not let my friends know any thing. For I never did want to have to ask for any help but when sickness and Hospital bills comes on you will do lots of things to help a poor Daddy that is trying to work sick hisself and trying to run a job to hard for him. I have to brothers younger than I. Dad is just running any Ice job be cause he cant do any better at presant time. So please write to me. Dont let any one else know a thing. There isnt enough words to express how much I would appreciate just a little help. Because we are up against it so. It is not on account of not working and trying. We have both worked hard and put every thing on it we dont even have enough Clothes on acont of trying to pay for our home. Know that my Hospital bill is on us we are going to loose our home if we can't get some help.

Sincerely yours —

■ Galena, Kansas
February 5, 1936
Mr Mrs Franklin D Roosvelt
Dear sir I am riting you about my Little Brother who sick see if could get you help send him to some hospial i see in paper where help other Little children i dont see how could Be any worse of then my Little Brother is my Little Brother be 5 years old June he cant walk are talk Are he cant feed his self he suck a Bottle only when mother feed him he just sit propt in chair that is all the county Dr said is just had him took where Be operated he thought get all rite some says he got Pralizes of Bone some say it from his spine he had Rickct when he Little never grew very much he had very Big now my dady had got any money send to hospital I thought rite ask you help send him mamma take up Capper hospital if had money pay way up there . . . hate see go through Life way he is my dady was on Relif roll Last Year . . . i am just 11 year old go stone school cherkee couty Kansas and our county seat Clombis Kansas and our county Dr name is Dr H. H. B. Clumbis Kansas if dont Believe about my Little Brother you write ask him . . . that reason riting you see help raise money for mamma take him away

hoping hear from you soon

tell me what think about him as do hate see him go through Life way he is i thought maby you might help as you other Little Children so will close hoping hear you soon send my Letters to T. L. Galena Kansas R 2 in care E. L. Galena Kansas R 2 that my dady name i be shore get your Letter from T. L. to Mr Mrs Roosevelt

ans soon

T. L.

■ Stillmore, Ga.
October 14, 1936
Dear Mrs. Roosevelt,
Probably, you are wondering who is writing you.
I am W. S. I was born in Louisiana and lived there until the year of 1933

when we moved to Georgia. I am in the eleveth grade. The reason I am writing you is because I wish to ask you to loan me one hundred dollars ($100). *Please* if you can lend it to me because I really need it. I will pay you back. I wish you would give me three years from the year 1937 to pay it back. You may charge your on rate of interest if you wish to. The reasons for my asking you to lend it to me are these. First, I wish to have my teeth attended to. I'm having a terrible time with two of my teeth. One I keep filled with a piece of cotton with camphor on it, the other I can't because it won't stay in and under my jaw on that side there is a hard ball in the inside caused whenever my tooth gets sore and it hurts all the time. All my teeth are decayed except my front teeth and they are starting to decay. I can't have them fixed because my daddy hasn't the money to fix them and he only says teeth are supposed to come out sometimes, but this is the only teeth I'll ever have, I've shedded all the teeth I'm supposed to. The second reason is I want to buy me some clothes. I haven't bought any this year. All I have except two were given me by my sisters, they are married. Papa and won't buy me any. It's always wait, take your time. Anyway I can't get along with them and its not my fault. Papa hates me and every time he gets angry, he takes it out on me. Anything that gets lost he blames on me and he says that I hid it. I'm not that kind of a person and I don't. Mama and me are always quarreling and its her, she's always picking at me and I can't help but answer her back when she talks to me. She sure believes in whipping. We've been in fusses her lately and she told me that she wasn't going to have anything more to do with me, papa said so also. Papa is always threatening to whip me and tells me that he is going to use his shoe on me, that he'll ruin my face. He'll try it too, he has a terrible temper and doesn't care what he does when he gets angry. He got angry with my brother and smashed a glass mug in his face near his eye. My brother is married now. I need a pair of shoes now, I know I'll have to have them by next week and I don't know where they are going to come from because my daddy hasn't the money. I need some winter clothes and I know I'm not going to get them. The third reason is that I want to have money enough to buy my clothes when I graduate. I will have to buy invitations and my diploma also. The fourth reason is that when I graduate I'm going to go in training to be a nurse. To enter I will need about $15.00. Mama and Papa do not intend for me to work, they expect me to stay home, the rest of my life unless I get married. Mama says a decent girl cannot get a job.

The reason my daddy cannot help me is because he hasn't the money. When we lived in Louisiana, he had a job on the railroad. He was roadmaster, he saw that the work was done and told how it should be done. He made around $200 a month from his job, besides what he made from trapping, pulling logs and selling wood. He bought what he pleased and he also saved his money and put in the two largest banks in New Orleans. He quit working and moved to Georgia, to live on one of his three farms. He also had built a grist mill. His farms did not pay him because he let one of his brothers live on it free. His brother had lost the farm, he bought it for his brother to get back sometime. His brother didn't have the money and doesn't pay taxes or pay him anything for living on it. The other farm, he had bought the parts of his brothers and had given it to his daddy as a place of his own to live on as long as he lives. It was his daddys home place. His mill has always been an expense, first it is a dry year, with no water to grind corn with and next a leak in the dam. Then in the year 1933 when he had moved here, the banks closed in February, he lost everything he had except the check for a few hundred dollars that the bank sent him.

I hate my daddy, a hate you can never know. He makes us (me, my sister — 15 years old and my little brother — 11 years old) stay home from school whenever he gets angry at anything. He picks at me all the time. He gets angry and then thinking he'll scare me, tells me he'll whip me if I don't get out and cut some wood. I never had to do that before we moved here, because I never knew anything about doing that or did anything like that. I work at home in the house, do the things I have to do but still they're not satisfied. I don't know now what the reason was, but papa got mad at me. He told mama to run me off, or he would do it himself, that he'd kill me. So later on mama was whipping me and I was mad and I left and went up to my uncle's, who lives about a ½ mile from us. Anyway they came and got me that was in 1934. Now a few days ago he got mad at something and I hadn't done a thing, it was my sister and brother, he took it out on me tho. He said to me that I had started to leave one time so now for me to leave and that he wouldn't walk a step after me. That next time he heard me say anything he was going to make me leave and whip me besides. Now he won't buy me clothes or anything and says that he isn't going to have a thing to do with me. I've got to work to get me some clothes and have my teeth fixed. The way they treat me now, I'm going to leave home and I am going to stay with my brother who lives in the city and I'm going to keep going to school and see if I can't get me some work to do in the evenings after school to earn me some money. If you won't lend me the money I have asked you to, I guess I'll have to leave home without any, because I've got to work and also keep going to school. My family is not a low class, they are among the nicest people of the town, but nobody knows what is under the surface of a family. So please do not ever mention this to any one. I trusted that you wouldn't ever tell this, so please destroy this letter. I have told mama I'm going to leave, she doesn't know where I'm going, she said I was crazy and doesn't believe I'll leave. Even after I told her that, she said she wasn't going to have anything to do with me. I'm a good student in school, my marks are A's and B's, mostly A's. I'm leaving home next week so won't you lend me this money and try and send it to me the next day after you receive this letter. Please, please won't you lend me this money a hundred dollars. Now don't think you'll ever see that money again, but trust me and give me a chance to show you I will pay it back. Answer as quick as you can, cause I don't know what I'll do if I don't get my teeth fixed in the next few days.

Listen, I can't receive a letter at home because they would open it, so if you send me the money send it to . . . and mark in the corner of the envelope this mark so she'll know its for me. . . . This mark . . .

Please answer the next day after you receive this letter and send me that money. I am enclosing a picture of me so that you'll know about what I look like. I wish to thank you very much if you will lend it to me.

P.S. I don't know what kind of a girl you think I am but I can say that I am nice. Mama would never let us go anywhere, and we never gave them a reason for keeping us home.

P.S. Excuse my writing on the back of the page. It's because I hadn't the money to mail this. I only have six cents.

■ Verona, N.J.

November 10, 1938

Dear Mrs Roosevelt;

I am writing to you as my last and only means of salvation. Please keep this confidential between you and me.

I am a young girl nineteen (19) years old, I have had a lot of sickness in my younger day which delayed my schooling. I am finishing High school in February. Dad has been out of work since last June. We lost our house in Newark through the Home owners Loan, which we had for almost twenty (20) years. Unable to find any houses in Newark, we moved to Verona. I have an older brother who is the only one working, and he makes only $15 a week, which is just about enough to keep up the rent. There are six (6) children in the family, a sister and brother in Vocational schools and a younger one in grammar school. We have little to eat and we tried to get relief but

Verona wouldn't help us because we had lived so long in Newark. Newark wouldn't help us, they said to come back to Newark to live, but in the 20 years we were there when we did need help we couldn't get it, now we have no money to move back.

My eyes have been bad since I received my sight, and now I need my glasses changed I don't have the money and it is very difficult for me to continue my studies. We have had no money to buy clothing and use only what people give us.

Graduation is very expensive because there are so many things to get and pay for. Could you loan me me twenty-five dollars so I can graduate. I am trying to get a job after school, but I need my extra time for studies, and the only work I can get is day work, or part time (half a day) and either would take more of my time then I have. After graduation I will try and get a job, for I have but one ambition, to be a nurse. I will save and send you back your money then I wll help my family, and if I can save a little maby by September, I will have enough for my entrance fee, into some Hospital. It is very embarrissing not to be able to dress like the other girls, and not have money for my class dress.

At home mother has always taken the responsibility of everything, she is not old, but very grey worrying how to make ends meet and keep us in school. Mother has always talked over her business with me, and I know everything is very hard, and now we are about at the end of our rope and having no one else to turn to I am asking you, can't you help us or tell us something to do. I will be waiting to hear from you and please keep this personal between the two of us.

Yours very truly

EVICTIONS

. . . .

▪ Swartz Creek, Michigan
August 6, 1936
Dear Mrs. Roosevelt:
I am a girl, 12 yrs. of age. I would like very much if you would send me a bicycle. My family is too poor to buy me one.

We live in a house made over from a chicken coop and a garage. We now lost our farm because it was on a contract with another farm. Although we paid in it an $8000 house and $8036.87, $36.87 more than what we were supposed to pay in it.

I hope you will recieve this letter if you would be as kind as to send me a bicycle and to let us have back our farm because we haven't any money to take it to a higher court. I do not want to tell my mother or anyone else to whom I am sending this letter for fear I would be laughed at.

Good-bye

Yours truly

P.S. I will be waiting every day for a bicycle and a reply about the farm.

[Boston, Massachusetts

acknowledged Apr. 27, 1938]

My dear Lady,

I am a little girl 9 years of age, I have a mother, and father, and two smaller sisters.

About four months now, my father opened a small grocery store . . . It isn't easy for him to pay all of his bills, because his money is very little. Nobody seems to help us. And sometimes my mother cryes because maybe we'll loose the store. I'm always sorry because I'm still young and I can't help much. I was thinking of You, because I always see You in the paper with a smile in Your face. And I know that You have a kind heart. I thought if I wrote to You, maybe You would help us, with a little money and then with Your help I can help my father.

Your's truly,

M. K.

Cleveland, Ohio

November 10, 1940

Dear Mrs. Roosevelt:

I am a boy of 17, I quit school 2 years ago in order to find a job. Since my dad died 3 years ago we haven't been able to do so good. We stretched his insurance money so far as it would go, but now we have to face it.

We are behind 2 months in our rent and the 3rd falling due this Wednesday, the 13th. We pay $15 a month for 4 rooms. There are 5 of us, mother, 3 boys and myself. I really wouldn't be writing this, but I can't see ourselves evicted from our house. We've got till Wednesday to get either all or at least a half of our rent paid up. It would be all right if it was only me because I could take care of myself one way or another. My mother can't get work because she just recovered from tuberculosis and must rest. I am afraid that if nothing comes up I will turn to crime as a means of getting financial help.

My little brothers are shoeshiners. They go out at night and shine shoes. They go mostly in beer gardens. Their little money even helps. You might say, why don't we go on relief, well you just can't convince my mother on that. She said she would rather starve than get relief.

I am working as a grocery store clerk at $8.00 a week. We could get along on this in summer but not in winter on account of the coal problem.

I was wondering that maybe you could loan us about $35.00 or more, we could get on our feet again and once again hold up our heads. We will greatly appreciate this second start in life with all our hearts.

Will you please be so kind as to answer this letter in some way. And will you please congratulate your husband for us for winning the election. I read all about how angry Hoover and all the rest were about not letting your husband have a 3rd term. The reason for that is because they weren't even good enough to be re-elected for a second term and are angry. We all have faith in our president.

Thanks Ever So Much

V. B. F.

P.S. Please, again I say, try to answer this letter before Wednesday somehow. I'll be praying every night for your loan. I'll give you $1.00 a month with interest until it is all paid up.

P.S., The reason I marked it peronel is that I was afraid it might be thrown out by your secretaries before you even read it.

[Brooklyn, New York
acknowledged June 25, 1941]
My Dear Mrs Roosevelt,

Have you ever gone thru a disgrace a personal shame. Have you ever had to sit back and listen while people who you had claim as friends were talking about you. Have you ever had to be pointed at and as you walk by their wispers float back to you. Mrs Roosevelt we have exactly ten days to live in our house for today our Landlord gave us a disspisis. It isn't that I don't won't to move in fact I really do won't to go but my family & I hate to move without paying our debts. And I feel so ashame and humble to ask you but I feel your the one I can only ask, the only one I can trust my secret to unless Tony That's the body who gave us the never too be forgotten document has not pass it already. I'd feel ashamed to go to school even though I know I cannot help if a just was unfortunate to have a jobless father and four brothers & a sister which are all younger then me and I am 14 years so you can imagine the burden my father & mother have to carry. My father use to have a good job a mail carrier but I never did find out the reason he lost it my father & mother don't wish too discuss it so I feel it is none of my business. We are 3 months behine the rent is $23.00 a month which is a very large amount for the meager allowance the *relief* allows us.

So we owe the L. L. $69.00 I'd appriciet even if you send me $25 dollars I swear on the soul of grandmother & grandfather B. I will pay you back. My father tries to be gay about it saying as lightly as possible "Who cares who wants to live here anyway." But under all his jokes I can see he is suffering terrible my pop is very sensitive. If you canot help us with mony can you see if you can get him some kind of a job. All my friend's father's work and receive good pay except my father at times I think our name is cursed. All my friend home are furnished with lovely furniture except ours the C.'s. I am not ashame of ourselves it's just I'm sick & tierd of being treated as the underdog I don't mind saying so either Mrs Roosevelt please help us someway.

Thank you very kindly

P.S. This happens to be a secret I don't want my mother's hopes to raise only to collapse again so will you please address it to me & mark the enevelope personal I would appricient it very mucho.

Muchas Gracias Senora

DEBTS

. . . .

■ Salem, Virginia

Sept. 9, 1934

Dear Mrs. Roosevelt,

Please excuse me for addressing you, but I have a very important matter to lay before you. I am a girl eighteen years old and I have my mother who is unable to work and a little Brother eight years old to Support and I Owe $28.67 twenty eight dollars and sixty seven cents on my furniture which I bought over a year ago and I haven't been able to pay anything on it for over four months, the collection was here and told me they would have to take the furniture up, if they do it will leave me with out a bed or anything in the house to do with and I just can't get a job anywhere I have tried everywhere that I could get to see about work but have been unable to get any. You may know we are in a hard place when we don't have bread in the house, and my little brother is begging for something to eat, we get a order from the relief every two weeks but we only get $3.00 or $3.50 every two weeks but everything is so high you can't get anything that will last for the amount we get. I tried to get the relief to pay a payment on my furniture but they said they could not. I am going to ask you to do me a kindness by helping me out of this hard place. As I don't know any other step to take, and have felt led to write you. And if I am ever lucky enough to do I will return the kindness along as I can. I will also enclose the furniture Co. address so that you will know I am telling the truth. I will be glad to hear from you by return mail in regard to my request.

Very Truly,

P. C.

■ Cleveland, Ohio

[acknowledged Jan. 17, 1935]

Mrs. Roosevelt:

You may think I am very bold to write to you but since you seem so kind and everything I ever read about seems pleasant I thought it would not be so very wrong to ask you for a little advice.

I am writting this secretly my father and mother don't know and I wondered If I could suprise them with your answer if you would possibly & kindly be able to send me one.

My father was not working for 5 years this being the cause of the great debt which are now in.

My father started working now and since he works only two days a week we could barely keep up with our present needs.

But now the landlord whom we owe $312.00 and the grocer whom we owe close to $500.00 are constantly asking for money which we positively cannot afford to pay now I wonder if you could advise me and give a little information to whom I could turn for these bills. Who would be willing to help but we cannot repay right away?

I just can't stand anymore to look at the crying & thinking my parents do.

I am 15 years old and entered High-school. The teacher gave me a job through which I earn my schooling. If I ever succeed I would gladly pay back every cent to anyone who would possibly be able to help.

Please keep this letter a secret Mrs. Roosevelt and please, if possible soon & if it won't intefere with your affairs answer me.

Maybe you know of a contest or anything which would help me win. I could at least try.

Trusting in the confidence of God and in your kindness I will await an answer soon.

Oh please do not think I'm terrible for writing to you but I can't help. My heart just seems ready to burst.

May God Bless You

Honestly Yours

■ Greenville, S.C.

March 18, 1937

Dear Mrs. Roosevelt,

I am writing you because I believe you can help me. I am thirteen years old and have three sisters and one brother. I have one brother and sister married. My sister is ill with pneumonia though she is better than she has been. My father did not get to work for sometimes this summer so we are behind in our bills. I was wondering if you could let me have $127.50 or if not that $60.00. I have and always will I believe have an ambition to be one of the following:

(1) movie star (2) lawyer (3) opera singer

If you send me a check for the money asked you will be risking losing it. If ever when I am grown and am making a lot of money I will send you amt. borrowed plus twenty dollars. if ambition not fulfilled then I suppose you out of the money, but if you send it you will know you have made one family the happiest at Easter time in U.S. I wrote you one letter, but thought it might be wrong so I did not send it. I am not telling any one about this and never will I don't suppose unless you send the money. My father is working now but there is such an expense and he the only one working his wages do not go very far.

Thank You,

(Miss) B. M.

■ Tiffin, Ohio

Oct. 30, 1937

Mrs. Roosevelt:

I am writing to you to ask you for a little help. But first let me tell you a little more. I am a junior in high school. I have a brother and sister that are married, one a senior and a brother and sister smaller than myself.

My father works on the Pennsylvainia R. R. He has very hard work and receives little pay. His wages average about $55 a month. In the winter he has to many nights over time. Our coal bill at the present is $75.

About a month ago my little brother fell and broke his arm. They have taken seven xras, broken it over, but still it will not heal. The doctor has decided that he must be taken to a special doctor in Toledo. This will cost a great deal of money.

What I am writing to you about is our grocery bill which is $65. If this is not paid within this next month we will not be allowed to get any more groceries. There is no one from whom we can borrow money and my brother and sister that are married cannot help us. Would you please help us to paid our bill so that we can have some thing to eat. I read in the newspaper that you helped to buy an iron lung for a boy or a girl. I have always known you to have many fine characteristics. Because of this I am sure you will not let me down. Thank You.

J. M.

■ Greensboro, N.C.
February 12, 1938
Dear Mrs. Roosevelt,

On January 1st I was layed off from my work leaving my brother the whole support of our family. Just recently he was cut down to 3 days a week with a cut in salary. With seven of us in the family it is just about impossible for us to live on this amount.

My mother has been sick for over two months having had a nervous breakdown, and we are unable to buy or furnish her with the medicine required for her recovery.

I am 18 years of age the oldest girl in the family, and it just seems impossible for me to get a job any where. I have been to Mills, Stores and Firms of all sorts. I am willing and able to work. Can furnish excellent references but at this time of the year it just seems impossible to find work.

We are so in debt and each week the bills are piling higher and higher that it just seems as if there was no way out.

We must make a payment on our furniture bill, and if it isn't paid soon they will be out any day for our furniture. And on top of this we are behind in our rent.

It would be a big help if we could get some of our bills paid on as they are already impatient for their money.

If you could help us out with from $35.00 to $50.00 I believe we would be the happiest family in the world.

We have a good respectable family, none of us have ever been in any kind of trouble, and our characters are above reproach.

Just as soon as I get back to work and the family on their feet again I will pay you back as much a week as possible until your kind favor has been fully repaid.

My Father's work has been very poor for the past year, he is an advertising saleman, and his work right now is practically nothing; and as he has had kidney trouble for some time, taking more than he could make, for medicine. He has been improving recently, since he has his teeth extracted, and is looking forward to a job but which will not be available for a month or more. We went through the depression without asking for relief. I registered January 14th for unemployment compensation, and although promised $6.25 per week, have not received a cent as yet.

Won't you please grant me the afore mentioned favor, please make it a personal favor, Mrs. Roosevelt, for if you would refer it to a local agency, I would suffer untold delay, and embarrassment.

Though we are poor, we try to hold off embarrassment, for you know it is "hard to be broke, and harder to admit it."

Please grant me this favor and I will ever be,

Gratefully yours,

This is not intended for *publication.*

■ Flat Rock, Ala.

Oct 7, 1939

dear Mrs Rosevelt

i thought i would write you this letter you may laugh at it and thank i am crazy but i am not, we are a family of eight my self being the oldest well we are finding a very hard way of makeing a liveing my mother and us children works all the time untill winter and then they is not any work to do but we get very small pay sixty cts a day for farm work and at cotton picking time sixty cts a hundred for picking cotton now my mother is very interested in getting us through school and she has Borrowed from Stevenson Bank forty five dollars and my sister forty five and it is due in now and we cant pay it and my mother is almost crazy and as she had me to write to the president once a bout a year a go a bout our condition but as he couldnt help us any i thought i would write you and see if you would help us well what i want to know is would you loan me sixty dollars and let me give you a good note and get it sined by good Relife people now i am a shamed to write this to you a stranger but i have heard so much talk a bout how good you and the president are and i just wondered if you would help us a little now if you was to see your mother a walking the floor crying over debts after she had worked her self almost to death for you you wouldent be a shamed to do almost any thing that was honest and if you had to work so hard you couldent sleep at night and then couldent have any thing hardly to eat nor wear you would know our condition now if you will let me have sixty dollars to pay off part of what we owe at the Bank i will make you a good security note and will pay it back next fall now if you can let me have it by the fourth of next month i will more than appriciate it i am not begging but if you know what this means to me i know you will let me have it well you may wonder why i dont get this closer home well the people a Round that could help us we have ask for so many commidations we are a shamed to ask for any more and most of the people that we know is poor people to now if you should doubt our conditions just write our Rural mail carrier Mr M. R. T. we dont want on relief what we are so bad in need of is money to pay off what we owe at the Bank please let me hear from you by Return mail and oblige

E. L.

■ Joplin, Missouri
October 27, 1939
Dear Mrs. Roosevelt,

I am a 17 year old girl. I am writing to you for help in solving a very serious problem.

My mother is very ill she may not live long. She has been sick for about 8 years. My step-dad is also sick. My mother has cancers. My step-dad has T.B. He has been sick for a long time too. There is only my sister who is 15 years old and myself to take care of them. My step-dad is a World's War Veteran. He gets $100.00 a month. But that isn't enough to keep us on. It would be enough if we weren't in debt. We are in debt about $500. Everything we get we get on *Credit*. We have gotten in so deep in debt that we can't get out. We are desperate. We can't think of any way out. Me and my sister has given up trying to ever have a good time. We can't go to school because we are in debt. We can't do anything to have a good time because we have to stay at home to take care of mother. We don't even have decent clothes to wear. and with winter coming on we don't know what we're going to do for bed clothes. Nothing we have is paid for. We do not own our own home. We rent. We don't have a nice modern home but we would be satisfied if what we do have was paid for. I could go on and on telling of our plight but I will not. We are worse off than a W.P.A. worker. We could be so happy if we was just out of debt so we could get a fresh start. sometimes it makes me so blue just thinking of it I cry and sometimes think I'll kill myself but that wouldn't solve anything for the rest of them. Collectors come every day wanting their money but we haven't got it. When pay day comes we have about ¹⁄₁₀ of what it takes to pay up. It is about to run me crazy. You can investigate us if you want to. We have no friend because of debt. I need glasses but I can't get them because I haven't any money. We didn't have any Christmas last year and I guess we won't this year.

You have heard my story so please please please help us if you can because you don't know what it's like to be in debt.

If you want a list of the people we owe I will send them.

Respectivly Yours.

N. C.

HOUSEHOLD CONVENIENCES

. . . .

■ Euclid, Ohio

[acknowledged Apr. 12, 1934]

Dear Mrs. Roosevelt:

I am in a very great need of $100 dollars. If I had that much money now, I would make my older sister very happy. Her birthday is coming soon and I would like to give to her, if I were only able, a gift which she has always wanted and longed for. She always wanted a certain kind of electric sweeper—"Premier Duplex Cleaner." I don't think that the electric sweeper would cost exactly one hundred dollars. With the money that would remain, I would buy some clothes for my younger sister and myself.

My younger sister and I go to a public high school where many girls of well-to-do parents wear the most beautiful clothes. My parents are poor for neither of them has worked for three years now. The help that we get is from my older sister who is married. That is why I would like to give her this particular gift if I were only able to. But I guess this idea of mine, must be dismissed for where can I get one hundred dollars? I am unable to go to work for I still have another year to go to school before I graduate from high school.

Dear Mrs. Roosevelt can you in any way please help me?

Sincerely yours,

M. C.

■ December 22, 1936

Grand Rapids, Mich.

Dear Mr. & Mrs. Roosevelt:

I am writing you a few lines to ask a favor of you all. My name is M. L. I am fifteen years old. This letter I do not just know how to word it. But this is it.

We live on the South end of town and my two girlfriends live on the West Side. I have been in both their homes and they have nice furniture in it. They are not rich or any thing like that, but their furniture is nice. They have the kind that should go with a room. Now may be you see my side of the story. We are not able to buy furniture. I wonder if you wouldn't help us get some. That is if you where to put one of your daughters my place. Could you picture her, how she would feel. I have never had the two girls over to my home. There are seven of us and father makes about fifteen dollars a week. Miss Roosevelt this is a personal letter to you and your husband and I wish no one else to see it.

But in making Your decision I do Pray that you will help me in this problem.

May God help you and Mr. Roosevelt.

Sincerely Yours

Please ans. in some way.

■ Nov. 30, 1937

Springfield Mass

Dear Mrs. Roosevelt:

I am a girl sixteen years old. Last May I beg my father to buy an electric refrigerator for mother on mother's day. We had talked about buying one with her. She thought it was not a very wise thing to do, because we could not afford to pay cash. I wanted it so very bad that my father bought it. He agreed to pay montly payments of seven dollars and twenty two cents. What mother had sayed proved to be right. For two weeks after we bought the refrigerator I took sick with a serious kidney ailment which confined me to my bed from May twenty until Nov. twenty-second. I am just recovering from a delicate operation. I came home from the hospital Nov. eighth and my father was layed off after working for the railroad fifteen years. Many a girl of my age is hoping that on Chrismas morn they will find a wrist watch, a handbag, or even a fur coat. But my one and only wish is to have father and mother spend a happy Christmas Mrs. Roosevelt I am asking of you a favor which can make this wish come true. I am asking you to keep up our payments until my father get's back to work as a Christmas gift to me. Though father worked part time for quite a while we never lost anything for the lack of payments. If the refrigerator was taken away from us father and mother would think it a disgrace.

I close hoping with all my heart that my letter will be consider.

Mrs Roosevelt you may rest assure that I have learnt my lesson

I am respectfully yours

J. B.

■ [Chicago]

Aug. 3, 1938

Dear Mrs. Roosevelt:

It has taken me a month to get up enough courage to write to you. Please forgive me if this is not written the way you are accustomed to being written to, but I have never written to a President's wife before, therefore am not sure how it should be done, particularly this kind of a letter.

I am going to ask you for money. I wrote that first so you need not read further if you do not care to, but, please Mrs. Roosevelt read my letter. I want to tell you what I need the money for. We have lived in this house for sixteen years & we do not *yet* have a bathtub. That is what I want $200 for. Please don't laugh. I know it must sound impossible to you that anyone should have the colossal nerve to ask the President's wife for $200 to have a bathtub put in her home, but that's just what I am asking. I am the oldest of seven children & my father works for the W.P.A. With his salary & the small one I make you can readily see that it would take forever for us to put a tub in. It has been my dream for sixteen years to have a tub put into our house but I just can't make it come true. I am doing this as a last resort, believe me. Last year I made a vow that by my twenty third birthday I would have saved enough to have the plumbing done, but the twelfth of this month I will be twenty-three & am no closer to my dream than a year ago. It seems that as soon as I have even a little bank-account someone either gets ill or an urgent bill comes up that must be paid. I have never been able to say "no" to my mother even if it was my last dollar.

Dear Mrs. Roosevelt if you feel you cannot grant my request please just forget this because I have not told a soul about this so I will be the only one who will be disappointed.

You've always seemed so real & human to me that I can't help thinking you are like what I would be if I had the money. You give your earnings to charities can you consider me a charity. I won't promise to return the money because I may never possess that much money but if I ever have it I will certainly give it back to you.

I will mail this quickly before I lose courage & tear it up. Please forgive me if I've done something I shouldn't have.

Respectfully yours,

Miss A. V.

■ Gallipolis, Ohio

Nov. 22, 1939

(Personal to Mrs. Roosevelt)

(Please, Read)

My Dear Mrs. Roosevelt,

I don't know exactly how to begin to write you or just why I should, but my pen keeps moving on. Some where off I still hear a little of the words "hope" and "faith."

I am a girl 19 yrs. of age, I live with my mother and two sisters.

My father died when I was 12 yrs. old.

I did not complete 3d yr. high School because of insufficient food and clothing.

We have only one support in our family and that is my oldest sister. For six years I have taken over the work in the home, as my mother is not able to do it.

We have nothing convient in our house. It is rather cold and bare. Things that we can't get because of other things we just have to meet. Taxes, and Bills. We do own our home, Thank God!

My sister gives me an allowance of $2.00 a month, from which I get amusement and clothing. I make my clothes.

There is no person here that I could ask this question and feel that I could get a sweet yes or a kind no. So that's why I am writing to you.

It's an awful big question and rather odd, but it won't hurt trying.

Will you loan me $500?

I know it's a shock, but let me explain.

I don't want luxuries like a car or a refrididaire, but I would like to have some necessary things that would make life a little more easier. We haven't a washer, and it is really back breaking to wash on a board. We have to carry water and it makes a day's work seem like years.

I am not in very good health myself.

I keep the house spic and spane. I give my right hand to God, that I will pay you 25 cents a month out of my monthly allowance of $2.00. Mrs.

Roosevelt, I am asking you because I believe you will do it. I'll do any thing you want me to. I'd kiss your feet if I were near you. If I die before I finish, from my insurance you will be paid. I am about at wits end. Please, help me. We joined the Red Cross, we do it every year, to help those that are little less fortunate than we, Will you help some one that is a great deal less fortunate than you?

If you do or don't, please answer. It will be great cheer to hear from you. This will be a secret between you and me until death.

Tired

Your Friend

M. A. S.

(over)

Here is a list of what I had planned to buy.

Living Room.

Wall paper = $2.10

Rug 9 × 12 = $23.88

Piece of Linoluem = $.29

Covering for 2 chairs = 1.96

Curtains   3.56

(Bed Room)

Stove—49.95

Rug—8.75

Blinds—1.44

Curtains—1.12

Chair covers—1.12

Drapries—1.33

Wall paper—1.80

(Dining Room)

6 chairs—10.69

Rug—3.89

Blinds—.72

Curtains—.56

Wall paper—1.50

New Floor

————

Kitchen—Breakfast set—5.89

Linoluem—5.19

Oil stove—19.95
Sink—12.50
Dishes—Washer—Coffee pot
Iron
Toaster
2 teakettles
A Built in cupboard

———————

A Small Room Made in to Bath
Wall paper
Lavator   8.95
The closet   13.95
Tub   15.45
Small cupboard

———————

Small Bed Room
Linoleum $2.10
Wall paper—Curtains   54
Blind   .54
Small Rug   .95
Drapries   .54

———————

A Back Porch Built
Inside paint $14.45
Outside for house in spring $11.75

———————

Sheets
Spreads
towels
sweeper
Curtains and other needy things.
   We have six rooms in our house. I'll Buy the cheapest to make things
stretch.

. . . .

■ Sept. 15, 1934

Stratford, Conn.

Dear Mrs. Roosevelt,

I am a young girl of only fourteen years, and am writing to you to see if you won't help me, because you helped so many other people. Here is my trouble: My mother has been a cripple since she was five years old. She is a victim of osteomolytis through a Doctor's mistake. These last few years she has been getting worse. She has seven incisions to dress every-day and has had fifteen operations. It is all in her hips and a pus matter forms in some part of her hips and makes an absess. Then she has to get operated on to relieve her. I have recently left school to take care of her, while she is home because she has spent the better part of her life in the hospitals. It has cost most of my father's pay every week for medicine and we are up to our neck in hospital bills. I have a younger sister eleven years old who is going to school and must be properly clothed. Now my mother is in the hospital again and is on the danger list. The doctor says this is the end. She will never pull through this illness for the pus matter has gotten into her stomach and is eating it all away. When she was a little girl she learned to play the piano and is known widely among our friends as a most wonderful player. Since she could not do much around the house, she devoted much of her time to writing songs. She wrote one in particular which she called "Cheer Up Connecticut" and used the N.R.A. [National Recovery Administration] in it also President Roosevelts name. She had so much faith in the piece that she sent it to him, hoping to get enough money to put it across. But it came back signed by Early* so I am in doubt if it reached the President at all. We have kept the painful news from our mother because we are afraid it will be too much of a shock. We just pretend we haven't heard from him yet. Dear Mrs. Roosevelt, we all know that within a week or so we won't have our mother anymore and she was so good. Despite all her pains and suffering she still had a cheery disposition. And my dear father has always been so patient giving her everything in his power. We have no money and we know she is going to die. We don't know how we are going to bury her dear body. Please for God's sake help us. Don't let our mother be buried in a Potters Field. Please dear Mrs. Roosevelt I implore you help us. God will bless you. My daddy doesn't know I am writing this letter. I have written

* Steve Early, aide to FDR

one to President Roosevelt but recieved no answer. So please please help us. You are the only one I can go to now and I know you are kind. Thank You Mrs. Roosevelt and may God bless you.

Tearfully

Miss E. S.

■ Denver, Colo.

9-11-41

Dear Mrs. Roosevelt,

Mother and I are grieved so much about daddy that I am writting you to see if you will be so good and kind to help us a little so we can see daddy one more time our in come is four dollars and fifty cents a week so you see we can't do much.

My daddy went away one day to look for work. He was killed in Reno Nevada by a Southern Pacific freight train Aug. the 11th was burried Aug. the 18th. Mother and I didn't get the word until Aug. the 22nd. We didn't get to scc daddy. They didn't know daddy had mother and I. So they burried daddy in Reno Nevada. We are almost dead with grief. We can't sleep or eat very much. The undertaker there wrote us we could see daddy. They would open the grave for us to see daddy for the last time. but the cost will be fifty dollars and we have'nt the money to pay. Mother cries all the time she said she couldn't live if she couldn't see daddy one more time. It don't seem like daddy is dead daddy was a good man. He and mother loved me. I love my daddy. Mrs. Roosevelt I am asking you with all my heart will you please help us to see my daddy please don't turn us down. I pray to God to help us in the darkest hours of our trouble. You can write to Reno Nevada and you will know this is the truth. I will close for this time praying to hear from you at once with good news. I am a little boy and I go to school every day and I sell pappers after school is out.

A Friend

S. P.

P.S. My daddy's name is A. J. P.

I have a brother younger than I, and he's in the same grade with me. My mother would whant both of us to go to school, and be something when we grow up. Yet, she can't afford to send both of us. My brother being the youngest, he's also the lucky one. He would go to school while I will have to stay home. Oh I just hate to think of it. I just would love to go to school. I do not like to go to school just to spare time, like some do, but I would like to go to learn. . . . Maybe you will help a girl that doesn't whant to quit school. . . . If you could help me, nothing would be so dear to me than you. Education is more than anything in the world to me

—L. B., an eighth-grade student from Illinois,
to Eleanor Roosevelt, February 1934

Lacking a school bus, these students in West Virginia traveled to school on the back of a truck, 1935. (Photo by Ben Shahn, LC-USF 33-006147-B-M3)

chapter 2

Education

Teachers, administrators, and government officials wrote and said much about the shortcomings of American education during the Great Depression. They told of school closings, shortened academic terms, cuts in teacher salaries, and harsh retrenchment in many school budgets, especially during the early 1930s. Few school systems were unaffected by hard times. But as the report of President Roosevelt's Advisory Committee on Education revealed in 1938, the Depression's burdens were not equally distributed. Rural, southern, and black schools entered the Depression as the nation's most poorly funded, and they could least afford the declines in school budgets wrought by the economic crisis. The National Education Association estimated that by 1934 rural poverty had closed more than 20,000 schools. In 1935–36, white students attending school in Arkansas, Mississippi, Alabama, Georgia, and South Carolina received less than half the national average of per pupil spending (which then stood at $74.30), and less than a third of the spending on students in such better-funded states as New York. Black students in Georgia, Mississippi, and South Carolina received less than a tenth of the national average of per pupil spending.[1]

That these were hard times for schools, families, and the young becomes even clearer when one looks at the birth rate and grade school enrollments. The Depression decade was not one into which adults were eager to bring children, and the birth rate fell accordingly. Declining birth rates shrank primary school populations. Between 1930 and 1938 the number of five-year-old children in the United States declined by 17.3 percent, yielding a 16.1 percent decline in kindergarten enrollments. The number of students enrolled in the first four school grades dropped annually between 1930 and 1934, in the first seven grades between 1934 and 1938.[2]

The educational picture was not entirely gloomy, however. Because of the tremendous shortage of jobs for the young, the Depression kept students in school longer than their pre-Depression predecessors—in the 1930s they had nowhere else to go. This trend was accelerated by the student aid program of the National Youth Administration. High school enrollments rose from 4,399,422 at the opening of the Depression decade to 6,545,991 at the end of the decade. These same factors led (after a brief dip from 1932 to 1934) to a rise in college enrollments during the second half of the Depression decade: in 1939 the college population was 1.3 million, surpassing the pre-Depression peak of 1.1 million.[3]

These rather contradictory educational trends in Depression America must be kept in mind when one reads the letters that students of all grade levels sent to Mrs. Roosevelt. The letters reflect both trends: the economic stress and inadequate school resources of the 1930s, as school systems lacked the funds to transport their students to and from school, and could not provide them with free textbooks or even secondhand clothes; and, at the same time, the new expectations created by the surging school population in the upper grades.[4] With the rise in school retention rates and an increasing number of students staying in school longer, youths came to feel that continued academic enrollment, at least through high school, was the norm, and that it would be unfair for their own poverty to keep them from enjoying the educational opportunities available to so many other young Americans. Thus the students' letters reflect both the limited educational resources and the expansive educational aspirations of Depression youth.

The letters also reveal something of a generation gap between the students and the teachers of Depression America. Much of the writing of teachers in the 1930s constitutes a literature of complaint about poor salaries, inadequate school funding, and other resource problems in the nation's educational institutions.[5] The First Lady's young correspondents, on the other hand, say little about eliminating the inadequacies of the schools and rarely complain about, or express a desire to reform, their school systems; they focus instead on the youths' desperate struggles to keep their own place in those systems by staying in school.

At first glance the individualistic nature of these letters might seem a sign of a lack of sophistication. One could argue that these youths were essentially prepolitical, too young and naive to formulate a coherent critique of their schools or a reformist agenda for them. But this is at best only a half-truth. These low-income youths more often wrote of their individual plight than about solving their schools' problems because the schools seemed well off by comparison. Their teachers may have suffered through salary cuts, but at least they were working full-time jobs—unlike the parents of many of these poor youths. At a time when factories and farms were in decline, schools seemed a going concern, a place where an increasing number of teens were staying on longer. For the young, the schools were islands of stability in a turbulent world—and students wanted, above all, to avoid being thrown off of those islands by their own poverty.

. . . .

The opening letters in this chapter on education come from youths in their precollege years. Their letters contain a variety of requests, all stemming from their desire to stay in school. Clothing was the most common item that children and teens asked Mrs. Roosevelt to help them secure. The majority of requests came of dire necessity: as a relief worker from Arkansas observed in 1935, "I find so many children do not get to go to school because they simply haven't a rag that they can leave home in."[6]

Along with deficiencies caused by family poverty, the letters reflect shortcomings caused by the limitations of the educational system itself. The 1930s were a time when location, especially in poor rural areas, placed grave limitations on access to secondary schooling. Students who lived on isolated farms or in small towns often had to struggle to find ways to commute or move to the nearest large town—what one of the letter writers termed "a high school town"—so that they could continue their education.[7] This caused hardships when the towns were a long way off or had rents that proved too dear for low-income students, so students of high school age often asked Eleanor Roosevelt for help with these expenses. The letters offer another reminder of how different the Depression decade's educational world was from our own with regard to school books. Today the most frequent complaint one hears about school textbooks is that they are boring, but they are almost universally free; back in 1936, however, only fourteen states distributed all of their textbooks for free, and Mrs. Roosevelt was often asked for aid in purchasing these crucial educational materials.[8]

The Depression convinced some low-income youths that it would be impossible to stay in school long enough to acquire advanced academic skills. They were more inclined to think of vocational education as offering a quick escape from the grueling blue-collar occupations of their parents. Thus we find the daughters of mill workers and miners hoping to flee the world of factories and mines by training to become beauticians. This is not the kind of educational aspiration that historians usually write about, but as several letters in the section on vocational education attest, it was a poignant, blue-collar version of the American dream, in which just a little bit of job-related training was seen as a way out of the dehumanizing milieu of industrial work.[9]

When one thinks of the deprivation that the Depression imposed upon the young, piano lessons and art classes may seem like rather small things, even luxuries, compared to the necessities of clothing, food, and housing. But for young people with intense artistic interests and talents, the loss of educational opportunities in this area was one of the most disturbing effects of the economic crisis. The letters in this chapter's section on the arts and music capture the concerns of young people who were determined that the Depression not be allowed to bring their arts education to a halt.

Graduation is supposed to be a happy time for students. Few school days are more festive than those honoring the graduates' hard work, intellectual achievement, and successful completion of their required course of study. Although ostensibly academic events, graduations by the 1930s were just as much social occasions, with quite elaborate rituals. A survey of 204 high schools in Wisconsin in 1934 found that the schools offered an imposing array of graduation rituals in addition to the degree-granting ceremony: senior class plays, junior-senior proms, junior-senior banquets, senior picnics, senior trips, senior camera days, faculty receptions, senior pow-wows, senior pageants, senior-parent banquets, and junior-senior theater parties.[10]

These social occasions were very much linked to American consumer culture—and especially to the youth apparel market. According to a commencement manual from 1929, youthful competitiveness over dress had made "the clothes problem a bugbear of the commencement season," as students became involved in "the lavish extravagance, the ostentation, and the desire of those who can ill afford it to 'keep up with the Joneses.'"[11] Students needed dress clothes for the graduation ceremony itself and for the dances and other social events which accompanied it; they also needed money to buy school rings, yearbooks, pins, invitations, and a host of other items which went along with graduation rituals. These items, as much as the graduation ceremony, meant a great deal to the students who had labored for years to complete their schooling. Most students looked forward to graduation with a youthful intensity reinforced by the school peer culture that promoted these occasions as the paramount social events of school life.

Given all this, it should not be difficult to imagine what it was like for low-income youths of Depression America, who found as graduation season loomed that they lacked the funds to participate fully in these pivotal school rituals. Each spring, letters came pouring in to the First Lady from students who dreaded the onset of the graduation season. Many were heart-

Girls' Graduation Frocks

Sizes 12 to 16!

$5.95

℄ Georgette and flat crepe Frocks in white and soft pastel shades.

Girls' Coats

$5.95

Tweed Sports Coats in sizes 11 to 17.

Basement Economy Store

A fourteen-year-old "motherless colored girl" from St. Louis, whose father had been unemployed for almost two years, enclosed this advertisement with her letter in 1934, asking Mrs. Roosevelt to buy her graduation clothes.
(From the collection of the Franklin D. Roosevelt Library, Hyde Park, N.Y.)

sick and ashamed that their families could not afford even the clothing necessary for graduation ceremonies. They had no one to turn to for assistance, and so they asked the First Lady to pay for their graduation expenses. Moreover, since graduation reminded students of the problems of keeping in school for the next level of education, graduation letters also featured requests for aid for further schooling.

The graduation letters in this chapter also display the class tensions present in many of the nation's schools. Impoverished students knew only too well that the Depression had hurt them more than many of their schoolmates. It was because the bulk of their classmates could afford graduation expenses that low-income students felt such a stinging sense of deprivation as they grappled with their own inability to meet those expenses. It left them feeling like outsiders in their own schools, pariahs too poor and shabbily attired even to celebrate with their friends.

These heart-rending letters convey such a vivid picture of the problems facing low-income students during graduation seasons that it may come as a surprise to learn that the leading journals of school administrators and teachers largely ignored these problems. Educational journals did have much to say about graduation. But the graduation articles that ran each spring focused upon bigger and better graduation ceremonies rather than upon the hardships that the ceremonies inflicted upon the poor. Even educational progressives of the 1930s seemed a world away from these poor youths. Liberal school officials published articles urging that graduation ceremonies raise political issues and engage students in thought-provoking activities; but most ignored the consumerism of commencement season and the inability of lower-class students to participate fully in graduation rituals.[12]

Just how little concern educators had for the poor in their midst at graduation time is suggested by a telling statistic: according to the most thorough state study of commencement practices, only 1 percent of high schools imposed limits on how much students could spend on their graduation clothes. Only 30.8 percent of the high schools mandated the use of caps and gowns, an egalitarian requirement that could have provided some cover for shabbily attired students (at least in the academic processions, though not of course in the socials that went along with them).[13]

This inattention to social class and the inequities wrought at graduation time typified the classic common school ideology of teachers and school officials. They liked to think of the schools as places where social class did not matter and everyone had an equal opportunity to excel through hard work and intelligence. Indeed, a good deal of the American educational establishment opposed New Deal youth initiatives such as the work-study program of the National Youth Administration, because these initiatives directly subsidized poor students alone instead of pumping money into the schools—where it supposedly would benefit all.[14] With this kind of belief widespread and school officials often inattentive to indigent students' special problems, low-income youths found that they had no one in their school systems to appeal to for aid at graduation time. Thus they chose to look away from their schools, all the way to Washington and Eleanor Roosevelt for someone to confide in and to ask for help.

After graduation from secondary school only about 10 percent of college-age Americans were able to go on to college during the Depression. America's college population included a sizable minority, thousands of students, who pursued their dreams of higher education even though economically they could not really afford to do so. There was, for example, the University of Georgia student too poor to pay for housing, who in the winters roomed "in a converted poultry farm among the college's 49 chicken houses" and in fair weather "slept in the fields"; or the midwestern students who roomed in cold basements and lived on milk and crackers.[15] Even when cutting corners with room and board, poor college students had trouble meeting their tuition payments. New Deal dollars, especially through the campus work-study jobs of the NYA, helped these struggling students. Yet as several of the letters in the higher education section of this chapter suggest, the NYA funds sometimes proved inadequate.[16]

Perhaps above all these college letters showed that low-income youths were not passive victims of the Depression. They reveal a younger generation using great ingenuity to obtain part-time jobs and loans, and displaying the most intense determination to pursue a higher education that might have seemed financially out of reach. The Depression had decimated the stock market, devastated industrial production, and staggered the rural economy, but it could not still the longings of the young to improve themselves through formal education.

SCHOOL DAYS: PRE-COLLEGE EDUCATION

December 29, 1933
Duquesne, Pennsylvania
President Mrs. Roosevelt
I am a ten year old little girl turning towards your kind heart in the name of 140 children from Duquesne that go to the St. Stephens School McKeesport. I read in the paper of your kindness that what a kind Santa Claus you were towards your poor people. I'm too, turning towards you for some favor if you would please listen to me. We would like to buy a bus on which we could go to school from Duquesne to McKeesport. We have to walk and we cross the Monagohaila River. Some of the smaller children don't have good clothes, and we almost freeze when we cross that river in this kind of cold weather. We can't collect any money for the bus because the people are all poor. Our school has been built two years ago had has a big mortgage that can't help us eighter. Dear Mrs. Roosevelt I always think of your love and I know that you will help us. I know that your heart is kind to wards the poor. You did a lot for our country too. We will always remember you like we remember George Washington. Excuse me that I can't write you such a good letter that should be written to you because Im too young and no body didn't help me to write this letter. I know that you will help the children some. I thank you even before you help us. I hope that everybody

will remember you till this county stands and I will pray until you live so that you would be happier this new year than you were before. If you would listen to me for what I am asking than please notify Sister Mary F. . . .

Sincerely Yours

I. L.

■ Fallsville, Arkansas

Jan. 3, 1934

Dear Friend,

I call you friend, although you are many miles away, and I've never seen you. I want you to be my friend in time of need. I am a young girl sixteen years of age and want to start into High School. I have now completed the 8th grade in the country school, but haven't the money to buy books or pay tuition. We had three months of school here on account of insufficient funds.

It may be kind of hard to start in mid term but I am willing to study hard. My parents are poor and there are four more children. Tuition will be four or five dollars a month. There will be four months. Books four dollars. As to my clothes I'll manage as best I can. To get an education is my ambition.

I'll be anxiously awaiting your reply.

Your friend,

E. M.

■ Amarillo, Texas

Jan. 4, 1934

Dear Mrs. Roosevelt,

I am a young girl eighteen years of age and in the ninth grade. I have always had a hope of completing high school any way. When I was bearly fourteen I graduated from the 8th grade at Halister, Oklahoma. My folks then moved to New Mexico and have made four crop failures and have been unable to send me to school last year for 2½ months. I worked my way thro school, and by hard work studing and prayer I made four whole high school credits. . . . This year I wanted to go so bad I left home and came to Amarillo thinking I could find a place to work for my room and board. I succeeded up until Christmas but since more students came in I can't find a place any where and really don't know what I shall do. It takes $150 to go thro school. This pays for my tuition, cloths, board and books. I have sold candy for part of my books but only make 75 cents a week to my part this did not meet the full demand. In 3 years I can finish if I can go on which I hope to do. I just wander if you could help me some. It will only take $140 a year & I can finish in 3 years with this year.

I have always wanted to get an education but for so long (nearly four years) I had lost almost all hopes. A number of the people makes fun of me being so old & in such a low grade but I am willing to stand all the cuffs and huffs to get through school. I go to the S.O. 7 School in Amarillo. I hope to hear from you soon as I'm in great need. I have a place to stay until the 15th of Jan. then if I can't get some money somewhere to help me I can never make this term. Any thing you can do will be oh so much appreciated. For I see my need to schooling and I so long to get an education. I have been making from 90–100 on most everything.

Your unseen friend,

E. S.

East Point, Ky.

Jan. 31, 1934

Dear Mrs. Roosevelt,

I am a girl sixteen years old. In 1930 I was a freshman in the Painteville High School but had to quit going on account of the depression. Since then financial difficulties have kept me from going to school anywhere, even a public school. The Painteville High school was the nearest school to my home. And it was about seven miles away. When I was going I had to get out of bed at 5:30 ever morning at 6:45 I had to leave home. I live on the river so I had to cross it in a boat. Sometime when it would be raining or snowing I would have to change shoes when I got across. And in winter when I started from home it would be so dark I could hardly see. Then I had to walk one mile on the railroad before I could get to the bus line. My parents worked hard to keep me in school. I wanted a good education and a chance in the world. And they wanted me to have it but since we live on a farm and could sell nothing it wasn't long until I had to quit school. My father had many debts he had to pay so of course he could not pay them and send me to school even though I was going to a public school he found it hard to buy my clothes, books, pay for my bus fare, etc. so there was nothing left for me to do but quit. Mrs. Roosevelt I am writing the truth today there is only $2.07 in money that we can call our own. Of course, we have some things to sell but noone wants to buy anything.

And now I am going to ask a favor of you although I don't know what you will think of me for doing so. I want you to send me enough money so that I can finish High School. I will not ask you to give me any. I want you to know and believe I will pay it back when ever I can although it might be years before I could. I wouldn't ask you but I though that since it couldn't mean much to you but would mean everything to me may be you might. If you couldn't lend me much a small amount would help me more than I can tell you. I might never be able to pay it back but I hope so.

Please Mrs. Roosevelt let me hear from you.

Yours very truly

M. L. A.

■ Chicago, Illinois

[Feb. 1934]

Dear Mrs. Roosevelt,

I'm a girl of fourteen years old. I came from Italy, my native country, three years ago. Few days ago I was promoted to 8-A in the Haines School, at 231 West 20th Street, Chicago, Illinois. In June, when I graduate, I will be fifteen years old. I will be too young to stop going to school, yet, if a miracle doesn't happen I will have to stop.

I have no father and my mother doesn't know how to speak English very well. I have a brother younger than I, and he's in the same grade with me. My mother would whant both of us to go to school, and be something when we grow up. Yet, she can't afford, to send both of us. My brother being the youngest, he's also the lucky one. He would go to school while I will have to stay home. Oh, I just hate to think of it. I just would love to go to school. I do not like to go to school just to spare time, like some do, but I would like to go to learn.

Dear Mrs. Roosevelt, you might have wondered until now, why do I tell you all these things. Well, you see I thought perhaps you could help me. I can not even think of how you could help me. But maybe there's some way. You have been so kind to every body, and maybe you will help a girl that doesn't whant to quit school. I can embrodrei very good, and my mother thinks I could get work to do at home, after I graduate. If you could help me, nothing would be so dear to me, than you. Education is more than anything in the world to me.

For the present I only have to thank you, with all my heart.

Sincerely yours,

L. B.

■ Youngstown, Ohio

Feb. 3, 1934

Respectable Madam,

I am very sorry to disturb you with my letter but the immediate need of help forces me to do so.

I am 14 years of age and was promoted to the 10th grade Friday, January 26th 1934. I have always been a good student and I am awfully sorry to think that I shall be forced to not attend school unless I get my books.

My father has always been a travelling salesman for Italian wholesale groceries. On January 30th 1932, he lost his job on account of the depression and from that time on has been unemployed. He had once worked for the Rome Importing Company of New York City. During these two years, he borrowed all he could from his insurance policy and with the small amount of cash he had on hand we were able to get along due to the fact that he had earned up to $50 a week and had fully equipped us in clothes etc.

Our landlord, knowing my father's honesty, has permitted us to remain in his house and dad will pay the rent when he works. . . . Now dad is completely broke and cannot buy my books. The books I need are:

First Spanish Course—Hills and Ford
Easy Spanish Reader—Tardy
English—Tanner
Modern Biography—Hyde
New Plane Geometry—Durrell & Arnold
Second Latin Book—Ullman & Henry

I have gone to the Board of Education with my parents several times but the only answer I get is that they won't help me because they have no funds for new books and the ones that they have will be given to those who got them from the Board last year. The woman in charge also told me that I was well-dressed. As I told you before my dad had equipped me pretty well but it just happened this skirt I had on was given to me by an aunt for Christmas. I told her this but of course she probably didn't believe me.

Last year I borrowed books from a friend of mine because she has finished using them but now she is using the same books that I need, and so is unable to help me in any way. My father has been a very honest U.S. citizen for over 22 years and mother for over 18 years.

I would like to explain our situation more fully but I won't annoy you any longer. Please help me as much as you possibly can as I shall be ever grateful to you.

Most respectfully yours,

C. S.

P.S. I have heard and read of your many kind and magnanimous acts and I feel sure to have your valuable support in this matter.

My wish for the betterment of this glorious conuntry is that Franklin D. Roosevelt could be President forever. Long Live the President & his Entire Family!!

Big Rock, Tennessee

[acknowledged Aug. 3, 1934]

Mrs. Franklin D. Roosevelt

Don't cast this away unread. Its not a sob story though it does sound pretty sobby.

Whether writing you is the thing I should, or should not do, I don't know, but I feel as if you'll not be offended because you were a school teacher once—Were you not?

My trouble is this—I am eighteen years of age and ready to enter school as a sophomore this term which begins Sept. 3. But the main thing is I *cant* attend. With me life has always been just a day to day existance, but I've managed (or Dad has) to be in school this far. As a studious girl I've always made good. My grades in my final exams last term were 97-98-99-100-. My friends and teachers encourage me to finish school, and, oh, I do want to—but it seems impossible, and is impossible with us. I thought perhaps you'd understand and would help me, well I'm ashamed to ask it but if I have to fall out of school it means the last of my hopes, for my one ambition is to be a writer.

I've always wanted to write and have tried both poetry and short stories. I have a collection of these on hand but writers are not made overnight and I know the road to authorship is a hard one. With an education it would be hard for a poor country girl like me but without even a high school education it means "you're just a flop." My English teacher said that I had talent and if I would keep on I could reach success but how can I "keep on keeping on" with no backing?

I hope you understand, I hope you help me, yet do you understand, how could you? You've never been a farm girl like me. Can you imagine getting up before "Sun-up" and going to work in the tobacco patch and all the time be thinking of school days comming when there'll be no school for you, thinking of the hundreds of old memories and things that happen in school life, thinking of the old pals you've been separated from so long, thinking of the gossips that will wag their tongues when you drop from the school gang and thinking last, *What will I ever amount to?* No, you can't imagine it, who could unless they've had experience as I have?

Can you imagine how hard it is to be eighteen—just in the morning of womanhood when life should be at its highest, to have all your plans and hopes crushed, To have to refuse all the gaiety and pleasure that a young girl should have just because your clothing is not sufficient? Well that's how it is with me. Last week a friend asked me why I had quit coming to church—it embarrassed me but I told the truth. My shoes were not fit to be seen in public!

Dad can't buy for me. He can't get the necessary things for home life—Why? He and I have all that we can do to keep our crop worked, Mother's pregnant, and Dad would have to desert his crop if he could find work.

I hope you don't think me a crank for I really am not. It hurts me to ask but could you—would you, help me personally, to attend school? Surely a woman like you can understand.

Respectfully,

R. C. T.

■ Humboldt, Kansas

Jan. 5, 1935

My Dear Mrs. Roosevelt:

Would you have time to read a letter from just a country girl? I will be sixteen years old March 22. I am a senior in High School.

We worked hard during the campaign for Mr. Roosevelt, our Democratic club (young peoples) had meetings and gave short programs before the speaking. I was on the programs all over the county for tap dances.

Here is my problem. We raised no grain and money is scarce. My father was seriously injured two months ago, which made it still harder. I need clothes for school but haven't funds to buy them. I just wondered if you might have some I could make over, as I do all my own sewing—which is mostly madeover. I would appreciate anything as I have to go ten miles to school and I have no overshoes or not very good shoes.

Dresses, hose that can be mended and used, shoes, overshoes or underwear. I wear 6½ shoes and a 16 dress.

If you can help me—write me.

Thank you.

Sincerely

P.S. Please do not let this be put in the newspapers.

■ Drumright, Okla.

January 16, 1935

Mrs. Roosevelt:

I am a girl, age fourteen (14), and in the eleventh grade. I am five feet, three inches tall, have brown hair and blue eyes, and weigh about 130 pounds. I have gone to school eight years, all of which my mother has paid for. My parents were divorced before I started to school, and my father, who is married again and has children, does not help us any. I have 1 brother, aged sixteen (16) who is also in the eleventh grade. He is taller than I am but weighs several pounds less. We are both at the head of our class, and have been exempted from all our semester "exams" so far.

We desire to go to college when we finish high school, and if we can manage the clothes and money, maybe have to work our way through, we will, if at all possible. My brother wishes to be a lawyer and enter politics, and I want to be a primary school teacher, an author, and a church and Welfare worker. I teach a class of girls, age 4 to 8 each Sunday and my brother, a class of boys, 4 to 9.

We lived in town for a while and Mother worked, but we had to come to the country over four years ago. My brother and I pick cotton each year for our clothes and Mother keeps house for a man, who surely does like, Mr. Roosevelt's new Deal. Since there was so little cotton this year we didn't have very much money to buy the clothes that we *have* to have.

We go to a high school six miles from home, and walk two miles waiting in the cold till the truck comes. We have no car, no radio, or any other musical instrument.

I am writing this letter to ask if you have any cast-off clothing or any wearing apparel you don't want. I would certainly appreciate them and Mother could make them over to fit me. If you have anything which isn't already spoken for, it would be new to me and I could surely use it. It costs a "lot of money" to keep in dresses, hats, slippers, hose, coats, underthings and everything else that a person needs and I don't have that "lot of money" to spare because it takes so much to go to school.

I would always remember you for the kindness you would be sharing, if you would send me some of your things that you have no longer any use for. I don't want you to think I am begging you for anything, but I'm merely asking for some cast-offs you don't want. I could use *anything* and it would surely make my Senior year in high school, much easier.

Your friend,

S. A.

P.S. — I'll tell all our friends what fine people you Roosevelts are in the next Presidential Election.

■ Albertville, Ala.
January 1, 1936
Dear Mrs. Roosevelt,

For some time I have wished to be aqainted with you. Or merly to receive a letter from you. I haved wish much to see you, but as I am a poor girl and have never been out of our state that will be impossible I guess.

Mrs. Roosevelt since I have been in high school I have been studing modern things and conveniences. I took your family for my study. I have found the study to be the most interesting subjects I could have found. In the study I at all times know where you are, by reading all papers I find at school and elsewhere. I find what you are doing. You may never had given this a thought, but to think over our daily lives there is a good story to it.

My life has been a story to me and most of the time a miserable one. When I was 7 years old my father left for a law school and never returned. This leaving my mother and 4 children. He left us a small farm but it could not keep us up. . . .

I am now 15 years old and in the 10th grade. I have always been smart but I never had a chance as all of us is so poor. I hope to complete my education, but I will have to quit school I guess if there is no clothes can be bought. (Don't think that we are on the relief) Mother has been a faithful servent for us to keep us to gether. I don't see how she has made it.

Mrs. Roosevelt, don't think I am just begging, but that is all you can call it I guess. There is no harm in asking I guess either. Do you have any old clothes you have throwed back. You don't realize how honored I would feel to be wearing your clothes. I don't have a coat at all to wear. The clothes may be too large but I can cut them down so I can wear them. Not only clothes but old shoes, hats, hose and under wear would be appreciated so much. I have 3 brothers that would appreciate any old clothes of your boys or husband.

I wish you could see the part of North Alabama now. The trees, ground and every thing is covered with ice and snow. It is a very pretty scene. But Oh, how cold it is here. People can hardly stay comfortable.

I will close now as it about mail time. I hope to hear from you soon. (ans real soon)
Your friend,
M. I.

■ Phila., Penna.

Sept. 7, 1936

Dear Mrs. Roosevelt,

I am a young girl of thirteen and I have great ambitions. My parents are very devout, but poor people. During the past eight years, we have always lived very close to the school and we still do, but I graduated from grammar and I have a great distance to walk every day. Therefore I have to be well equipped. My parents have six other children. It is extremely hard to provide our family with food, shelter, and clothing on an income of $19.60. It is my heart's desire to become a school teacher. I often think of giving my parents all the luxuries I am denied. For instance a lovely home with everything a couple of old folks could want. I only hope they will live that long. My object for writing this letter is ask your aid in helping me to get a lovely coat to wear to school. Won't you help me Mrs. Roosevelt? I need one so badly. If I don't get one soon I will have to miss school and I dread the ordeal. Just any kind you feel I should have. Will you kindly send it. Oh Mrs. Roosevelt you don't know how much we will appreciate your gift. I live in the rural part of North Philadelphia and I have to walk to 15th & Wallace Streets. I beseech you to help me please. I do believe you will help me.

Prayerfully yours,

G. H.

P.S.

I forgot my size

Sweet sixteen

■ Granette, Ark.

Nov. 6 1936

Dear Mrs Roosevelt

I am writing to you for some of your old soiled dresses if you have any. As I am a poor girl who has to stay out of school. On account of dresses & slips and a coat. I am in the seventh grade in school but I have to stay out of school because I have no books or clothes to ware. I am in need of dresses & slips and a coat very bad. If you have any soiled clothes that you don't want to ware I would be very glad to get them. But please do not let the news paper reporters get hold of this in any way and I will keep it from geting out here so there will be no one else get hold of it. But do not let my name get out in the paper. I am 13 year old.

Yours Truly

■ Comanche, Texas
[received Sept. 3, 1940]
Dear Mrs. Roosevelt.

I am a thirteen (13) year old Farm girl from down in Comanche Texas. School will start this next Monday Sept. 2.

And I have no clothes or shoes to wear to school. My Father (G. C. P.) is Seventy two years of age and gets on Old Age pension of $14 a month, but there are eight (8) of us so it takes All that to live on.

I am the oldest child of our Family.

My mother is sick all time, and can't work. And Oh, Mrs. Roosevelt I do want to go to school. I will be in the seventh grade when school starts. I would have been in the eighth grade but I did not get to go to school last term. I always make exilent grades on all my work in school when I can go, and this is the reason. Every time I get to start I always stay in after school and at recess for fear I will have to stop school and wont get to make all my grades. And while I am trying so hard to go to school, Others are being made go to school and are wishing they would not have to go. Mrs. Roosevelt why is it that way?

Why can't I find a way to get me some clothes and shoes. Mrs. Roosevelt can you help me? I have written an order to Sears RoeBuck and Co. Dallas Texas for clothes and shoes and I am sending it to you. And if you will help me you can send the order on to Sears RoeBuck and Comapany. Mrs. Roosevelt if you have a kind heart (which I'm sure you do) you will help me. Its hard to write this, with tears rolling down ones cheeks. But this was my only chanch Mrs Roosevelt, I am wondering if Monday morning will be a happy day for a little girl who is now sad. And I have great Faith in you helping me. If you send the Order (which I'm sure you will) all you have to do is send the money and your name and address But have the order sent to me.

Mrs Roosevelt I can't believe you will fail me.

Please, Mrs Roosevelt help me

I'm not wanting much just what I think you can afford. May God Bless You

GP

GRADUATIONS/PROMS

- Harrodsburg, Ky.
  December 18, 1933
  Dear Mrs. Roosevelt,

  I wrote you more than a week ago but, never recieve any responds from you. Please help me, if you think that much I ask you were to much Why not Loan me the amount of $18.75 for Debt on Sewing ring, Pin and invitation cards and if you have any old white dress, an old crep dress I can rite for my class dress an old dress for the senior, and junior prom, an old grey cap and sward you know what I am trying to explain to you. Your husband, son, daughter, and your self have been through the same thing of what I am going through, I mean graduation but, still not like me, you all of high class could finance yours and look forward to a happy graduation why I am of poor class no parents, no means by which to finance my graduation in any way. It is a pleasure to graduate but, it gives me more heart aches than pleasure. At night it is a constance worry with me wondering just what to do, or how to do, to go about doing some thing. I haven't any job and can't get one, holding the class back, who have their money for their things and waiting on me to bring mine. Please shut your eyes for a while just imaging you are in my predictment. Please understand and help me. If you would send the clothes to I can make them over during the holidays and pay for my things just as soon as I can give the secretary of my class the money to send to Lexington, Ky.

  Mr. E. our superintendent of Harrodsburg, Ky, Mr. J. R. of Frankfort Ky our superintendent and Mrs. S. have been very good to give me my books and a few clothes Please help me and please don't disappoint me as I know no one else to help me, write in care of Mrs. M. E. C. old lady I stay with for food and room

  A very anxious poor girl
  H. L. M.
  P.S.
  Hopen to hear from you at once (Please)

- Briscoe, Texas
  February 28, 1934
  Dear Mrs. Roosevelt:

  I dont know but I supose you probably get lots of letters like this but here is my trouble. School will close some time in April. I am in the eleventh

*The Faculty and Senior Class
of the
Wicomico High School
announce the
Graduating Exercises
Friday evening, May thirty-first
nineteen hundred thirty-five
eight o'clock
High School Auditorium*

This graduation announcement accompanied a letter that an eight-year-old girl from Maryland sent to Mrs. Roosevelt in 1935, asking for "a dark blue suit size 35" so that her oldest brother could attend his graduation ceremonies. "If you could find an old suit one of your boys used to wear mother could mend it as I think she is the best mother in the world."
(From the collection of the Franklin D. Roosevelt Library, Hyde Park, N.Y.)

grade and will graduate when school is out. But I have no nice dress or slippers to wear I don't know I supose it is pride but all the other girls will have new dresses & shoes and I could not attend to either the banquet or graduation ceremonies with out looking like the rest of the kids Daddy is a renter we lost our home in Oklahoma eight years ago. We have been renting ever since. Daddy is good to us kids but money has run so short he said he couldnt afford to spend so much money for a dress and pair of shoes. But he nor Mama, either, ever went to school long enough to graduate they do not know what it means to a young person Daddy had always promised me when I graduated he would get me a guitar for a graduation present but he said the other day he couldnt. I have always wanted to play and sing. But I can't see no way through Mama isent the kind that believes in girls working out. She said when I went to working out I stayed out so thats that. I have no hopes that way. Can you manage to send me enough to get me a dress and slippers. If you had rather I'll send my size and you can pick a dress your self. But I've got to have one some way or I cant bear to face an audience and my classmates with these I supose you know how I feel I supose you were all along this line I dont know you may just laugh and throw this in a waste paper basket But please do not. Won't you help me some way. I wear 4½ slippers and 34 Bust measure. 51 in. length. Mrs. Roosevelt when you answer this (I want you to answer whether you do any thing else or not) wont you send me one of your pictures. I've got one I cut out of a paper and I nearly worship it but I want a real one. Well I must close and study my English so hoping you can help me some way. Wont you answer real soon.

Your true friend

I. M.

P.S.

If you send money send any amount you want to. I supose you know about what they cost.

■ Seiling, Oklahoma

April 12, [1934]

Dear Mrs. Roosevelt,

I am writing to you only because I need help. I am a fifteen year old girl and am in the eighth grade. This year I am looking forward to my graduation out of the eighth grade into high school.

The thing I am worrying about now is how I am going to get the money to buy my graduation clothes. My folks are poor and cannot afford to buy my graduation clothes. It takes every cent they get to buy food. There is a big family to support and therefore it takes quite a bit to keep us.

I've tried to get a job working, but I can't seem to be lucky enough to get one. If I can't soon get some money I'm left out. School is out May 15 and that isn't so far off. I know that you probly get letters every day like this asking for help, that maybe are false. But this one is not. I can send proof if necessary. Mrs. Roosevelt could you send me $20. for my graduation?? I figure that isn't very much to you, but it certainly would mean a lot to me. I would certainly appreciate it very much. If you could only know how bad I really need it.

I think you could spare $20. very easlly and never miss it.

My folks nor no one else knows I'm writing to you asking for money, I don't want any one to know it.

No one on earth knows my heart aches. I have been looking forward to my graduation for a long time and studying hard to make it. I didn't know then what I do now. I wouldn't ask any one for help if I didn't need it. But I guess I should be thankful for what I have.

Mrs. Roosevelt its awful to have graduation so near then be wondering how on earth you can get any money to buy clothes. God only knows what I go through with and I feel that he is with me and is going to help me. Please help me out. I'll promise to keep it secret. Please give it a thought. I hope and pray you will not make fun of this letter. Hoping to hear from you real soon.

Yours truely

P.S.

Please help me because we only have 5 more weeks of school. Answer real soon and I promise not to tell anyone.

■ Meadow view, Virginia
April 17, 1934
Dear Mrs Roosevelt.

I am writing you in regard to helping me get my Graduation Clothes I have tried my best to get an Education but have had a struggle going to school. We are so poor. My father was once a railroader but has been out of Employment for 4 years And there's 6 of us children. Im the oldest. We've been in such hard luck. I'm 14 years old and finish free school the 10th of May All the other girls in my Grade are boasting about their nice white dresses and shoes they're wearing for the commencement. While I've nothing. I've often heard of how good and kind you were to poor folks especially Children that I thought I would ask you for some help. I would appreciate it so much and then I could enjoy going to the closing of school. In case you could send me something (second Handed) if you care to send me anything I'm large to my age I'm 5 ft. 6 in. wear a *no* 6 shoe but only weigh 127 pounds. So you see I'm tall and slender. We girls are all supposed to wear white. So anything will be greatly appreciated and will thank you for what you've done for other folks I've read about. Kindly consider this as it will mean a lot to a girl like me.

Your grateful and Thankful Friend

M. S.

■ Haynes, Arkansas

December 30, 1934

Dear First Lady,

I guess you get lots of letters similar to this, but I thought I'd try writing you anyway.

I'm twenty and a Senior in High School. I know I'm rather old to still be in High School but there have been years in which I haven't been able to go. My parents are old, my mother is fifty-five and my father is seventy-one, and we are very poor. My father is a farmer—a share-cropper and there have been years when we haven't made enough money to send me and my sister to school. During those years we picked cotton and bought clothes to go the next term of school. Even this year we stayed out the first three weeks of school to pick cotton to help pay our way through this term, though we have some cousins who have been generous in sending us dresses, which they can no longer wear and even sent a coat, which was still wearable.

During the summer before the depression shut down too tight I worked in a factory and saved my wages to buy books and clothes for the fall term.

I've never been able to attend parties given by my class due to the lack of money and the fact that we've lived so far from town. Now commencement is on its way and I'd like to have clothes I wouldn't be ashamed of to wear to the parties and dinners given in honor of the Seniors, and especially the Junior-Senior Banquet.

There are other expenses, too—the invitations and cards, the cap and gown and the pictures. My mother is the only one in the family working and she gets only five days a month in the F.E.R.A. Sewing room. So I see no way of making my wishes come true.

I had intended working in the Five and Ten during the week before Christmas but I was ill with the "Flu." This caused the end of my hopes of possessing a class ring.

After graduation I intend to enter training for a nurse.

Wondering if you can help me make my wish of graduating as the other girls in my class will, I am

Sincerely yours

A. R.

Following is a series of five letters from the same teen.

◼ Graniteville, Mass.

Mar. 18, 1935

My Dearest Mrs. Roosevlt,

Just a line to let you know if you can help me out a little, if you dont mind. There is nine of us in the family & no one working I'm the oldest (15 yrs.) My father hasn't been working for 3 yrs. He got hurt up the quarrel where he was a stone cutter. This coming June I have to graduate grammer school and I suppose I can't. So I thought I would write to you & let you know if you can send at least a small check that I could get every thing for graduation & if any is left over I'd get a dress, & coat for Easter. This is the first time that I gratuating and I'd like to graduate as the other girls. Well I hope I will received what I told you. When I'm working I will send you a lovely gift. Dear Mrs. Roosvelt Please, please don't say anything to anyone because I wrote for help. Please don't. Please don't even put this letter in the newspaper. Because I know you will help me account of being the President wife. You are a lovely, lovely lady. I'll pray to God every minute I think of it and ask him that I will receive the check. If you do send a check please write a letter also to be sure that you send it. I thank you very much if you send it. I'll be expecting to receive a envelope from Washington D.C.

Thank You.

Yours truly

P.S. Please don't forget. Please don't let me worry about graduating

◼ Dear Mrs. Roosevelt

Would you kindly send me a wraist watch *please?* Don't forget now. For *Easter.* Don't forget what I told you about the money. Please. I'll be expecting by *Friday.*

■ Dear Mrs. Roosevelt another word I would like to write is, that no one in the world expect you and I knows that I wrote. So please don't say any thing to any one. Please send me what I told you.

■ Graniteville, Mass.
[no date]
My Dearest Mrs. Roosevelt
I wrote you a letter & haven't received the money nor the wraist watch. Graduation is drawing nearer & nearer every day and yet I didn't receive a cent from you. I made a whole list of things that I needed for graduation including the ring and the amount was 22.83. Please send me $30.00 that I can get Mother something for Mothers Day Please Please send me a wraist watch. Because I never had one. I'll be expecting the money and the wraist watch by Tuesday without disppointed. I always cry because I can't gradu-ate and even cry because you didn't send me the money & the wraist watch. Other people won't know if you send the money or not. Just my mother.

My father said that I had to leave school next week. and that makes me very weak. Please send the money that I could graduate. No one will know if you will send it to me. Tell the President & see what he says. I bet he'll send it to me. Please tell him if he would that I won't worry of graduating. I hate to leave school because school is very interesting to me. Please send what I told you or the President will. If you send it Tuesday. well it will be a luckie day for me. I will remember you until I died, if you send what I told you.

I been waiting & waiting to get the money and wraist watch from you and I never heard yet. Two weeks ago I wrote to you. Please help me.

Thank you.
Yours truly
P.S. Tuesday will be my lucky day. without disppointed.

■ Graniteville, Mass.
April 16, 1935
My Dearest Mrs. Roosevelt,
I received the letter that you send me and you found it impossible to help me out a tiny bit. There might be a lot of people that write to you but I don't know. I thought I would have good luck from you but I didn't. I had bad luck. I read in the newspaper that a girl send you a cherry pie and the President send her a hundred dollars. Well if I received that much or even half I think I'd be million air. Please my dear Mrs. Roosevelt just try your best to send me as much as you can. Because no one will know if you

send it to me or not just you and I. and I also told my mother about it, she said the only thing is that I can't graduate. I really thought that I was going to graduate by you, if you send it to me. I need new Easter clothes and I didn't get anything yet. I need a coat, shoes, dress, stockings and hat and even the underclothes for Easter. For graduation I need the same and even more without the coat. So please Mrs. Roosevelt try and send it by Friday that Saturday I can go down town and do my Easter shopping and get my graduation clothes. When I received the letter yesterday morning I was so happy I thought you send it to me but you didn't. When I look in the envelope to see, I was so disppointed that I couldn't hardly read it. Of cause I need the clothes very badly, I don't even go to church sometimes. And that is a very bad sin, but what am I going to do. When I am working I will send you a lovely gift. I won't forget. Don't you forget to send the *check*. I'll be expecting it Friday without disppointed please

Your truly

◼ Bartlesville, Oklahoma

May 5-1935

Dear Mr. & Mrs. Roosevelt:

In regard to my project, I am writing you, for help.

I am an Eighth Grade Student of Fish Creek School, Washington County.

Now as School is near an end I have Graduated to High School, and I am not able to get my Graduation clothes or to supply my needs to enter High School and my parents are not able to help me. I am at the age of 16 years, and I haven't been able to get a job yet.

Any favors returned would certainly be appreciated by,

Your ever lasting citizen

O. E.

A few words to Mrs. Roosevelt, as I have read some of the articles published by you.

You must be a kind hearted woman, and understand the needs of the poor class of people, and also our President has done many great favors for his citizens.

◼ [Westphalia, Kan.]

March 30, 1936

Dear Mrs. Roosevelt—

I am sending in a reading or a song I composed one night after supper.

I hope u and the President will like it.

Of course u can tell by it that we are Democrats. All of our entire connections are.

My name is L. R. W. I was 18 the 7th of last Sept. There are 12 in our family and I am the oldest living

We haven't made any crops here for three straight in very poor circumstances

I go to High School and am a Jr. this year.

I contracted lobar Pneumonia during the Xmas holidays and came near dying. I was out of School 9 weeks Seven of those wks I was bedfast

The third wk I was taken to the hospital and a operation was performed to drean my lungs in order to save my life. They taken out a part of my rib & put tubes in to drean the puss off

I started back to H.S. the first day of March and I have the most of my work made up. However I am still very weak. The Dr's didn't think I would live at all.

My folks are very poor & I am sure striving hard trying to receive a good education and live right as I journey along my way.

We will have our Jr. & Sr. Banquet the week following Easter but I will just stay at home and miss it all . . .

I think I can make out with other things I have if only I had a presentable dress.

I thought of u maybe u would help me out along this line. I have read different times u are the best dressed woman in America. And I know u have a mighty big heart

Some pretty lt color pink rose gold or tan or even blue I think would be swell. I don't care for anything so expensive I will enclose u a picture. . . . I can wear a 32 Bust but 34 will be better. I am five ft & 4 inches tall and weigh 120 lbs. Am a brunette with naturally curly hair

If u would send me any thing I would be tickled with anything but I wouldn't want a sun back as I have terrible scars from my operation and I don't like those anyway. I wear 5½ cc shoes.

I am sending this all by myself. I do so want to go to the Banquet but I know my folks can't get me the necessary things. the stork again next mth in our family. I have 1 sister the rest are brothers.

Let's keep this a secret as I am afraid it would hurt my folks if they knw I wrote u. They are willing to do if they only could.

There are five in school besides me. My brother 16 a Freshman & the rest in the grades.

Respectively
Your True Friend

[Her song:]
1.
O, come now all ye people
And listen while I tell
About Franklin D Roosevelt
A man u all know well.
2.
His face is fair and handsome
His heart is brave and true
And he's doing all for the
Common people
That any man can do.
3.
The republicans they do cuss him
I'll tell u it is a sight
And when I hear them cuss him
It makes me want to fight
4.
For I know they are jealous
Of the grand things he has done
For they do not like to see
The little man with more
5.
And when the fight is ended
And Franklin D has won
You sure will hear them cussing
About how it was done
6.
They'll say he bought his way in
With all those Federal funds
And will not once admitt it
Twas the greatest thing he done.
Author L. R. W.

[The writer also encloses two advertisements for dresses.]

■ Linden, New Jersey

May 10, 1936

Dear Mrs. Roosevelt,

I am a young girl in high school (16 years old) and I realize that I can't have everything because I come from a large family. Father works but he doesn't make much, so mother works to help out. My older sister and brother work but they have intentions of getting married soon so ————. I have another brother (I hate to call him a brother) he's *so* lazy. He sleeps every minute and eats like a pig. We all hate him from the youngest to the oldest. Mother works so hard but he doesn't care; he curses her and all. He just won't work because he has it good at home doing nothing (and I *mean nothing* because he wouldn't think of chopping wood or fixing the place up.) Whenever he has a chance, he smacks the kids around but now he's afraid to because we said if he hits anyone of us, we're going to the police and have him arrested. He always gives my married sister and my mother a "sob story" of how he looks for work and can't find it. This isn't true because we leave for school & he's sleeping; when we come home he's still sleeping. My married sister said we should try to make friends with him—but how can we—he makes our home such a "hell."

Mother is wise to his game now and wants him to get out. She won't throw him out 'cause she says it's a shame. She says God will fix him. (I'm still waiting)

I'm not writing to ask you to give him a job. He wouldn't work if all he had to do was push a pencil. He's just a plain ordinary bum, and I despise him.

I'm asking if you have an old (not old—modern style) gown of your daughter's that would fit me. (I take a size 12 (sometimes 14). My boy-friend (yes I have one. Perhaps sixteen is young to have boy-friends but I'm much older mentally—and he's so good to me.) wants me to go to the Prom with him, (The High School Prom) and I've disappointed him so many times that I just hate to tell him no. He knows all about my home and realizes that it is hard for me to get a gown. I've been saving for two months to get it and had five dollars, but I had to send for another one of my sister's typewriter. So now I only have two dollars left. I don't mind so much *giving* her the money but she said that if she got a job after school she'll *loan* me the money. That's what hurts. I practically paid for the typewriter myself. She doesn't worry about it very much—I do.

I *do* want to go because I never go anywhere. The prom is May 20 so I know I'll never have enough money by then. If I hadn't sent for the type-writer I could have bought a gown for five dollars but now I can't. Please Mrs. Roosevelt look around you may have one somewhere. If you don't, please write me a note because I would like to know if you recieved my letter. I've been disappointed so much that—oh well what's the sense of talking. Thank you if you try to help me and thank you if you don't. At least it helped being able to pour my troubles into someone's ear other than my boy friend's Please send the answer to this to I. H. c/o N. M. Jr. (That's my boy-friend)

Yours truly

I. H.

Thanks again

HIGHER EDUCATION

. . . .

■ Brooklyn, New York

May 14, 1934

Dear Mrs. Roosevelt:

I trust you will not misunderstand the writer and please help him out of the rest. I am an admitted freshman student to the University of Wisconsin but have not enough funds with which to matriculate. I need about two hundred and fifty dollars. Now, I've been reading a great deal of your activities on the radio and heard you on the radio. My parents haven't the money because my father does not earn enough on the C.W.A. [Civil Works Administration] Before he had the position he now holds with the C.W.A. he had a position with a big welfare organization. We had some money saved up for my education. I am ambitious to, and want to study medicine. My father was hurt in an automobile accident about ten months ago and was incapacitated as a result of it. I had a position but the salary was so little I just barely got along on it. . . . Before the C.W.A. job my father had a position and with a little part of each of our earnings we were able to put aside a few dollars. Of course, this entailed a great deal of self denial and scrimping. Recently the old injury was reopened in an unfortunate incident and we paid the doctor some of the money. We don't like charity. I was wondering if you would care to help a young man get started on his educational desire by giving him a helping hand? The proceeds of your money from the radio talks are to be used for education purposes? Why not an

Franklin D. Roosevelt scholarship for a needy student? Surely, the President deserves that! Or, better still, and further, why not, as the R.F.C. [Reconstruction Finance Corporation] has loaned money to industry (we construe it as education) an R.F.C. Student Aid Loan Fund as a dedicatory measure to the President of the United States? It can be designated as the Franklin D. Roosevelt Memorial Fund for needy students. Leaving the rest to your discretion and looking forward to spending the year 1934 at the University of Wisconsin,

Yours Very Truly,

L. L.

P.S. I have been in Washington before, but have never seen a President or First Lady. R.S.V.P.

■ Church Point, La.

June 18, 1934

Dear Mrs. Roosevelt:

We have read of numerous enterprizes of charities you have helped in and many other good things you have done to help the unfortunate class.

We are two young girls who are being denied the privelege of attending college. Our parents are unable to send us on to school. Prices have been low on farm produce, hence our farms have become heavily indebeted, and of course there is no money to send us to college.

If some way could be made for us to secure loans of about $350.00 each per semester for two years, until we could secure positions and repay the loans. We thought you might be able to give us the proper assistance in securing these. We are interested in attending Hillman College, at Clinton, Mississippi.

Louisiana ranks among the lowest of the States in illiteracy. Of course, we are not proud of this fact, it is a reflection on our people. But, Louisiana has been forgotten in lots of things. Our public school system has improved greatly, but nothing has been done to help the student after finishing high school.

Should you be able to help us, of course you would want references of dependable people. We could give you these to assure you we aren't in for any cheat or graft.

Please see that this letter and our names does not get published, for we would be looked on as "jokes," when we are really sincere. No one knows what it is to be denied the privelege of attending school unless you have known yourself—and, but for a few hundred dollars. There is very little work offered to an individual unless she has a college education.

Hoping this will receive the proper attention, we thank you.

Sincerely,

■ Medina, N.Y.

Nov. 1, 1934

Dear Mrs. Roosevelt,

In today's Buffalo Evening News I read where you were contemplating buying a set of dishes worth fifteen thousand dollars.

I am a young girl eighteen years old and would like very much to train for a nurse at the Presbyterian Hospital in New York City. This would cost between seven hundred and a thousand dollars. Because of the depression my parents are unable to send me there.

Couldn't you buy a fourteen hundred dollar set of dishes and lend me the other thousand so I might prepare myself to earn my living?

Yours truly,

A. B.

■ Allen University Columbia, S.C.

March 5, 1937

Dear Madam:

I suppose it is quite shocking to hear from a poor insignificant student, but I felt that you were just the person for me to bring my troubles to. I believe that you are one person who has the American Youth at heart. I do not feel that you are too blasé to consider my appeal.

The president of this institution has offered me a scholarship under the N.Y.A. which pays all of my expenses but $40.00. I entered school with the expectation of being to pay this amount at the end of the first semester, but I have not succeeded and the bill is past due. So I am writing you to ask you to please help me. By helping, I mean to lend me this amount until the summer months when I can work and pay it back. I promise to pay every cent of it back if I have to work my fingers to the bone.

First of all, I suppose this seems rather disgusting to you, but if you actually knew my financial circumstances and the little illiterate village from which I came you would be able to understand. There is nothing there that would inspire one to attempt to further his education, and yet I've reached my junior college year by honest hard work.

May I have the pleasure of hearing from you as early as possible? Thanks in advance.

Very respectfully yours,

M. E. P.

▦ University of Tennessee

Knoxville, Tennessee

December 30, 1937

Dear Mrs. Roosevelt:

What would you do: If you had a $60. note due today? If you were expecting to register for the second quarter at the university next week and had to have $40. to do so? If already you owed $300. for past schooling expenses? If you owed $100. for clothing and maintenance? If you couldn't pay your voice teacher and she wouldn't let you give up your lessons? If the job you were expecting hadn't materialized because you were not quite prepared? If you hadn't any money and no one to fall back on? What would you do?

I've asked myself that question until I'm sick. I didn't want to appeal to you or to anyone, but I was impelled to. By all the rules of finesse, etc. my pride shouldn't allow me to write to you, but after all isn't that false pride?

It is my real pride that prompts me to such presumption. I can't let down the friends who signed my notes, the stores who gave me credit, and my parents who can give me only a home.

You probably wonder how a young girl can be in such a mess. I hardly know myself. I'm sure I've made many mistakes, but not intentionally. When I have obligated myself I've have always looked ahead and believed that I would work things out, but "the best laid plans o' mice and men gang aft agley."

I swept floors, washed dishes, took care of babies, and ironed shirts in a small junior college in order to have an education. However, I had to make notes for part of my expenses.

I graduated in the middle of the depression. No work was available but school teaching, for which I was not very well suited. However, I was glad to get a position. One would suppose that I would have paid off my notes immediately. I had thought I would, but there was the rent, groceries, and upkeep of a family of eight, four of which were in school. My father had three small country churches that hardly paid for the gasoline required to reach them. There was no other work for him. My debts had to wait awhile.

At the end of three years of school teaching I knew I would have to quit.

My nerves wouldn't stand the strain any longer. No one but myself realizes how necessary it was for me to resign last summer.

My family was now in better circumstances and agreed to help me get a new start in the school of commerce at the University of Tennessee this fall and help take care of my debts. However, in their generosity, they overestimated. (But we've always lived on hope—there was never quite enough to be entirely practical. We've had to put up a respectable front. Our position in the community demanded it.) Anyway, their help just barely covered carefare and lunch money. I paid my maintenance fee at school with an N.Y.A. job. (I worked in an office when not in classes.)

So here I am, at the threshold of a new year, eager and hopeful, but feeling somewhat like a spider tangled up in his own web. I would rather have a job than anything, but I can't get one until I've had a little more training and I don't see how I can go to school, owing as much as I do.

I'm not asking for the future. I can take care of that, if only I can have respite from the past for just a little while.

I am not writing you merely as Mrs. Roosevelt, First Lady of the Land but as Mrs. R., "friend of the people." You will understand and hold in confidence what I have told you; you will not laugh at my seriousness, nor ignore my request. Everything you do and write speaks kindness. You have shown your appreciation for human worth regardless of rank. That is why I can appeal to you.

You have every reason to doubt my word and question the sincerity of my need, but I'm asking you to pay me the greatest compliment—just by believing in me. I could send you references, but investigation would mean delay and publicity. And can't you see how desperately I'm trying to keep my chin up. My friends and family would be shocked at my audacity in appealing to you but I'd feel myself a coward if I saw a way out and had not the courage to venture.

Mrs. Roosevelt, I do not ask you for a gift. I merely need a loan that will enable me to go on and keep my self respect. It will be a pleasure to repay you when I am able.

Neither do I ask for sympathy. I couldn't stand to be pitied. If I were hungry and in rags someone would give me a pittance. If I were a genius someone would invest in me, but as Miss L., Citizen, I can't promise anything except to contribute my share to the world's happiness.

This letter is already too long and now I hesitate to finish. Perhaps it sounds presumptuous, mercenary, begging—but it is sincere with no complaint or blame intended. I have shown you my heart. Please believe in me and forgive my mistakes and audacity.

I read these lines a few days ago: "There is one thing stronger than fear, dear. Faith. Fear is the chasm between our prayer and its answer, and faith is the bridge that crosses it." Until I hear from you my faith shall keep me strong.

And may you and yours have the happiest, most satisfying New Year ever.

Very respectfully,

The next letter, from R. L. W., is one of the few in this book that clearly came to Eleanor Roosevelt's personal attention. It is followed by the response from her secretary, Malvina T. ("Tommy") Scheider, then by a second letter from R. L. W.

■ Santa Rosa, Texas

August 8, 1939

Dear Mrs. Roosevelt:

This letter when you have finished reading it will probably be just another letter, but to me it will or will not be the turning point of my life.

I finished High School in Santa Rosa a small town near Mexico, which has only one Drug Store and no place that a girl could obtain work enough to lay up enough money to enter any college. I graduated as Honor Girl and I think that I would be able to make fair grades if I could afford to attend college. There is eleven at our house now and I am afraid that it will be impossible for me to attend college as my father's occupation is driving a school bus at seventy-five dollars a month.

I would like to borrow enough money to go to school four years at a nice college, and I would like to pay it back when I get a job. At a bank you are not allowed to do this and at all the other loaning firms they will not let you borrow money on this plan.

You are in a position to where it would be hardly any trouble at all because you are more fortunate in having plenty of money. Do not think I resent your having so much money, I think it is grand for anyone to be so fortunate, but I do envy you.

You know about what it costs to go respectably to college and if you are not afraid to trust me it would be my one aim to finish college with honors and pay your money back. I hope you will think the matter over before you discard this letter.

Sincerely yours,

R. L. W.

■ August 15, 1939

My dear Miss W:

Mrs. Roosevelt has asked me to acknowledge your letter which she read with sympathy. She is indeed sorry to know of your difficult situation, but regrets that she is unable to lend you the money you need. The number of demands on her resources make it impossible for her to respond to request for loans, much as she would like to do so.

Mrs. Roosevelt suggests, however, that you write to the National Youth Administration, Washington, D.C., as this agency may be able to help you in some way.

■ Santa Rosa, Texas

August 20, 1939

Dear Mrs. Roosevelt:

I was delighted to receive your letter which your secretary said you had requested she write me. Of course I was disappointed to learn that you would be unable to lend me the money which I requested but I understand how impossible it would be for you to meet all the requests you receive.

I had already investigated the NYA before I wrote you the letter. I can get twelve dollars a month working two hours every day. I will have to pay eleven dollars and fifty cents a month for tuiton. After I have payed my tuiton what will I have for clothing and my food. I plan to stay at home and ride twenty-two miles a day with some classmates who are going to attend the same college. I will have to pay seven dollars and fifty cents a month for transportation. Father said he would be able to help me in paying the transportation but he would not be able to help me get any clothing.

I thought I would let you know how everything was because I can't go to school with out clothing and I will not have time to do any extra work besides the NYA for I will have to study some times.

Thanks again for answering my letter.

Sincerely yours,

R. W.

■ Memphis, New York

Jan. 28, 1940

My dear Mrs. Roosevelt,

The article concerning yourself in the February Reader's Digest prompted this letter. I realize that the article said that you receive many such letters, as this one. However, I should like to tell you my story.

I am asking you to help me financially, toward my education. I must be a doctor! I have been two years trying to amass enough money to finance a seven-year medical course at Syracuse Medical College. It is a great medical center, and has the seven-year course, as an advantage over other eight-year courses.

At the present time I could furnish only one years's tuition ($375). I shall not enter any college unless I have the knowledge that my study need not be interrupted only because of lack of money.

I am willing to work and realize that I would have to do so, if I did go to college. The medical years (four) have a tuition of $500. Thus making the necessary fund to begin college with, $3,500.

I am now twenty years old, and I realize that the path I have chosen means seven years of hard study. Thus you see, the necessity of my beginning college soon.

I realize that a common person, such as myself, should not expect such a great thing as a college career! I rebel against that opinion. It is said that you, and many people such as yourself, have given to many charitable organizations. Why, then, am I not to be considered such an organization? I have the great ambition, and I believe the initiative, if its given an equal chance.

United States is supposed to be a nation of no narrow-mindedness. We have no "lower class" so to speak. But—how many have had great desires unfulfilled because others, better off, were unwilling to help less fortunate people?

I for one, shall ask for what I am unable to give myself. And if I can not be given a chance, I shall demand the reasons why.

I'm sorry if I have caused you pain by anything I have said. I sincerely hope that you are able to understand me and my desire. So few do.

I am Miss R. L.

◼ Marion, Alabama
September 15, 1940
Dear Mrs. Roosevelt:
I feel that I do not have the right to write to you, as you have never heard of me, but if you will be kind enough to read this letter I will be fully repaid for the time you spend in reading it. In case you need any question cleared up as to my character I shall refer you to Senator Lister Hill and Congressman Frank Boykin, both of the state of Alabama. You may ask them any question you like but that is for you to decide.

Mrs. Roosevelt somehow when you try to do something and do not obtain success it behooves one to try other places. I shall give you a word description of myself. I am the son of a widowed mother. I am five feet 6½ inches tall, weigh about 120 pounds, have dark blue eyes and dark black hair and as personality goes I rate myself as fair.

I am writing to you with the hopes that you may know of some way that you could help a very ambitious boy.

During the early part of January 1939, I received a letter from the Alabama State Department of Education which stated that upon my completion of my high school work at Murphy High School in Mobile, I would be eligible for aid in college—in any college of my choice—in the state of Alabama. This aid I learned later would pay for all supplies, tuition, and books, my junior and senior year. The fees and other expenses for the first two years would have to be met by me.

I am the son of a widowed mother, and the second oldest child in a family of four. Mrs. President—Mrs. Roosevelt have you ever really wanted any thing so badly in your life and try every way you knew to achieve that which you have set out to do only to find that the more you try the less the way seems clear? I am earnestly hoping that I may find a solution to my problem without turning to others but I have not succeeded. I am and have written to three of the leading schools in Alabama stating I was willing to give all my time and energy during the summer months aiding in any way I could professors in the colleges to which I had written, only to find that there was no provision made for young men who were financially unable to go to college.

I have hoped that I would be able somehow to get aid from *somewhere* to go to school for two years and then be able to take care of my own expenses for my last two years. During the months following my graduation from high school in Mobile last May 30, I worked my way through Marion Institute but I found that I could not meet expenses for the fall term. I finished Murphy High School in Mobile with an average of B in a four year academic course, during which time I worked an N.Y.A. school aid which kept me in school. I find that if I could get aid from anyone *for one year* I could attend Alabama Polytechnic Institute at Auburn, Alabama for the following amount

Uniform for R.O.T.C. Books—tuition,—room & board for a year—in fact all expenses for $500.00. I would also need clothes and two important pieces of equipment—a slide rule & Mechanical Drawing set which I would purchase from Montgomery Ward, Chicago for $16.00 which would save me about $10.00. What I would like to know is — (I know that due to conditions in Europe and the conditions in this country that you might think it absurd that a boy you have never heard of before you received this letter should write to you but Mrs. Roosevelt I earnestly *want an college education* and I am willing to work hard to prove that you could or anyone could depend on me) — would you be interested in aiding a young man to get a start in life who really wants to amount to something but cannot because he has no one who is interested enough in him to help him along? I would like to know also would you be interested in loaning a boy about $11.00. I know that is a lot of money for a boy who has no way of paying it back until completion of his college work but Mrs. Roosevelt I can assure you that I am dependable. I am neary 21 and I do not gamble, drink, curse, run around lie or cheat in any thing that I do.

I sincerely hope that you may answer this letter personally as I should like to have a letter from you to remember the wife of the greatest President the United States has ever had.

I sincerely hope that the people of the United States will not let the coming election and politics cause them to forget that our forefathers fought and died that this nation might under God flourish upon the face of the earth and that in its borders "men may know the truth and that it shall make one free." The last is taken from the Holy Bible.

For references I refer you to Dr. R. G., Pastor Siloam Baptist Church Marion, Alabama Dr. R. B. Dean Judson College, Marion, Alabama, Mr. K. J. C., Principal Murphy High School Mobile, Alabama, Miss M. E. Assistant Principal Murphy High School Mobile, Alabama

May we all feel the need of God during these troubled days and may God give you and yours many days upon the face of this earth and may strength & supreme wisdom be give to the President.

Yours very truly

J. D. E. II

P.S.

May God bless and keep you
May he cause his radiance to fall upon you
And give you power and peace
And may your life be filled with happiness and the peace that passeth
   all understanding

Mrs President —
A Prayer — dedicated to you.

Dear Father in Heaven
On this thy day do I send
Up a prayer of petition
and thankfulness.
Dear Lord on this thy day
I Humbly pray that peace
May come once again
Unto all men upon the face of the earth
May the people of this great land
O God realize that wealth
and pleasure are not
the things to bring peace to the body and soul
Or that quarreling beween nations over land
in wars which destroy
Can bring peace to the world.
Dear Lord I humbly pray that
Thou will grant wisdom
and a clear vision to
the President of the United States
and Dear Lord may we the
people of the United States
Keep forever the flame of Independence
and the freedom of all men
alive on the face of the Earth.
In the Name of thy Son who
died for the sins of the world
do we ask this
    Amen

◼ Penn State University
   [State College, Pa.]
   Nov 6, 1940
   Dear Mrs. Roosevelt,

I have suffered severe, crushing, heartrendering blows from life because of poverty. And I am still suffering. I am going to become a great social worker like you some day & dedicate my life in the fight against it.

My father is dead. My mother is seriously ill & my brother is dying with cancer. Last year my brother and I were probably the *only two in the state* to go to college while the *family was on relief.* It was too much for our pride so this year the family is not on relief. As you know it takes a great deal of money to go to college & keep a family at the same time. I am writing you this letter as a last resort, because I am supremely confident you will help me when you know how worthy my case is. I want to borrow as much money as you will lend me.

If you want more particulars or proof write & let me know. My father was a minister and I do not lie. Please, Please, help me so that I can make the life of my family a more happy one.

Very truly yours

C. H. S.

ARTS AND MUSIC

. . . .

■ Girard, Ohio

[no date]

Honorable Mrs. Franklin D. Roosevelt:

I am a girl twelve years of age and have always wanted to study piano, dancing, singing, and acting but I am not able to study these subjects because of lack of money. My father works but does not earn very much and we have many other debts and my mother is very ill at the present. All these things are preventing me to study these professions.

I am writing this letter with tears in my eyes to think that I have to beg for money from such a fine and noble lady as you. I am sure that if I could get the opportunity of learning these professions I would be very studious and would tell you where I'm studying, and how I'm studying. I am sure I would study just as good as I study in school. I am always on the honor roll in school and I enjoy studying.

I am sorry that I have to ask this of you but I have much faith in you and I am sure you will understand. I have two girl friends who are fortunate and take lessons and when they go on the stages and sing and dance and then get congragulations I cry to think that I can't be that fortunate.

Please forgive me for asking you to help me in these professions. Even if you do not help me please send me an answer and if possible please send me a picture of yourself. I am proud to say that I have a large picture of your honorable husband, President Franklin D. Roosevelt.

An unfortunate friend,

E. B. D.

■ Moorhead, Minn.

March 26, 1934

Dear Mrs. Franklin D. Roosevelt

I have been very interested in you because I read in the papers how much you were doing for the poor children and crippled children. I want to thank you for doing so much good for these little children cause I know how tough it is now.

I am thirteen years old and am going to school with my twin brother, and little sister M. who is eleven years old.

As daddy has been having kind of hard luck and is trying to get a letter through to President Roosevelt. I had to quit music lessons about two years ago as we had to sell the piano daddy bought me, to get clothes and stuff to eat.

Daddy used to teach school about twenty-five years ago Mamma has been making all the old clothes over for us for the last two years

I do hope that President Roosevelt can make those big money guys loosen up the money so daddy can get some carpenter work. I am going to send you a picture of my twin brother and I taken about three years ago. I would like if you would write to me when you have time.

H. S.

■ Paola Kans.

May 16, 1934

Dear Mrs. Roosevelt.

I am a little boy 10 years old. When I was seven I took piano lessons. Daddy has been out of work and we have not been to afford a piano. I could manage to take a few piano lessons this summer. If I had a piano on which to practice. I enjoy reading about you in the papers & I know you are kind & understand children.

Now would it be to much to ask of you the mony for a cheap piano. I dont ask for a expensive one. A cheap piano will do to practice one. I hope I do hear from you soon. I thanking you so much.

I am you little friend

B. B. T.

■ Basom, New York

Jan. 19, 1935

Madame,

I am a girl going to school. After exams I will be entering high school. I am also taking lessons on a Hawaiin Guitar. My father is sick and he is not able to work. Therefore we have no money to pay for these lessons. I am very interested in my lessons and wouldn't like to stop.

I have heard you have helped many other people who are interested in different things. I would like you to help me also. If you can.

I am an Indian living on the Tawanda Reservation and am very interested in you. I do not care what amount of money you send me but I will be very grateful to you. In all, these lessons amount to $52. Before my father became sick we had paid a little.

I hope you will consider my plea or even answer me. I am 15 years old.

Yours very truly,

C. S.

■ La Moure, N. Dak.

October 12, 1936

Dear Pres. and Mrs Roosevelt,

Well I relize that you are too busy to consider my letter but I am going to send it anyway. My brother is eight and I am twelve. This may sound awful funny to you but our whole future depends on your presidency. If you don't get in I don't know what we will do. My Dad is only a W.P.A. worker and we are certainly thankful for that. Every day after work and Friday and Sat. he's out campaigning for you. He certainly has wonderful results. He's convinced many of people that if it wouldn't of been for you only the Lord knows what would have happened to all the poor people including us. I can remember Hoover was pres. We were hungry many times and without warm clothes and actually froze. Now this may seem a little think to you but its my whole future. I dream so much of a piano that it seems that I can't work when I think of it. My dream is growing bigger every day but it seems as though they are to be shattered. My Dad and Mother can't buy it out of $40.00 a month. I'm not complaining. I'm so thankful for that. Please, Kind Sir don't think I'm begging for I'm not. But seems that I had to tell my troubles to some one. Next to God I thought you would be best. We certainly hope you'll be president the next four years. By the way I'm in the seventh Grade. I've had A's for 4 yrs straight that is being on the honor roll. I've been on since we moved to town. I'm hoping you are pres. the next four years. If not my dreams will die with election day. God bless you and Mrs. Roosevelt. If you aren't to busy won't you *please* answer our letter.

Yours truly,

A hundred per cent democrat

B. T.

■ Chester, Pennsylvania

January 30, 1939

Mrs. Roosevelt,

I do not have any way to go, so I come to you againest the hungry depression of today

I have study the violin for two years and I cannot go on studying, because the violin is too small and I am too big for it. I am 15 years of age.

I need a full size good violin complete to continue with the study of the violin.

My father does not work not because he does not want to work but he cannot find work, so I wrote to you to see if you could get me one so I could continue with the study of it.

The violin that you will sent me will be remember all the rest of my life.

This picture that I am sending to you is when I just me and my small violin were just starting to play.

That is all I have to say. If you are going to sent it I will be appreciated for it. Best regards to all.

Thank you

Sincerely yours

B. S.

[The writer encloses a photograph of himself and his tiny violin.]

■ Davy. West V.

April. 15, 1939.

Dear Mrs. Roosevelt:—

As I hardly know how to be-gin my letter to you. As you see I am going to ask a favor of you. I guess it is rather unusual. And then you may get letters like it every day. I am a boy 14 yrs old and will graudate from Junior high school next month. And I am more enterested in drawing. And as I anaswered several adds in magazines I selected the Washington school of art. And I thought you would help me with this course as my mother just cant afford to give it to me. I am sure I could make good. As I want to do this more than any thing. And if you will help me. I am sure some time I will pay you back every penny of it. I have heard you would help folks like me. But it sounds too good to be true. I have tried to go to the CCC Camps but am not old enough. My family is not on the WPA are Relief and never has been. I am sending you a sample of my drawing. I can just sit for hours and draw. Mother wants me to take it. She worries so much because she cant give it to me. And I make her think that I dont care. But no body knows how much I do. No one not even Mother knows I am writing you this letter. I am send you this blank and envelope if you decide to help me. I have read how kind you were. You see $89.00 on time are $69.00 cash you see that seems like a lot of money to us. You see we have always been rather hard up. But respectable. But Mrs Roosevelt if you dont help me you see I will not feel hard are mad at you For I know you cant help every one who asks for help. So I guess I will close

With Best Regards

D. C.

[The writer encloses two drawings.]

■ Grand Marais, Minn.

Jan. 16, [1940]

Dear Mrs. Roosevelt,

I know that this isn't a proper way of writing to you, but I have no other choice.

I have always thought well of you ever since I first heard of you. And that was when the President was running for his first term of office. About a week ago, I read a long article about you in the Harpers Magazine, which made me like and admire you much more. On the same day, I show my feelings toward you, I wrote a poem for you. I know it isn't at all good, but at least it's sincere. I guess it's a poor excuse for a poem, but I could do no better right then.

I suppose you're wondering who I am, and so forth. Well, to start out with, my name is E. E., I live in the most northern part of Minnesota — Grand Marais to be exact. I live on a little 40-acre farm five and one-half miles from Grand Marais. I'm a Swedish girl (by parentage) of sixteen years of age. I'm a senior in High School at Grand Marais, and will graduate next spring.

All of my life I have been a lover of music, love to sing, and like to play instruments — but the trouble is that, I haven't a chance. I know I'm not the only one that hasn't, however. Ever since I was old enough to have desires, I've wanted a piano. I've never received it as we are too poor to afford such luxuries. So I next have wished for a guitar, because I thought that maybe I might get that as that is cheaper and love it a lot too. Nevertheless, I still have nothing whatever to play on. Once in awhile when I go to a neighbor's house or to the grade school I practice a little. I know only a very little of notes, but play by ear a little. I know could do much better if I had something to practice on. I also love to sing while I play. I have a good voice—a high soprano—at least people say it's very good. I don't try any fancy singing though, like yodeling or opera—I just plain sing. I especially like Stephen Collin Foster's songs. My favorite being, "Beautiful Dreamer."

My father is a janitor in the rural grade school in Maple Hill and earns 75 dollars a month sometimes less. I have two sisters and had four brothers until recently on last Dec. 10, a Sunday morning, my dearest of all brothers, J., nineteen years old, died of acute Leukemia. He was in the hospital for only thirteen days when he died. To say that I miss him—means nothing. To say that I, now am a lonesome being, not caring at all for the world without J. means something. I have no happiness left now that he is gone. I have many relatives and friends yes—but he was dearer to me than life itself— more than that even, because that doesn't mean much anymore. My only little piece of happiness, I have now is listening to songs on the radio, and they sometimes make me cry because they remind me of J. I want a piano so bad, but I know I'll never get one, so now I hope and pray for a guitar. Whether I will get it or not, I don't know. All I know is, is that life means nothing without music. One ambition of mine is, is that when I finish high school I might get a chance to sing old, sweet songs on the radio—or somewhere else. Singing is as natural as breathing for me. Whether I'll ever have a chance to show it is another thing. Another favorite of mine is "Brahm's Lullaby" or "Cradle Song"—

It was thirty-five degrees below zero this morning. We have no school today as the heating system froze up or something. We received snow only a week ago—the first snow to stay, which is unusual for our part of the country.

Please, Mrs. Roosevelt, can't you help me to get some music? Oh! Please!
Respectfully, and sincerely yours,
E. E.

P.S. I am sending a picture of my father, mother, J., B. and me taken two years ago—J. is the best-looking one—curly-haired—the one that died— our angel in heaven.

To Eleanor, The First Lady of America.
The First Lady of the air, the press, and the nation
Is practical, reasonable, loving, and kind.
She is like one's best friend, advisor, or relation,
Who thinks of your troubles, believes in your live.
When poor people write to her, begging for aid,
Some reasonable thing, quite easy to give
She give it to them if possible, and sends her love,
To keep healthy, & wise, to live and let live.

■ Ironton Ohio
Nov 21, 1940
Dear Mrs. Roosevelt—
I am a little girl 11 years old and in the 6th Grade at school. I go to church and Sunday School with mother now we are poor and mother and I live alone she does work for folks and what I want to tell you is I play a saxaphone in the orchestra where we go and it is a borrowed one and when we are done playing I have to give it up to our instructor untill the next sunday. and I would love so very much to have one of my own to take home with me and play all the time but mother says she is very thankful to have the comforts and cannot afford to buy me one. I do want one so much and I hear you on our little Radio and you sound so kind and nice and mother votes for Mr. Roosevelt all the time we have his picture right by the sewing machine and mother thinks God sent him to lead us out, like he did Mose with the children of Isreal she talks to me all the time about the bible and things she is awful good. and I try not to worry her by asking for a horn but its very hard. Now I would like you to see if some of the band boys has a saxaphone or the orchestra from the whitehouse what they don't want or something like and please send it to me now don't do any thing so mother will know I wrote this as she don't like very much to accept charity, she never complains. but you can just send it to me and say Santa Clause sent it for she would spank me if she knew I wrote to you for she says you 2 people are very big and gots lots to think of but still I want to play and be somebody someday and so I don't know any other person to ask so if you find one please send it to me and I will be oh ever so thankful this is Thanksgiving after noon and mother went to see a sick lady and I must hurry and finish this and run out and put it in the box my name is same as yours so please forgive me for asking and I thank you a million. I want an E flat Alto saxaphone

Your little friend

E. D. H.

VOCATIONAL EDUCATION

- -

■ Chicago, Illinois

January 4, [1934]

My Dear Mrs Roosevelt: —

This is not a begging letter Mrs Roosevelt please do not think that. But I hope that it gets past your secretary for I'd like for you to read it.

I am a girl of nineteen, reared in a good family. A family that at one time had social position money, everything. We still have social position in the south — particularly in Kentucky — a state where family background is pratically all one needs to be in "the inner circle" I might say.

I don't wish to bore you, but will you read my story?

My mother and father seperated when I was five years of age. I was sent to my grandparents (my mother's parents) my father visited me regularly until I was ten. Since then I haven't seen him. I started to school in that small town of Horse Cane, Ky. where my grandfather was city judge (and still is) In my seven years of school there I wasn't allowed to associate with but a few of the children. My grandmother, a typical old southern lady of "high birth" did not consider the family background of most of them quite good enough for me. And so I formed but two real friendships.

At the conclusion of my seventh year, my mother sent for me. She had married when I was ten but we had never seen her husband. At the age of 13 I left my grandparents and the home I had learned to love, came to Chicago and entered a life that I did not know existed. It was hard those first few weeks to adjust myself to my new home. My mother I loved, but her husband I both resented and didn't like. I, who had been reared in an atmosphere of love, music and good literature and southern hospitality found myself thrown in contact with a man who cared nothing for good music, nor good books; who cared for little except himself and how many arguments he could make in one day. My mother worked also and as far as clothing, and something to cat I was satisfied. I went to the eighth grade here. The next year I went back to my grandparents. My freshman year only served to emphasize the great difference in the two households. I returned to Chicago for my sophmore year and a more miserable year I never spent. My mother realizing how difficult it was for me helped me in every way she could. I made but one friend for I wouldn't bring anyone home with me. It was at this time that mother and her husband lost their jobs. That winter was a hard one for us all. In October of 1930 my grandmother wrote asking me to come back and sent for me. I went and in 1932 I graduated from high school. I remained with them until February 1933. My mother wanted so that my grandfather sent me back. I have been here almost a year. We have been on Relief the entire time. It has been a bitter pill for me but I have tried my best to accept it. But the time has come when I can stand it no longer. It has been impossible to find a job. My mother and her husband are on the verge of separation. I seem to have the alternative of going to my grandparents (which I won't do for they are old, my grandmother 68 and my grandfather 81, and I won't be a burden on them. They own their home but the town pays it's officers little (he is city judge and has been for almost 20 years) and they can't bear any extra expenses. The other was writing to you for help to do something I have wanted to do for 4 years. I am the only one of the family for years that has not gone to college. But it was impossible. It has taken me a long time to reach the objective of this letter, Mrs Roosevelt, but here it is. I want very much to take a business course. I know I'd make good for I like the work. There is a Business College in Chilecothe Mo. which offers a complete secretarial course in six months for $350. This includes room and board. The college guarantees a position in 90 days to its graduates or they refund all money given them. For $475. I could take the course, buy clothes, I have none, have train fare and buy the necessary books etc needed for the 6 months, and in a short time be in a position to not only help myself but my mother and grandparents.

I am not asking you to *give* me the money but would you consider loaning it to me. I can not possible say how much I would appreciate it if you would help me do this. You could be certain of getting your money returned for I would have a position and would pay you as soon as possible after finishing my course. It would be giving me the chance to make something of myself. I can give you any number of references if you wish. My grandfather is Judge J. F. P. of Horse Cane, Ky.

Respectfully yours

H. P.

■ Twila, Kentucky
May 16, 1934
Dear President & Wife:

It is indeed a great pleasure to write to the most beloved President and First Lady that the United States has ever had.

We are two girls age 17 years and have just finished our Junior Course at Wallins High School, Wallins Creek, Ky.

We had our hearts set on going to Knoxville, Tenn. this summer to take a beauty course, but as our fathers are miners and the mines here in the South-eastern coal fields have closed down it now looks impossible to obtain the necessary finance.

As the closest Beauty training school is in Knoxville, Tennessee it will be necessary to pay board buy uniforms, books and other necessities, we would also have to pay for our training. So wont you please help us? We are not begging for money, we are just asking for a small loan. You can judge for yourself how much it would take to finance both of us.

Mr. & Mrs. Roosevelt we are two 100% girls and if you care to find out what kind of girls we are we refer you to:

Mr. L. P. M.—Principal of
Wallins High School
Wallins Creek, Ky.

also

Miss M. L. J., Teacher
Wallins High School
Wallins Creek, Ky.

As soon as we have finished our training and recieved our first pay we will begin sending small payments to you.

Won't you please give this, careful consideration? As the Summer Session begins May 28th. Please let us know at once if you can Help us.

Thanking you,
Miss R. S., Miss M. J. M

■ Mingo Junction, Ohio
[received Feb. 21, 1939]
Dear Madam:

You may think it absurded, me writing to you this way when you have never seen or heard of me. But I would like to make you a proposition, I would like to know if you would loan me $2,800 (Two thousand eight hundred) so that I can take a course in aviation at the Lincoln Flying School at Lincoln Nebraska. The course takes two years to complete, it prepares the student to start out as a co-pilot on a commercial airlines or as a mechanic on a commercial airlines, the school has a part time employment plan to pay for room and board.

I would not be writing to you, asking for a loan, but our town is about dead, they are going to take the mill out of our town, thus putting a lot of men out of work, including my father. There are nine persons in our familey at home and work is scarce, only my father is working now and he isnt getting much money, he is a watchman at the mill.

If you will loan me this money to continue my schooling, I will pay you back double your money when I get a job upon completing the flying course.

I will graduate from Mingo High School in June, 1939 I am seventeen years old, and I have a good character, I am also honest. For character references you can send a telegram to M. L. D. Superintendent of Mingo schools.

It is necessary to send the tuition to Lincoln Flying School immediatly so as to get the benefit of the part time employment plan for room and board.

Please let me know if you will make the investment (because it is really an investment) so that I can complete arrangments for going to school.

Yours truely,

L. T.

◼ Cramerton, N.C.

April 5, 1940

Dear Mrs Roosevelt;

May I borrow a few minutes of your most valuable time? I'll try to make my subject as breif as possible if you will if you will give this your personal attention.

I am a 18teen year old high school graduate of a little small mill community in dear old "North Carolina." I worked in the mill in the evenings & went to school in the morning because I wonted to help my parents and not be a burden to them. Now my reason for writting.

All my life I've been interested in beauty culture. I wont to take a course in this feild but havn't got the money to pay for it. I know you have never been asked such a question before & will laugh at me if this letter ever gets to you. But will you please, loan me $115.00 to pay for it? I wont to borrow it for one year. I'm going to work in the mill in the evenings & go to this beauty school in the mornings if I can borrow this money. It take's 3 mo.

to complete the course going all day but it will take me 6 the way I'll have to do. Mrs Roosevelt, I don't wont to spend my life working in a cotton mill. My parents before me have had to do that, and I've seen what they have gone threw. I wont to get a job to make enough, so my dear mother wont have to stand on her tired legs and work until she dies. I'd like to repay her for some of the things she done for me.

I'll sign any paper's or any thing you wont signed. Also you can write my pastor as I am a Christian and an active church worker. I can also furnish reference from the sheriff of this county and police of this community. Also the school supt., owner of mill . . . & business houses.

Maybe you say why dont you try borrowing from some one you know. Because, I dont have any personal freinds who have that much money. Another reason they would make it public, and please for mercy sake, dont make this public. If it has to be made public, just drop it. Again may I beg you to take this up with in your heart and maybe some day in my small way I can return the favor because this small world never gets to big that some time or other we dont need a friend. Hoping & Praying that Our God in Heaven will answer my Prayers I remain here hoping & Praying to hear from this letter soon.

A friend always

Hospital Bill $2.00
Transportation to School $3.50
Pade on loan (if I get it) $3.00
Uniforms   .50
Parents $4.00

My salary is $13.00 per week and this is how it will be divided.
Again my I ask, please do not make this public.

We live five miles from town, and we are poor we have no money for
boughten amusements. There is not a radio around in the country and
I get terribly lonesome in summer. If you could in any way help
me to obtain one it would mean enjoyment for all of my
friends as well as me.

—M. N. C., a thirteen-year-old from Oklahoma,
to Eleanor Roosevelt, April 1935

Boys outside a movie theater, Scott's Run, W.Va., 1935.
(Photo by Ben Shahn, LC-USF-USF33-006204-MI)

chapter 3

Social Life

In the early years of the Great Depression, the Federal Emergency Relief Administration (FERA) was among the New Deal agencies most intimately connected with the poor. Headed by Harry L. Hopkins, a veteran social worker, FERA hired masses of unemployed Americans who built thousands of bridges and public buildings from coast to coast. FERA loaned money to desperate farmers, taught more than a million adults to read, established nursery schools for poor children, and gave 100,000 low-income students part-time jobs that enabled them to attend college. Through his work with FERA Hopkins had come to understand how the economic crisis disrupted the social lives of millions of Americans who had lost jobs and status. His sensitivity to the pain that this disruption caused was nowhere more evident than in the Christmas message he released in 1934.[1]

Hopkins noted in this message "how lacking in the traditional pleasures this Christmas is for many American people." He pointed out that Americans had traditionally greeted Christmas merrily by exchanging presents, holding family reunions, taking time off from their jobs, and "turning aside from workday preoccupations to celebrate the warmth of home." But the Great Depression placed such celebrations out of reach for many low-income Americans. "Gifts," Hopkins said, "can be few. Families are broken. They have no workdays from which to turn and cold homes to turn to. Unless we are blind we cannot send these greetings in terms of those things which people have always expressed when they say 'Merry Christmas.' . . . For millions of people these have become barren words."[2]

Using Christian imagery, Hopkins turned his Christmas message into a call for a war on poverty. He argued that though traditional modes of holiday celebration were unattainable for the poor, "the deeper significance of Christmas cannot be taken away from the destitute. It means more to them than even to those who have known no discomfort. It is the birthday of one who disliked poverty and injustice and who taught us we are our brother's keeper." Invoking the idealism of the New Deal, Hopkins pointed out that "today there are more men and women than ever before who believe that poverty is wrong and . . . unnecessary . . . and [are] fighting it with no intention of letting up . . . until not only the new poverty but the old poverty are beaten out." Hopkins concluded by pledging to work for that day when poverty would be banished, so that "Christmas will come for the first time into the lives of" the poor who could not previously afford to celebrate it "as well as return to those who have lately lost it. In those terms may I express a Merry Christmas."[3]

Two years later Hopkins again demonstrated his sensitivity to the suffering of the poor at Christmastime. During Christmas week 1936, Hopkins, who by then headed the giant work relief programs administered by the Works Progress Administration, announced that 30,000 relief workers would produce gifts for 725,000 children. Toys would be made from scraps in WPA sewing rooms and carpenter shops. Mrs. Roosevelt would for this reason send some of the Christmas requests she received from the poor to the WPA. Hopkins hoped to further spread Christmas cheer by dispatching 15,000 musicians from the WPA and hundreds of thousands of children and adults in Federal Music Project classes to orchestrate "Christmas caroling on a nationwide scale." Thus Hopkins assured a reporter that "during four hours on Christmas Eve there will be no moment in which voices will not be raised some place in America."[4]

Although thousands benefited from such New Deal generosity, millions of impoverished Americans, especially the unemployed and their children, were not reached by Hopkins's Christmas gifts. The letters from poor youths to Eleanor Roosevelt affirm Hopkins's words in 1934 about the barrenness of Christmas for those unable to afford to celebrate it; they speak of a holiday without gifts, children being told that Santa Claus could not reach their houses, and despair that a festive time of year had become joyless. The volume of what Eleanor Roosevelt called her "Santa Claus" letters requesting holiday gifts was such that they were something of a barometer of economic conditions. In the short span of the two weeks preceding Christmas in 1934, for example, the First Lady received 7,358 "Santa Claus letters." In the following year the number of such letters in the same two-week span declined to 4,946, which the press took as a welcome sign of "greater prosperity throughout the country."[5] Of course for the young who wrote to Mrs. Roosevelt for Christmas aid it mattered not at all whether the White House mail contained nearly 5,000 or 7,000 similar requests, for in

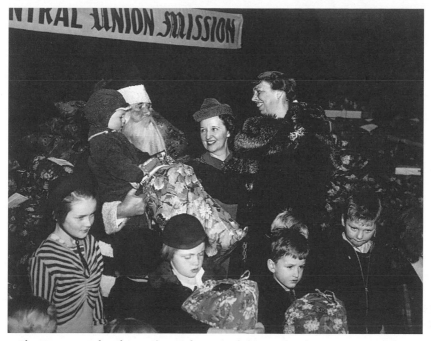

Eleanor Roosevelt, who as First Lady received thousands of "Santa Claus" letters from needy children and teens hoping for Christmas gifts, assists a Salvation Army Santa at a Christmas party for underprivileged children, Washington, 1939. (Photo courtesy of United Press International)

either case they had been driven by despair and by the writers' love of their families.

The Christmas letters are among the most touching in Mrs. Roosevelt's collection because they are among the most selfless. Except in the case of the youngest children, most of these letters were from youths asking for gifts not for themselves but for their family members. One most often finds teens writing for gifts to give to their siblings and sometimes asking for similar aid for their parents. Along with requests for toys or dolls were others which underscored just how hard the times were, as youths asked for necessities such as clothes that children needed to wear to school or a winter coat that their mother needed. This is not to say that lower-class youths were immune to the temptations of consumer culture. Some of the teens' Christmas letters to Mrs. Roosevelt included advertisements, showing the items that the writers hoped to receive from the First Lady. But as if to again remind us of the gravity of the economic crisis, there are letters from youths who seemed to be living out of the reach of Madison Avenue and consumer culture, in which they ask the First Lady not for pristine goods from stores or catalogues but for modest, secondhand items, especially used or discarded clothing—the barest necessities needed to cope with hard times.

Although there was undoubtedly something uniquely oppressive about the combination of Christmas and poverty, since the poor often had to go giftless in a holiday centered on gift giving, at least this suffering was visible. Christmas, after all, was a time of year when the press and public spotlighted the problems of the poor (as Hopkins's Christmas message and the WPA's gift-production drive exemplify), displayed sensitivity to their difficulties, and raised money for charity. Easter, by contrast, was a holiday celebrated with much less attention to the problems of the poor. One would never know from reading the press of Depression America that Easter was, at least for female teens and preteens, a holiday whose material demands bred as much heartache among the poor as those of Christmas did. The problem with Easter was that its celebration traditionally involved purchasing and wearing new clothes, and for women and girls this meant new spring outfits. With the approach of every spring in the New Deal era, Eleanor Roosevelt was swamped with letters from mostly female teens and children, upset that they could not afford Easter clothes. The letters reflect the importance of clothing to the self-esteem of these young girls and the extent to which they felt marginalized by their inability to dress nearly as well as their friends and schoolmates.

Much as the Depression disrupted holiday celebrations, it also interfered with other central parts of American social life, including courtship and marriage. From 1930 to 1934 the marriage rate fell by 9 percent. Public concern about this decline was so strong that according to a Roper poll one out of three Americans supported the idea of "governmental subsidies to help young couples marry." [6] The central reason for the slumping marriage rate, as the letters to Mrs. Roosevelt make evident, is that young couples hit by unemployment and diminished career prospects could not afford to go off on their own and establish independent households, which had traditionally been a prerequisite for marriage in America. Nor could they afford the kind of church weddings they had envisioned (which is why the proportion of marriages performed in civil services and in homes increased). However, while the young postponed marriage, most did not give up on it altogether, which is why in the mid- and late 1930s the marriage rate recovered. One could see in this recovery an inspiring tale of love and romance triumphing over adversity, as Americans determined to get married after some delay did not let the Depression stop them. This may offset some of the gloom reflected in the letters that Eleanor Roosevelt received from young people frustrated over the way the economic crisis had delayed their marriage plans. But on the other hand the very first marriage letter to appear in this chapter suggests that the Depression led at least some needy youths to give up on the romantic ideal, to embrace marriage as a purely economic proposition—and we find a nineteen-year-old girl from upstate New York ready to resign herself to a loveless marriage in order to pull herself out of poverty. The letter suggests that in at least some cases the Depression disrupted not only the timing but the nature of marriage itself.

In mass consumer society one tends to think of the Depression as a collective experience which hurt whole classes of people. But with regard to social life, the Depression's impact was often experienced individually as an isolating event or process. Youths unable to date for lack of funds felt hard times as an impediment to being with others, to socializing and having fun. Similarly, one encounters this sense of loneliness in letters from young people asking the First Lady to send them radios. Despite the Depression, radio had become the central form of home entertainment—much as the television would do two decades later. By 1938 radios had been purchased by nearly 27 million American households, of a total of nearly 34 million. Owning a radio allowed Americans to feel connected to popular culture, to tune in to what the historian T. H. Watkins has aptly described as "a daily aural kaleidoscope of serials, soap operas, comedy shows, serious drama, farm reports, country music, big band music, symphony music, opinion shows, amateur hour contests, breakfast shows, sermons, political speeches, and millions of hours of commercial pitches, jingles, and promotions that spilled out of 743 individual stations."[7] With radios so widely owned and radio culture so pervasive, youths who could not afford radios felt as if there was a big party going on continually over the airwaves, but one to which they had not been invited. These letters are a reminder that the Depression bred deprivation of not merely material goods, but also of spirit, and that this was a form of deprivation which needy youth felt was especially cruel.

Here again youth culture reared its ugly head, making things more difficult for low-income youths in their social lives much as it did in their school lives discussed in chapter 2 (and in the section on clothing in chapter 1). Youth culture heightened the sense of deprivation felt by poor teens and children regarding the part of their lives that was supposed to be devoted to recreation. The materialism and competitiveness of the larger society was internalized into the dominant culture of youth in 1930s America and made all the worse by the immaturity of the young. Despite the Depression, children and teens who possessed recreational items valued by youth culture felt no qualms about lording it over those who lacked them. Thus in the letters by poor youths asking for recreational items—bicycles, ice skates, even scouting uniforms—one reads repeatedly about their being laughed at, even shunned by those in their schools and neighborhoods who could afford such things. The desire to be able to buy their way out of this kind of derision was clearly one of the main impulses motivating these youths to write to the First Lady. It seems that only the very youngest of Mrs. Roosevelt's correspondents, the grade school children requesting sports equipment, dolls, and other toys, had not yet been touched by this shaming from other youths; they were still too young and homebound to have been mistreated by the larger youth culture.

But if the letters related to recreation often reveal the mean side of Depression America's youth culture, some also show lower-class youth at their most altruistic. A number of the letters about bicycles make evident how eager these poor youths were to be helpful to their families. In these letters the bicycles are not a status symbol or toy. Instead they serve two functions: a literal one, as they enable the children to take themselves to and from school, and a symbolic one, as they represent the children's desire to be useful and not burdensome to their parents.

This desire to be useful also manifested itself in a group of letters which rank as the most surprising of those connected to the social life of Depression youth. These were the letters that young people wrote asking the First Lady to help them become movie stars. At first glance such letters seem nothing more than sad, even pathetic expressions of Hollywood fantasies. During the Great Depression, as historians have often noted, the film industry specialized in gaudy musicals and escapist rags-to-riches stories, enabling Americans to have fun, fantasize, and at least temporarily forget their hard times. The youths who wrote to Mrs. Roosevelt can be said to have fallen for a Hollywood fantasy. But on the other hand, the writers come close to transcending escapism, in that they seek to use Hollywood not to retreat from reality but to overcome it. Those who were too young to work in their home towns and thus were unable to help pay the bills hoped that by achieving stardom they could, despite their youth, give their ailing, impoverished parents and their families a Hollywood-style happy ending.

The letters about automobiles offer examples of both the cruelty of well-off youth to their more needy schoolmates and the desire of lower-class youths to be helpful to their families and not to be a burden. The image from one letter in this chapter, of a North Carolina farm boy who got up at dawn to do his chores and walked miles to school only to be mocked en route by laughing classmates as they sped by honking their car horns, is one of the more memorable testaments to the cruelty of consumer society. While in this context the automobile was surely a status symbol, in the majority of letters it seems desired only as a necessary mode of transport for work, parents, and access to school (all but one requested a used car). However, the most significant fact about these letters may be that there were so few of them. In Mrs. Roosevelt's files of requests for material assistance are fewer than a dozen requests from youths for autos over the course of the Depression decade. It seems that a car, even a used car, was simply too expensive an item for a needy youth to request from the First Lady or to imagine owning. This relative absence of cars in the discourse of needy youth sets them apart not only from the dominant consumer culture that emerged in America during the 1920s, which was centered around widespread auto ownership, but also from youth culture in much of the twentieth century, in which dating and social life were tied so closely to the automobile.

CHRISTMAS

· ·

■ [Jersey City, N.J.]

Dec. 14, 1933

Our good Friend Mrs. & Mr. Roosevelt:

Hope this reach you & your good husband Mr. Roosevelt in the best of health. Well Mrs. Roosevelt I am a little girl 12 years old. My mother has 7 small children and my father just started on to work in one of those job your good Husband started for the poor people and we were sure glad to see him working as he did not work in ycar hc is only makeing $15 a week. But thank God he is getting that so my Good Friend you see he will recived he first cheack. Just the time our rent is due so my poor mother will not be able to get my little sisters & Brother a little doll or a toy for Christmas so if your little granchildren have any little things from last year I will be thankful to see you send them to us Hope God send you Plenty luck & Health and Hope you have a Happy Christmas & New Year.

C. H.

This is Jesus. I draw it.

After asking Mrs. Roosevelt for a toy and wishing her a merry Christmas in 1934, a ten-year-old Puerto Rican girl from New York City enclosed these sketches, signing her note "Kisses for you."
(From the collection of the Franklin D. Roosevelt Library, Hyde Park, N.Y.)

■ Keegan, Maine
Dec. 23, 1933
Dear Friend:
Mrs. Roosevelt I am writing you to ask you a little favor. Please if you have some old cloth to send us, we would be very glade. For we are a poor

I draw this from Carmen for Miss Roosevelt.

family. I am the oldest one I am 16 years old. The oldest of my sister is 12 years old. We are 14 children in the family. My father works, he earns only $14 a week. With fourteen dollars we can't spear any money to dress ourselves. I tried to have some work but they wouldnt give me some work because there is more married man that they can't employ. If you have some old clothes that you have spear. If you please send a part of it to us. If you send us anything you can spear we'll pray for you. We're in need so much that three of my sisters would go to school, but they're not dress to go. We are six that goes to school. We're trying to have help in town but the people are as poor as we are. We are writing you because every person in town that talks of you say that you're the only woman to look for the poor as much as you. Yesterday we were reading on the newspaper in the first page was written in black, "Mrs. Roosevelt looks for the poor." We read that about you and it says that since last Christmas that you were picing cloths and toys for the poor. I don't ask you any toys but I ask you clothes that you have spear. It makes three years that we didn't see christmas and my little sisters don't know what's christmas. Your the first president's wife that looks for the poor. It's nearly insulting for a poor little boy like me to a person like you. We didn't write to other president's wifes because they only try to owns money, but not you. I am asking you some old clothes that can be remade for my sisters and brothers. If you want information to know if it's true, write to the priest of our church. His name is, Rev. Father St. Martin S. M. Keegan Maine. I'm wishing you a Merry Christmas and a Happy new year.

Your friend,

J. B. Jr.

■ Powell Wyo.

Dec. 26, 1933

Dear Mrs. & Mr. Roosevelt

Thought I would write you a few lines to tell you how I spent Christmas. I didnt spend Christmas like most girls & boys. I stayed at home & didnt get any thing because my father wasent able to get me any thing he works hard but it takes every thing he makes to keep us something to eat he doesent know that I am writing you & please dont say any thing about it to any one because he would get me for writing this. We have enough that the county dont half to keep us up. I would like for you to help me just a little if you will I have two orders made out & I wonder if you would get them for me. If you will I know there is some one that will help me & I thought I might be you they say you are helping poor girls & boys thank you very much & please dont write any thing to Dad because he would get me for writing to you. I dont have any mother & I am 16 years old.

Yours

G. R.

[two orders follow]

■ Powell, Wyo.

Dec. 24, 1933

Dear Sir:

You will find enclosed a money order for $17.70 Whil please send me these things.

Wool & Silk tweed dress no. 31D4340 size 20 color brown Plaid
    price 3.98.
Rayon crepe dress no. 31D4435 color Medium Green size 20 price $2.98
Warm Blanket cloth no. 27D4922 color med Blue & Tan size 38
    Price $1.79
hat no. 78D6624 color Black size 22¼ price $1.69
all in one Softie no. 18D491 color Peach size 34 price $3.69
gloves no 33D3600 color Black size 8 price $1.98
dance set no. 38D2602 color Tea rose size 36 price $1.29 a set.
all rayon Taffeta slip no. 38D3545 color white size 36 price $1.00

Yours Truely
G. R.

■ Powell Wyo.

Dec. 24, 1933

Dear Sir:

You will find enclosed a money order for $28.45 which please send me these things

Jacket no. 910D2258 color Bright Blue size 19 price $3.79.
Silk crepeback Satin dress no. 914D9190 color black size 20 price $5.98.
Transparent Velvet dress no. 914D9160 color black size 20 price $8.98.
Swede shoes no. 24D303 color black swede size 7 1⅞ cuban heel
    price $2.00
Hand laccd oxford no 24D3036 color Black calf-grain size 7 price $1.98
Hosiery no 30D900 size 10 colors Light Taupe & Beige Brown.
    price 2.00 for two pair
dance set no 39D918 colors Flesh & Tea Rose size 34 2 sets for 96 cents
Gown no. 32D1360 color blue size 38 price $1.89 slip no. 32D119E
    color Flesh size 36 price 87 cents.

Yours Truely

■ Mason, Wis.

January 9, 1934

Dear Mrs. Roosevelt,

I suppose you'll be kind of surprised to hear from a poor little girl. I am ten years old. On Christmas eve I had waited for Santa Clause to come but my mama said the chimney was blocked & he couldn't come, so I had a poor Christmas. I was expecting Santa to bring me some things.

I lost my daddy when I was two years old.

I have read in the papers how good you are to the poor and thought maybe you can help me some. I will appriciate it all my life.

To-day we have started school from our Christmas vacation & all the children talk about how many presants Santa has brought them & I felt so bad cause I had nothing to say. I guess that is all. . . .

Yours truely

M. A.

■ Chicago, Illinois

November 4, 1936

Dear Mrs. Roosevelt,

Please accept my heartiest congratulations for being the wife of such a great man as the President.

As you go on to read this peculiar letter, you will see that it is from a girl of parents with rather small means of livelihood.

I am a young girl of 18 years, graduated in June, and second eldest of 7 children. After graduation I proceeded to look for work, with high hopes, but these high hopes were banished after two months of failure to secure a position of any kind. Now, for a few months I cannot go out and try, because my Mother is expecting a new arrival around Christmas or first week of January. I don't know whether to be happy or whether to cry for this new event; because after a 10 years lapse, two baby girls have come into my life in three years and I don't know if I should consider it a happy event.

You probably think I am a very selfish person, but I think my parents are the selfish ones. Since my second year in high school I have been denied the good times girls and boys of my age enjoy. When I reached the age of 10 I was told that my playing days were over and they were.

For two years, Father was out of work and when he has worked it has been for $30 a week or less and all we have ever had is bills, bills, and bills. We have to take turns, each year, to get new clothes.

I hope my troubles haven't given you a headache, although I know they have bored you to death, but please forgive me for this outburst and I assure you it shall never happen, again.

The real reason for this letter is to ask you to help me earn some money for Christmas gifts for the kiddies. I want you to help me by mailing a pink card, (for cream, which I will send to you from the Belle Co.), with 60 cents and in return I will receive 30 cents. Please send me the names of others, whom you think will be interested.

Please dissappoint me in this plea for aid.

Thanks a million for your aid in the future.

From one who needs help,

M. B.

St Paul Minn

Jan 20 1937

Dear Mrs. Lady

Please dont be mad at me for riteing to you. but I have been reding how good you are to every body so I thot mabe you can help me out. my mother ant got no winter coat and it is alful cold here. She works so hard to get us kids cloths and eats that there is nothing left for her so I thot mabe that you having to have new coats for the ineurashion boll and things that you mite have one of your old ones you dont need and you would send it to my ma. I ask Santa Claus to bring her one but there is no such person because she did not get one ples dont tell any one I rote to you as the kids would lafe at me I will have to stop riteing as my ma is comeing home and I dont want her to see this but if you got a coat you dont want I will pray for you all my life no fooling if you make my ma hapy it dont have to be so swell just so its warm. I go to the blind school as I cant see very good but mabe somday my eyes will get better. I want you to know that I love you and our president.

Your Friend

D. R.

I am 11 years old only in 4th grade becaus my eyes are not good. so please excus this Letter

Pittsburgh, Pa.

December 1, 1937

Dear Mrs. Roosevelt,

I am a young man employed on the W.P.A. I also attend night school, thru the N.Y.A., taking a course in welding. Words cannot express my gratitude to our President who has made this possible for me and the thousands of others.

I read in the "Press" that you had bought the President gloves for Xmas. Pardon me for being so bold, but would you please send me a pair of His discarded gloves? I assure you that there will be no publicity or boasting on my part altho I would be mighty proud to posess something which belonged to so great a man.

I trust that you and the President will continue your good work and remain at the White House for a "long time." And that you continue in good health. I want to wish you and our President a Happy New Year.

Yours very sincerely,

F. D. H.

■ Wallingford, Connecticut
[received Dec. 9, 1937]
My dear Mrs. Roosevelt:

I just read recently about your trip out west, to visit those miners. I saw your picture as you were dancing (block) with Mrs. Cromwell. You looked fancy indeed! You looked so nice; and you seemed to have such a kind face. And, Mrs. Roosevelt, this is the purpose of my writing this letter. I saw your kind face in that picture; I have it in front of me now to help me write this letter; and so I'm not afraid to ask you. Mrs. Roosevelt, Christmas is here, and I'm dispondent. I have no money to buy anything. I'm not a poor girl on relief, but I'm not a girl well-off, either. Oh! Mrs. Roosevelt you have too much money, why won't you please help me? You can have the pleasure of buying anything, anytime you want, but that isn't so with me. Oh! Mrs. Roosevelt, I feel so ashamed. No one knows of this letter I have written to you. It is one secret I shall cherish by myself for the rest of my life. I'm so scared that I might get into trouble writing you this letter. Please Mrs. Roosevelt do not let anyone see this letter, not even The President. My sister is going to be married soon, and I have nothing to give her. My other sister teaches first grade in a grammar school and she would like some locking chairs for her room, but I have no money to buy them for her. My mother was going to buy me a winter coat, but if she did she wouldn't have any money to carry us over the holiday, and so I told her not to bother buying me any. My father owns our house, but he pays so much tax money, that we have none for ourselves. But we don't mind. We get along fine. And can't you see Mrs. Roosevelt, that its just for Christmas that I need this money? I read in the paper last year at Christmas time, you bought this girl out West, a Christmas outfit. But its not clothes for myself that I'm worrying about, but for my dear people and friends, for whom I want to buy gifts. Please Mrs. Roosevelt do not think me a vulgar ignorant child. I'm seventeen years old and a senior in high school. I graduate next June and have no hope of going away to some school. Please Mrs. Roosevelt answer my letter. I want to see if you have received my letter. I thank you for your kind attention and I'll still love you regardless of what you think of me and my letter.

Thank you.

■ December 18th 1937
Washington, D.C.
Dear Mrs. Roosevelt,

I'am sending you with this, my love to you, Your dear husband and your Son for the benefits we have received through Your husband administration; We have been living on relief and W.P.A. since the storm of 1933. Now my father has been out of work for over four months on account of being sick of his back and can not do hard work. I believe we will not have a Christmas tree this year. My father says that he believes he will have a decent job with the city this coming year because he helped the Democratic party on election day and won. But in the mean time he has no money to buy anything for me or my sisters. I have eight sisters no brothers, one is 18 year old, her name is M., she don't neet any toys and another is 17, other 15, other 13, 11, and I'am 10 years old, and H.,8, M. R. 5, and S. 3 for this last ones I wish you could be our Santa Claus and send us a few toys for me and my little sisters also if you have some old clothes of yourself and wish to send them to mother she will fix them for my other sisters. Please, madam do not say anything to no body because my father don't like for us to ask for anything. I know you have many little children to take care of but you are a very kind lady and I believe you will send my little sister S. a doll, which she wishes to have: please excuse me for bothering you so much. We all wish you a very happy Christmas to you all with love.

■ [address lost]
[received Dec. 27, 1937]
Dear Sir and Madam,

I guess you don't know what this is,
or what's this all about
But I'll tell you in no time
So you can find out.

Im a girl who's very poor
And in the age of twelve
I never have anything
Not even underwear.

I don't have pretty dresses
Like the rich girls do
I only have ragged ones
That's because I'm poor

I asked my mother
What for Christmas I would get
But she says
I haven't the money yet.

Even if she would have
I wouldn't get nothing
Because my daddy only gets
44 a month.

Then comes a light bill
And the rent
And the grocer bill
And the milk
Oh help me if you will

Ther's five in the whole family
And like "hobos" we all look
Oh help the poor if you could

Thank You
L. C.

■ Watkins Glen, N.Y.
Dec. 15, 1939
Dear Mrs. Roosevelt
I am writhing to tell you I am so sad I dont know how to tell you I had a
yellow persian male cat and I loved him with all my heart a man with a car
ran over him and killed him I want another one and my father says he cant
get one I want one like him. My dad works on the W.P.A. and he only get
$39.00 a month and he says Roosevelt will help you get one will you send
me a yellow Persian kitten for my Christmas Please I dont expect anything

for Christmas I cant sleep I cant eat we buried my kitten in a hole I got a box put a little Blanket around him every boddy loved my cat he would sit up and wash his face every time I told him he would mind better than I do I think I am 8 years old in the fifth grade and on the Honor roll I go to church every Sunday I have a song to sing and a piece to speck and a play I am in to church Please send me a kitten.

M. B.

Georgetown La
Dec 18 1939
Dear Mrs Roosvelt

I am going to drop you a few lines to see if you would please help me I am a little boy 10 years old and in the 4th grade I would like for Santa Clause to come to see me and my sister but Mother has told me that he wont for my daddy has been hurt over 2 months and we are to poor to let Santy know. Mother said she would write to Santa but he had quit coming to see her and she could not give him anything.

Mrs Roosvelt if you see him will you please tell him I have done my best to be good and to please please come this year. I will stop with love and a Happy Christmas to you with my love to

A. A.

Dec. 28, 1939
Logan, Utah
Dear Mrs. Roosevelt

I am a boy 13 years old & I deliver newspapers to help make my part of the money to keep us. My daddy died when I was 8 months old, she was left with 5 little children my mother has been working on the Adult Ed. program. She got laid of on the middle of December. Wich was the worst part of the year. I want a pair of hockey shoe Skates so bad but Santa Claus couldnt bring them to me, I hope the President Roosevelt goes in for a third term. He has done so much to give the people that needed work, imployment. he has helped us a great deal to. two of my brothers have worked there way through school, & my brother & I are going to school now. My brothers are married. Mother is just laid of for a month—we hope, I ware a size 8 Skate, I would like Hockey shoe skates very much if you have any at the White House. I read in the paper that you were giving gifts to the poor people in & around Washington.

I Hope you all keep Well

Yours truly

J. W. J.

■ C.R., New Brunswick

[acknowledged Dec. 5, 1940]

Dear Lady and Santa Claus,

A few words to tell you if you are kind enough to make me a favor to Santa Claus. Maman was telling me that Santa Clause is not coming for me this year a Xmas because we are too poor. And Santa Clause left his bag of toys over to Lady Roosevelt in America. Today that I am all alone I thought I would write you to tell you to see in Santa Clause toy bag If you can find a little phonograph with a dozen records. Would you kindly send it to me. It would be a great pass time. I would also like to have a doll. During the winter nights. Tell Santa Claus for me that I was good all the year. I did not go to school this year because I was too poor to go. If you will send me a phonograph I will send you a rug I made for a present I will send it to put near your bed. I also got some to sell and I would like to sell them I would try to sell them $3.00 each I would like to sell them so I can buy Some Clothes to go to school. If you want to buy them I would be awful glad we are five children in the family and are poor people Tell Santa Im ten years of age not to forget me And In payment I will pray God for you to be blessed your family.

Yours truly

N. L.

EASTER

· ·

■ Port Morris, N.J.

March 20, 1934

My Dear Mrs. Roosevelt:

Do you realize that "Easter" is at hand? Do you realize how many hearts are broken on this account? Do you realize how hard its going to be for most people? Like me, for instance, I am a young girl of fifeteen and I need a coat, so bad I have no money, nor any means of getting any. My father has been out of work for two years.

My brother works on the C.W.A. but he is, or rather has been, insane in an asylum and has taken most of our money. My mother gets "fits" when I ask her to buy me something new Poor mother, I sypathize with her because it has been very hard on her, this depression, and no money at all but debts piling up on us. I want to tell you something: We were once the richest people in our town but now, we are the lowest, considered, the worst people of Port Morris.

For Easter some friends of mine are thinking of getting new out-fits and I just have to listen to them. How I wish I could have at least a coat. That would cost about $5.00 at least. I need a dress. I want one and it only costs $.79 cents Dear Eleanor how I wish I had the coat and dress for Easter I would be the happiest girl. I love you so much.

Please send me about $6.50

I thank you so much

A. C.

■ March 27, 1935
Philadelphia, Pa
Dear Mrs. Roosevelt:

I am asking you for your charity, asking you to send me and my two sisters suits for Easter. It is not only that we have nothing to eat but also nothing to get dressed into.

Easter is coming nearer and nearer but I do not think it will be an Easter for me. It will be another dull and unpleasant Easter like last year. It is supposed to be a time of rejoicing but I know I shall not rejoice for I have nothing to rejoice about. Mrs. Roosevelt I do hope you shall send the suits. If you do I would like you to send them in these sizes. J. 15 years old size 20 a shadow check S. 14 years old size 20 in a shadow check A. 10 years old size 14 in a color of blue You notice the big sizes, that is to last us for a few years I hope you will send them and make our Easter a time of rejoicing at least once I hope you shall send them about a week from Easter. During this time I shall pray for you and pray that you do send them. If you do send them just let it be a secret between me and you, please do not tell anyone.

During this time God Bless You A thousand times

Yours truly

P.S. Mrs Roosevelt please send mother one of your old dresses that you do not wear now if it is a size 40 please!

■ New York, N.Y.
April 15, 1935
Dear Mrs Roosevelt,

As you know Easter is comming very soon, I thought I would write, and see if you had an old coat, or I would like a swagger suit. I am 13 years old, and take size 14 or 16, I am very stout. My mother is very poor, and my father has been out of work for 3 years. I havent any coat to wear to church Easter Sunday. If you can find an old coat or suit I will be thankful. I will be very thankful. Thank you.

Yours truly

A. B.

P.S.

I hate very much to ask you but I had because I havent anything to wear.

■ Washington D.C.
March 15, 1936
Dear Mrs. Roosvelt,

I am a fourteen year old girl of Washington, D.C. My mother gets me nice clothes and she goes without. It has been so long since she has been fixed up for Easter that I can't remember when it was. This year I have made up my mind she is going to get fixed up before I am. My father was in the World War as a head cook, so he will get a bonus, and I will get ten dollars. I need it next month so I can get my mother a little something for Easter. I asked my father if I could have it then instead of when he gets his bonus, but he doesn't have it to spare. I was wondering if you would help me out, by loaning me ten dollars until I get my bonus. I am considered very honest in school by my fellow students, and give you my promise to pay you back. I would just love to get a letter from you in your own hand writing, and also a picture of you. My father is a president but not of the U.S.A. He is President of Local 252 Federal Employees Union. P.S. You just can't imagine how much this would mean to me.

I thank You

V. G.

I often read your column in the Times Hearld and like it very much.

I am the great, great, great, great grand daughter of Gen. N. G., and was born on Lincolns birthday.

■ [Fairmont, W. Va.]

March 20, 1939

Dear Mrs. Roosevelt,

I know that you are extremely busy with pre-Easter functions, besides the other many things in which you participate. I suppose this is very foolish for me to bother you, but I have heard so much about your extreme kindness and desire to help your people. I felt that you would help me.

First, you might like to know something about me. I am nineteen years old, will be twenty Easter day; a sophomore in a small State college; have been burdened with an anemic condition, that makes it disagreeable to go to school and to help things I have an infected kidney, now. My mother and father are very hard working people. My father has a job but his salary is not too much. My mother is so economical that we get along exceptionally well. They will not let me work on account of my health. I have one sister and two brothers.

This is another "hard luck" story. You probably hear hundreds of them daily. This one is true. It is not serious, to the extent that it means life or death but it is terribly painful.

My sorority is going to church Easter Sunday in a body or group (which is my birthday). After services, I have an invitation to eat with my boy friend and some other friends. I simply cannot go wearing my old clothes. I have worn them so much.

Let your mind drift back to when you were a young lady in school. Remember? Easter Sunday came once more. All the girls in your crowd came to church in their new outfits, looking like fresh flowers on a pretty sunshiny morning in the spring—and there you were in the same old black and white dress. Imagine how terrible you would have felt.

Although my father is very kind and sacrifices everything he can for his children I can't expect him to pay my doctor bill which is $17.50 and get me new clothes, too. He is a person who pays all his bills and lives on what is left.

If it isn't asking too much I would like to borrow $25.00 from you, and pay it back when I get through school and get a job. This probably seems a very small amount, but you don't know how much it will mean to me. In case you are in doubt about my honesty here are a few people whom you may ask:

Miss D. P. (Dean of Women)
Fairmont State Teachers College,
Fairmont, W. Va.

Dr. J. P. H.
Deveny Building
Fairmont, W. Va.

I am praying that you will help me, then my dreams will come true and I can go to church on Easter Sunday. If you don't mail the money would you please send me a penny post card. I wish you and your family a very happy Easter. Thank you so much for everything. I feel that you will help.
Sincerely,
E. S.

■ Norfolk, Va.
[acknowledged Apr. 7, 1939]
Dear Mrs Roosevelt;
First Lady of the White House.
My name is A. K., and I am sixteen years old. My mother is out of job and my father is not making hardly any money at all. As I was sitting down thinking about the lovely things my friends would have for Easter, tears came into my eyes. But I am trying to be a heroine, by not leting my mother and father know that I am worring. Because I knew if they were able they would give me any thing they possible could. And I am writing to you for help, please send me a small amount of money or send me some clothes so that I too may look nice on Easter. I know you will help me. Please, pardon me for the unneatness of this letter. Please *keep it a secret.*
Sincerely Yours

■ York, Alabama
April 7, 1939
Dear Mrs Roosevelt:
This may sound like I am begging but if I get able I will someday return it. I am sixteen years old three is four children in our family. My daddy tried to get work for four months and now he is making $26 a month and we don't have enough to eat & hardly nothing to wear. I mean you to please sent me $5.00 to get me a dollar dress, a dollar hat a dollar and a half pair of shoes and a 50 cent pair of hose and a dollar bag. I never have had an Easter dress. If you will do this I won't ever tell a person we try to live right and I am going to be looking.
I respect you sincerely yours
M. M.

MARRIAGE

. . . .

■ Utica New York

April 20, 1934

To Mrs. Franklin Roosevelt

I am a girl of nineteen years of age. My parents are living. I am the only daughter. We have an income of only twelve dollars ($12.00) weekly, from the C.W.A. work bureau. Although we own our home we are way back on our payments, and life is so discouraging at times.

Wishing that I would find a job, but its in vain. I need clothes and my people cannot afford to buy them. I have been given a pair of silk stockings, by a friend, for street wear, so one can plainly see, that I don't wear stockings around the house. It isn't very long ago I have met a man in his thirties going to his forties. He is very much in love with me and wishes to marry me. By marrying him, I would be dressed up like a girl, but I do not love him, He has a good position, and has never married, and he wishes to get married, and he wishes to get married now. If I would be married to him, I would never be happy, I would be marrying him for clothes. Now, Mrs Roosevelt, I wonder if you can help me, avoid this unhappy marriage? I hope to hear from you,

Receive my best wishes

Your needy friend

Miss C. S.

■ Washington C.H., Ohio

April 30, 1936

Dearest Mrs. Franklin D. Roosevelt:

I sincerely hope you read this letter and give it just a small ounce of thought as I know you must receive so many you just discard them without perusing them.

By the way, I'm twenty-one and old enough to vote this year. Even if I didn't like President Roosevelt, which isn't true, my father said I had to vote for him. Even so, no one should have to be told to cast their ballot for him. They should know he *cannot* be beaten.

This isn't a plea, sob story, etc. I'm merely presenting my case which, no doubt, won't seem nearly so pathetic to you as it does to me.

Nevertheless, my boyfriend & I have been going together six years, and, cannot possibly get married. Why? No job, no money, & no place to get either one. You'll probably say to yourself, well, he could get a job if he tried hard enough, but he has been all over our town, all over adjacent towns, in fact, every nook & corner he can find to go to. We live in what you might term a village, went to a small town high school, and, of course, when you cannot afford to go on to college, you have no trade, whatsoever. Where does that put you? Simply in that lower class who yell "strawberries," or "Lady, do you want your trash hauled today?", etc. Mrs. Roosevelt, we are both from very decent and respectable families but are just of the middle class of people; can make a living comfortably but can give no help. We have tried to get small loans to get married and go to housekeeping on, but they say we are only young kids and can't take the responsibility of paying a loan. Then, too, they charge such a high rate of interest and make the payments so high, you just couldn't possibly do it. We both want to get married and raise one or two children, so that we can be young with them. We have wanted to marry for four years and still don't see a possible chance in view. Of course, we could go in with either parents. But tell me, what kind of life would that be? We would live peaceably for about six weeks, maybe less, then fighting & arguing would begin and it wouldn't be long before each one would be embittered toward the other one. I don't care how good natured you are, you simply cannot get along with two families *existing* in one home. For it isn't *living*, you know.

Well, last week my boyfriend got a job which varies from ten to twenty dollars a week, according to the weather. And, again we tried, but was turned down as we had to have fifty or seventy-five dollars, down payment on furniture.

I'm asking you, would you loan us two hundred dollars, make your own terms and interest, and you'll get every cent of it back? We would sign a note, or an I.O.U. or whatever you like. Please, please think this over. We counted, added, & did everything last night and found we could furnish a house very nicely for two hundred seventy eight dollars and fifty three cents. But we thought with a two hundred dollar loan we could pay that and carry the rest. This will probably seem very foolish to you but were you in our place, maybe you would do the same thing. Of course, you would never have such things to worry about. You can't possibly imagine our feelings but please try to. We are very much in love, but hopelessly so, I fear. We are both beginning to believe there is no peace and happiness on earth for middle class people, at least, there isn't for us. Just try to put yourself in my place and see what your thoughts would be.

I have listened to practically all of your talks, and also, the President's. I'm sure I could love you both if I had the chance.

My father is an architect & contractor and you know what chances they had, during the depression. Absolutely none. Well, since President Roosevelt has been in that work has picked up from year to year and is now good enough to make my parents a comfortable living. Daddy is sixty-three and Mother is sixty. They are the dearest, sweetest dad and mother in the world.

Well, I've probably bored you to death with troubles that don't mean a thing to you, of course, but please read this a second time before you refuse me.

Just remember that if you loan us the two hundred dollars, you'll get every cent in return and more, according to your rate of interest.

Please let me hear from you.

Sincerely yours

Miss W. D.

Brooklyn, N.Y.

March 21, 1939

Dear Mrs. Roosevelt,

I'm so confused so troubled—I don't know where to begin. I'm not trying to convince you with this letter. I'm asking—please—to believe and help me.

My problem is that—of most young folks—"Marriage."

It's easy enough for children of the wealthy—those—with permanent positions—but how about us—with only season jobs—are we not human too.

Mrs. Roosevelt—my girl friend and I planned to get married in September of 1939. Two months ago—she lost her job. I do season work—and although I've been out of work for four months—I'm working now and expect to until Easter—when my season ends.

We're young folks—I twenty six and my girl friend nineteen—and very much in love—and we don't want to live another day—apart from the other—feeling this way—we changed our wedding date to June 4th—we changed because I was getting sick waiting—we have the blessings of her family and mine but financially they can't help us.

Mrs. Roosevelt—I must give my girl friend some kind of a wedding. I had thought of borrowing—from a finance company—buying furniture on credit—but—it's all too much with the little job I have—I couldn't pay—when my season slackened—the sensible thing to do—would be to wait—until I accumulated enough money together—Mrs. Roosevelt—please believe me—I'm headed for consumption—if I wait another day—I have no friends from which I could borrow two or three hundred dollars—that's all I'd need—couldn't you—wouldn't you please help me Mrs. Roosevelt— you would never miss that amount—in time I'd pay you back—but I must have your help—if I wait any longer—my health is at stake—please—believe me.

Praying to God—that you will help me—I remain—
Respectfully,
J. T. M.

P.S. Mrs. Roosevelt—please forgive me—for daring to write—but I'm helpless—I wrote to Mr. Rockefeller—Mr. Rushmore and a Dr. Sauchelli —but my letters went ignored—Please Mrs. Roosevelt—give my letter thought.

BICYCLES

. . . .

The Bronx, N.Y.
December 28, 1934
Dear Mrs. Roosevelt,

I am a girl of fourteen years old and I have diabetes. You might not know much about this disease but it is most unpleasant and painful. I take needles twice a day which hurt extremely. As you see I havent gotten much fun out of life. I also cannot eat a bit of sweets. I have not tasted candy, cake, ice cream or pie for over 4 years. I have thought several times of committing suicide. I received nothing for Christmas because my father only makes $18 a week. I have two other sister who have to be provided for. My medicine cost $3 a week. This also takes up a lot of money. There is only one thing that my sister and I wanted for christmas that is a model 28 bicycle blue in color. If I had a bike I could ride to school and save carefare. If my sister had a bike she could run errands. The children around our neighborhood got one for christmas. They tease us until we almost cry. This makes my father feel bad and he will try to get us one. But out of his salary this is impossible. I will be most grateful to you if you will grant my most desired request. It will make me very happy. And if I ride to school it will use up some of the excess sugar in my blood. Please regard my request carefully. I desire a Model 28 bicycle blue in color.

Yours truly
M. G.

■ Methuen, Mass.

Mar. 31, 1935

Dear President & Mrs. Roosevelt:

The favor I am about to ask you is one which I consider a great one. I am asking you if you could possibly send me a girl's bycicle. The school which I attend is very far and as I am not very healthy I often get pains in my sides. My father only works two days a week, and there are six in my family, it is impossible in almost every way that I can get a bycicle! I am in the eighth grade and am very fond of school. Sometimes I have to miss school on account of the walk so far I have often thought things would pick up and father might be able to get me a bycicle, but instead they have grown worse. I assure you, that the bycicle shall not be used as a pleasure but as a necessity.

I shall be waiting patiently, for my greatest wish to be granted, as I feel sure you cannot and will not turn me down. *Please* try to send it to me.

I shall remain

Sincerely yours

M. B.

■ Niles, Mich

May 17, 1936

Dear Mrs. Roosevelt,

I have heard that you get lots of money and that you have life easy. Our way is quite different. I have wanted a bicycle for so long But my parents are two poor to get me one and I haven't any work anywhere.

At school I am the only one of the big boys who hasn't a bicycle. They make fun at me because I haven't a bicycle and haven't enough money to buy one. The little children don't want me and I get so lonesome I can't hardly get my lessons.

I will thank you ever so much if you would send me about $25.00 so I could just get a second hand one.

I am 12 years old and in the seventh grade.

I will be sure that my dad will vote for your husband the next term in the president election.

I will be very grateful to you if you will help me.

Goodbye

R. E. R.

I am interested in aviation and hope someday to be a pilot if my parents have the money to send me.

St. Louis, Mo

Aug. 13, 1936

Dear Mrs Roosevelt

I am a girl of 12 and my parents are poor I can not afford a bick. Some day I set at the window and cry to see other children with bicks. and long for one I save and save but I get so little and sometimes none and I have only 40 cents and I been saving for almost a half year. I would aperciate a bick. very much. The children around me won't let me ride and every body is still getting bicks and I like for you if it isn't to much trouble. All the girls are going bick riding now and I have to stay home. May name is O. T. Please send it soon before school starts.

As ever

O. T.

Please don't over look me.

Little Rock, Ark.

[received Sept. 26, 1936]

My Dear Mrs. Roosevelt,

I'm a boy 16 years old. I had the pleasure of seeing you, and our dear President while you were in Arkansas. Mrs Roosevelt, I hope I am doing the right thing by making this appeal to you. I have a mother, daddy, and five little brothers and sisters. My daddy is working on the W.P.A. of which he only gets to work 7 days a month. I don't see how we are going to exist very much longer. School is about to start again and my little brothers and sisters have'nt the clothes and the books to go to school with. Mrs Roosvelt will you please help me. I can go to work and help my mother and dad if I had a bycycle. My mother has tried to get me one, but she can't get that much money and no one will let her have one on credit on account of daddy on W.P.A. Will you please lend me the money or fix it so I could buy me a bycycle. I will send you every cent out of each payday I draw. I have tried to get work with-out needing a bycycle but I am not very strong and I have been unable to get anything to do. Mrs. Roosevelt we are all so thankful for what you have done for the suffering and depressed and mother and dad prays every night for our Dear President and wife. I will be watching each day for the Postman hoping you will answer my letter. Please help me, I will work and help mother and also send you every cent you send me, just as soon as I commence making any money.

I am sincerly your Friend

E. A.

Sikeston, Missouri
January 20, 1938
Dear Mrs. Roosevelt,
I am writing this letter in hopes you will answer in my favor.

My father, H. C., has been in bed from a stroke for almost a year. We have no money and my brother works but makes only $3.00 a week and there are eight in our family.

My step-mother is very good to me and I try to help her. She takes in washings and I have to walk for six or eight blocks and then carry the washings home . . . before school and it has been very cold here. If you could send me a bicycle to ride when I go after washings for her I shall appreciate it. I am in the eighth grade at school and work very hard to make passing grades. The Principal of the school bought two of my sisters and me a pair of slippers so we would not have to stay at home. If you would do this for me I shall be able to help my step-mother more. If you send me one I would like a girls bicycle. I am fourteen years old. I am about 4 foot 3 inches tall so if you send me one you can judge as to what size.

Loving and appreciating—
A. L. C.

Iron Mountain Michigan
May 12, 1938
Dear Mrs. Roosevelt:
I am writing you this letter to let you know I am dying to recieve a bycke. I have been wanting one since I was nine years old. now I am thirteen I am a very tall girl I am five feet six in. tall I weigh about 104 lbs. My dad is on W.P.A. which pays so little you can hardly live on it. I know I shouldn't be asking for shoes. But I really love a bycke more than anything else in the world. I had to take my last three cents to write to you, because no one would give me any money for a stamp they all said no it was only a foolish notion, but I take it seriously. I have told you once before that my dad was on W.P.A. Which I know if I don't get a bycke from you I'll never get one, so I am hoping, and praying that you will take pity on me, and send me a bycke. I have been trying my best to save enough money for a bycke, and every time I get about a dollar saved up I had to take it for some-thing to eat. I know I shouldn't write, and ask you for a bycke. So if you can't send me a bycke I do wish you would come to Iron Mountain for a visit, and see how we are getting along. We have eight in the family, and $44.00 a month is not enough to live on can't you please do any-thing about it. please speak to

your husband about, it he ought to be able to do some-thing for the people of the U.S. I want to ask you one more question do you think that's fair well I sure think its terrible. And I do wish you would do some-thing, and please let me know if you are, We are just about going hungry on $44.00 a month with eight people in the family—we have to pay our rent which is $9.00—water, and lights. if we need wood we have to pay for that, and the little bit of enjoy-ment we can get out of that, and beside that we have to buy cloths, There are many families who only have one child in the family getting $44.00 a month now that isn't fair, and I wish you would do some-thing about it for my sake Am I asking too much from you for a bycke, and to do the big favor of all to look after the things in Iron Mountain. I think there is some crooked work, don't you really think that we should get more then forty, four dollars a month on a whole. Well I am coming back to the bycke part of the letter again, Now don't get angry with me for asking you for the bycke, but I have been trying to get a bycke since, I was a young lad of course I am not so old now. I'll repeat again If you would do these two big favors for me you can ask as many favors from me as you wish. I do wish I could get to talk personally with you, and your husband. then I could tell you many other things that are going on in Iron Mountain. I am telling you if I don't recieve a bycke from you I'll never get one the rest of my life, and I will feel very disappointed. I wish you both could come down to Iron Mountain to visit, and don't be affraid to come to my house I'll repeat the address for you it is. . . . I have been wishing all my life to get to see, you, and talk to you, but I guess it is hopeless Well I must say good bye to you both, and I am hoping, and praying I will recieve a letter saying Flash! It is on its way now.

Well I wish you both the most happiest and successful time of the year and many years to come.

Yours very truly

E. F.

P.S. Your pal.

■ Endwell, New York

[received June 14, 1938]

Dear Mrs. and Mr. Roosevelt,

I am a girl of fourteen, whose hobby is to ride a bicycle. It has been four years that I wanted one but there isn't any signs of getting one yet. My father is a shoeworker and the shoeworks are very bad. My father is only working two and three days a week. The average wage my father makes is nine to twelve dollars.

His work has been poor for two years now. I have a long distance to school and I would like to have a bicycle then I would not have to walk. The walk tires me out so at night that I can hardly do my homework. I wish you could help me by getting me a bicycle. I see no other way out so I am asking you for one. I have seen a bright wine colored one in Montgomery Wards. That is in the city of Binghamton, N.Y. It is only a few miles away. Bicycle riding is what I dream about.

If you have a chance of getting me one. When I get bigger I'll pay you back for your kindness. I will be at Gettysburg to see you on the fourth of July. My mother and father are from Gettysburg and we like It very much there.

Someday we would like to go back. It is so beautiful around the battle-field since they have improved it. We went through it the last time we went down. I hope I will hear from you soon.

Thank you,

Sincerely Yours

Miss K. R. E.

Sharpsburgh, Pa.

May 2, 1939

My dear Mrs. Roosevelt:

Would you please give me thirty five dollars ($35.00) for a bicycle. All the kids on our street have bikes and they make fun of me because I don't have one. If you give me the money I will not know how to repay you. The reason I am writing to you and asking you for the money is because you have more money than you need. Just taking $35.00 out of your money wouldn't hurt your salary.

Also send me your autograph.

Dont forget to send me the money.

Yours very trulie,

P. S.

p.s. Dont forget to answer. If you cant afford to give me $35.00 give me whatever you can afford.

■ Star Route Mo

May 5 1939

Dear Mrs. Roosevelt,

I am a poor farm girl live down in the hills. and haft to walk 8 miles to school and my father is not able to work much he is 68 years old and my brothers dont want to stay home. I live on a 80 acre farm with my parents and we have a $168.50 morgage on this farm and we cant get it payed up and it libled to be sold any time then we wouldnt have no home. we are so hard up cant buy any clothe mother and I dont have but one dress to wear. havent no slippers to wear haft to wear old shoes. I go to sunday school when I can haft to walk about 6 miles. I have two brothers and a sister married. one of my Brothers is in Boise Idaho. last we hear from him he didnt have no job. he is 23 year old. and H. my youngest brother he 18 years old. I am 15 years old, mother is 54 years old, sister 28 years old. I would like to have a horse to ride to school. got two more years in grade school. my youngest brother wants to look for him a job but mother wont let him because he havent got no money to start out on. I shore get lonesome down here havent no place to go only a foot and then it so far to walk. when i go to school I haft to start about 5:0 clock in the morning and get home late after dark. I would be plased with bicycle to ride to school. we have had so much bad luck our house burnt down burnt every thing we had. lost Three cows an a cane patch. I my little poney broke her neck. papa was sick costed us $20 one horse got his leg broke and had it killed. well I will close hopng to hear from you soon. an if you are down in this part of the country come in and see us.

P.S. Excuse this writing.

From a lonesome farm girl

Miss M. L. D.

To Mrs. Roosevelt

P.S. again mrs Roosevelt recon you coulndt help me get a poney or bicycle to ride to school I sore would thank you if you could help me.

■ Lackawanna, N.Y.

June 15, 1939

Dear Mrs. Roosevelt,

Having heard of the many kind deeds you have done for the underprivileged children, we have deceided to ask for your aid.

We are both fifteen years of age and in June will complete our sophmore year in the Lackawanna High School.

If it is not asking for too much we would like to know if we are capable of receiving bicycles from you. In exchange we agree to do anything within our power.

We are asking this of you because it is not possible for our parents to purchase them for us. The reasons for this is because my father has been dead for several years and my girlfriends father is a cripple; therefore we are unable to be supplied with luxuries. In order to meet the expenses our mother's do outside housework and take in weekly washing.

We are not writing this to recieve your sympathy and pity but to obtain your aid and advice.

In our city mostly all the girls and boys of the younger generation enjoy the privilege of having a bicycle and we feel very out of place. For this reason we are mocked and scorned at and are left out of many social activities.

If you think that we are fit for your aid, please answer our letter as soon as possible and write us your decision of the matter.

We remain,

M. M. H. and E. A. B.

We Thank You

▨ [Warren, Ohio

acknowledged June 27, 1939]

Dear Mrs. Roosevelt

I am a little girl I am 11 years old. My name is G. P. I have no daddy. My mother is on relief. I want a girl's bike real bad. every time I see a girl riding a bike it makes me cry. And my mother cries to because she can't by it. if you will give me a bike. My mother will pay you back when she gets a job. I know she will pay you. because she is a good American Citizen. I know you will. because my mother said Mr. Roosevelt is so good he gives us food and clothing. I will wait for the answer days & nights.

Yours Truly

G. P.

▨ Denham Springs La

Nov. 11, 1939

Dear Friend

How are you getting along theas days find I hope. I heard about you how kind you were, and I thought I would write to you. I am in the 5th grade and I am 10 years old. I have black hair, 4 ft. high. My teachers name is Miss

D. L. M. she is a very find teacher and I love her very much. I make theas grades on my report

Reading	A+
Spelling	A+
History	A+
Geography	A+
Language	A+
Arithmetic	A+
Science	A+
Art	A+
Health	A+

I am studing very hard and trying to keep my good grades up. My teacher said if I keep my good grades up she will give me a prize at the end of the year. She love me very much to. Later on I will send you one of my drawings at the end of the year. Maybe I will send more than one if I can. I want a picture of you if you will give it to me. Today is my birthday and my mother said she is going to get me a dress maybe if she can. My aunt from Baton Rouge said she will give me something later on. I have wished for a bycicle all my life and still wishing for one but my Mother and Father is not albl to buy me one. I have even tried to sell books and save to get one but I couldn't sell them so I din't get the bycicle I was very sad and cried very much about it. My daddy is a painter but he just make enought money to pay our mounthly bills. Can I do anything for you to earn one if so let me know I will be glad to do it just let me know no matter it is I will try to do it. I want you to write back to me and let me know if there is anything I can do for you so you will send me a bycicle. Tell your husband hello for me. I love both of you, I will give you my name and address.

Your little friend

J. S.

CARS

. . . .

■ [Crisfield, Md.]

August 21, 1935

Dear Mrs. Roosevelt,

I have read so many editorials and articles you have written for books and magazines that I feel I almost know you through the feeling you put in your writing. But I suppose that first I should tell you something about myself.

Last Wednesday I was fifteen years old. When Crisfield High School starts in September, I enroll as a Senior. My one ambition is to be a surgeon and when I finish school next June, I intend to work my way through medical school. My parents are poor, both of them having to work for our living. My father grades tomatoes in the summer and opens oysters in the winter. In the spring and early fall he does anything he can find. My mother works in the factory and I help her with the cleaning, washing, ironing, etc. That is about all there is to know about our family.

I shall tell you now what I am writing to you about. Recently, my father traded his old car for a little better one. He has to have a car to go to his work in because it is so far from home. The other car would fail all the time even if Daddy just went from home to his work. We owe over $75 on the better one yet and I am afraid it is going to be taken from us. If it is taken from us, my father will have to give up his job because it is too far for him to walk and there are no trolley cars in Crisfield and taxis are so very expensive.

So, dear lady, I am asking if you won't send me $50. If you don't have it, maybe Mr. Roosevelt does, and I would appreciate it so much. I will not accept it as a gift but as soon as I receive it I shall send you my I.O.U. and upon my word of honor, I swear I shall pay it back, every penny of it.

Forever yours,

Miss M. E. B.

P.S. I saw Mr. Roosevelt when he came to Crisfield last summer. I truly admire him and I sympathize with both of you in regards to the sudden tragic death of Will Rogers and Wiley Post.

M. E. B.

◼ [Bourbon, Ind.]

February 27, 1936

Dear Mrs. Roosevelt:

I am G. S. was 16 years old on the 30th of January with President Roosevelt.

We live on a farm since a year at Bourbon, Ind. I my mother and my sister come from Chicago. My mother was working hard all these years in the hotels as maid. She broke down on her nerves, so couldn't do the hotel-work any longer. And so we moved out here on the farm, which we think will be much better for my mother and sister. My oldest sister is 18 years old, and is not very strong. Everybody think she is 12 or 14 years old. She was most of the time sick, and was over one year in the hospital. Now she is O.K. and likes it very well on the farm too.

We have no Team. I and my mother do the spading ourselves. Maybe next year we can buy a Team. We have a cow a calf 20 weeks old and 50 chickens.

My father is in Chicago, working in a Tannery. He doesn't make such good money either, has to send money to us for living, and to pay the farm. My father was twice in the hospital, and had an operation every time. He was also unemployed for two years, and all the working my mother had to do.

And now, Dear Mrs. Roosevelt, that's why I am writing to you. My father told we would get a car by the time Spring came. Now he wrote us he can't buy us a car yet, he has to save the money to pay taxes. He is not feeling well, both his hands are awful swollen, on account there is such strong stuff in the water in which he has to work.

And we need so badly a car, we don't care how old, just so it runs. We live 4½ miles from town, and it is too far to walk. We can't bother our neighbors all the time to take us to town to get food for our stock, and also for ourselves. If we had our own car, it would make it much easier for us. And, Dear Mrs. Roosevelt can I ask you for help, in getting us a car? We don't care how old it is. O, how I wish I could surprise my mother and sister! Theyve never been anyplace yet, since we're here.

Now Dear Mrs. Roosevelt don't get mad at me, you're the only one I can write to. Please will or can you kindly help us? Or is it too much both for you? I am sure that my mother father and sister will vote for President Roosevelt again. We have a very nice picture of President Roosevelt hanging in our front room.

Sincerely and respectfully Yours,

G. S.

■ Keltner Missouri

January 1, 1938

Dear Mr & Mrs Franklin D. Roosevelt:

I am writing to you to see if you will buy me a new car or pick-up. Here is what I want with it. I want one to drive to high school. As, for I live in the country where the school busses does not come. They will not come to my home where I live. I am a poor boy and if you will buy me a new pickup. Then I can earn some of my money to buy some of the gasoline with. If you will buy me a new pick-up it will mean and education to me. If, I had money enough to buy it I wouldn't be writing to you. For you to buy me one. If you will buy me one may be some day I will be president. And if you both are living I will buy you one. If you will buy me one to help get me through high school. For I love school.

I will never forget you if you will buy me one.

I will close.

Yours truly,

O. M.

The kind I want is a Dodge

P.S. I am only fifteen years old.

The pickups cost $677.00

The cars cost $875.00

■ Bryson City, N.C.

October 12, 1940

Dear Mrs. Roosevelt

I live on a farm about six and one half miles from Bryson City. I am eighteen and in the eleventh grade of Bryson high school. I live about four miles from where the school bus runs in a small neighborhood where there is four boys whitch all have cars but me. The boys will not have me to school becaus they think I am a sissy for working on the farm, they think I should loafer after school like they do. I hafto get up ever morning at five and milk six cows and carry in the water and cut wood and then eat breakfast and go to school when it rains I can't go to school and part of the time I am late. The boys will blow there horns at me and laugh as they pass me up. I have often heard people talk about how you have helped people who wanted to make something out of them selves. I want to finish school very much, so I though maybe you would help me. If I had $175 I could buy a farely good second hand car and I could finish school and not miss so much. If you could send me that much I would be so glad I would cry for I don't won't to quit school whitch I will hafto for I can't walk through the snow that far. If you could send me that mutch when I finished school I would get a Job and pay you back. I am not begging for I though you would help me out. If you could.

Excuse my writting for I am not a very good hand to write.

Truly yours,

F. J.

My address is just F. J.

Bryson City, N.C.

. . . .

■ [Milwaukee, Wis.]

Sept. 9, 1934.

Dear Mrs Roosevelt:

I would appreciate if you would kindly help us out in having a radio in our home. It is so lonesome without one! We have had a radio, but Mr. S. (county sheriff) took it away when we but a few dollars to pay. My father has been out of work three years, and have gone through two serious operations. The last one has taken place, but a few weeks ago, and is not able to work. I have tried in many ways to obtain one, but so far have not succeeded. I am but sixteen years of age, and have always loved music. Hoping you will do everything in your to obtain one. Hoping to hear from you soon!

I remain a noble Citizen

Miss D. H.

Parents: Mr. Mrs. J. S.

■ Wolfe City, Texas

Sept. 13, 1934

Dear First Lady:

Will you take time to read a letter from a lonely little country girl. I am fourteen years and will be in the junior class in high school this term. I have to ride five miles to school—on horse back when it is too muddy for the bus. Mrs. Roosevelt, I want you to tell me if you can some way by which I can get the thing I most want right now.

When I read how you get $3000 for each radio broadcast you make, I can't help but think how unjust this world is. Here I sit straining my ears trying to hear the sound of your voice we a little crystal set my uncle helped us to make last winter. It is about half the size of a ladies' shoe box and with the cheap head phones, I just hear enough to make me eager to hear more.

I have only heard your voice once or twice as we can only get the Dallas and Fort Worth stations.

I have so little pleasure and past time. We are just poor renters on a farm and there is no money for a radio or the books I like so much to read.

I have done a boy's work every since I was five years old. This week I have been breaking land with a sulky plow and three mules.

Dear First Lady, I have read of your kind heartedness and the cheer you have brought to so many. Can't you suggest some way that I can get a radio so I can hear the music and talks and news from outside my very small little world?

I could never thank you enough.

My daddy doesn't know I am writing this. He would think me foolish to expect a favor from a great lady. Any way I've had some pleasure from writing it.

Excuse this paper—there is no money for nice stationary either.

Your little friend

W. H.

■ Geary, Oklahoma

April 20, 1935

Dear Mrs. Roosevelt,

I am a thirteen year old girl and live on a farm with my mother and Step-Father we are very poor people I have lived here for five years and have wished each year for a radio but as the years go by our circumstances get worse and worse. I am wondering if I would be asking to much of you to help me obtain one. As we live in the country we would have to have a Battery Radio. We live five miles from town, and we are poor we have no money for boughten amusements. There is not a radio around in the country and I get terribly lonesome in summer. If you could in any way help me to obtain one it would mean enjoyment for all my friends as well as me.

If you can help me to get one my appreciation cannot be put into words.

Sincerely yours,

M. N. C.

■ Kansas City, Mo.

Jan 23, 1936

Dear Mrs. Rosevelt,

My name is A. S. I am 12 years old. I go to the Allen School and I am in the sixth grade. My sister D. is 11 years old. She and I both love to listen to raidio but we have none. The only time we have a chance is when we go to our aunts. And if you would send me some kind of a one I would be very happy. I know where I can get one for $14.00 but I have no money. The best program I like is the gang busters. And Eddie Cantor.

Yours truly,

A. S.

P.S.

Please do not put me in jail.

■ Elmer Mo

Nov. 15, 1937

Dear Mr & Mrs President Roosevelt

I am a girl age 15. But I am undersize. I only weigh 67 lb. I am 4 ft 5 ½ in tall. I can't attend School because of poor health. I have an absess on my right bronchial tube. I live on a farm and have five sisters and two brothers. They are all married but two sisters and one brother. All of them that are old enough vote the demicrat ticket I am also going to when I am old enough. And as I havn't any thang for intertainment while my only sister at home attends school I get very lonesome, so I'm writing to you to see if you will help me to get this radio, I am sending you the picture of. As we are poor people and cant afford to buy one ourselves. I'll be very thankfull to you if you can mandage to get it for me. If you cant mandage to get it for me. I would injoy hearing from you anyway. I am thanking you very much in advance. Hoping to hear from you soon

I am Very Truely Your Friend

Miss D. P.

[Advertisement for radio enclosed]

HOLLYWOOD

. . . .

■ Brooklyn, N.Y.

Dec. 16, 1934

My dear Mrs. Roosevelt,

Will you please excuse me for taking up your time. As I read in the papers and heard it discused in school, that you have a good heart for the children of the United States. I come to you know to tell you a little story of my life. I am a Jewish girl 9 years old. My name is I.M. I was born in N.Y., now I am a puple of Ned Wayburn studio. I take singing and dancing lessons. I which I am his future star. Now I have a chance to take a screen test. In the Long Island Paramount Studio N.Y., to play in the movies. This is an expance about $200. My father doesn't make very much, my mother also helps him out. My parents have to much pride to take relieve, my parents would rather starve then take relieve. That is why it brings me to ask for help. As you are the best woman of the U.S. I am coming to you to do something for me direct please do this through the studio. A good word sometimes does more than money. I don't expect to be disappointed. I expect to go through with my career. When I will pass, I will never forget in poor children. I will always give my talent and help to charity. I am enclosing my picture. I am expecting a good result.

Yours respectfully,

(Little) I. M.

■ Brooklyn, N.Y.

February 5, 1938

Dear Mrs. Roosevelt,

I write you this letter because I heard you was very good. I heard that you help poor children so much. I hope you'll try to help us too. My two sisters and I always bother my mother to go to Hollywood. She answers us in a very sad way like this, "I'm sorry but if I had some money I'll send you right away." She can't afford it because she is separated from my father and all she gets is twelve dollars a week of him. And this is the first week we started to get twenty dollars a month off the relief. And you wont believe it even if you saw what kind of a house we live in. Please try to make us go to Hollywood. Here are our names and ages, C., thats me the eldest one, eleven (11) years old and E., ten (10) years old, and F. six (6) years old, She the littleest one is just like a little doll. Please try to help us. And I'm sure you will try to help us and we want to try to make some money to help my mother. Thats the best thing I like to do, because I don't like to see my mother cry. I wont sleep until I get an answer. Thank you.

P.S.

Please Answer

C. I.,

E. I.

F. I.

■ Centerdale, R.I.

April 23, 1938

Dear Mrs. Roosvelt

I am writing to you to ask a big favor, the biggest favor any body can ask. I would like to know if you would pay my way to Hollywood. You may think me crazy but I'm not. I mean every word I say. I know you may write back and say, lots of people ask you to pay their way to Hollywood or for some other reason, but this is different honest it is you've just got to believe in me your the only one that can help. Or you may say what can I do child. Well you can tell them you sent me and you know I can act, I'm sure they would belive you, because you tell no fibes. Just think woulde'nt you be proud if

I became a great movie Star and you would say to your friends, She's the little girl who wrote to me and asked if she could go to Hollywood. And I've helped to make her a great Star. I would like to tell you all this in person and then you could see me, but I have no money for care fare and I dont want you to bother to give it to me. My Little mother is a sickly lady, she is lovely so small and sweet I love my Little mother dearly and I want to help her all I can so this is why I am writing to you, It will also give me a future and bring proudness to my relatives. my Little mother has something the matter with her heart which these small Doctors dont know although they do try their best. So I thought if I went to Hollywood and earned enough money I would be able to give my Little mother the best Doctors and proper care. I am not writing this letter to Mr. Roosvelt because men don't understand things like we laides do, so I am writing to you because I know you understand. I have read and heard so many nice things you Mrs. Roosvelt and Mr. Roosvelt that I have high hopes of you saying yes. Oh just think woulde'nt it be fun if we could both go together, I am a jolly little girl and never kill joy. I'm sure I woulde'nt be any nusenc and would be a very nice companion, I act like a little lady and I woulde'nt climbe all over you. We could have so much fun sailing on the boat reading books and talk long conversations together while we stroll along deck hand in hand. I think it would be heavenly I can just picture myself. And it would be much easier for me to get in the pictures if you were their I'm sure. I am not writing this letter in big words like other people do, I'm writing this letter from the bottom of my heart to the very top.

I know I can act because I make little plays which I get out of story books and act them out. Please tell Mr. Roosvelt that I'm terribly sorry he lost that Bill. I think Mr. Roosvelt is doing wonders. Please be sure and tell him this, it will make him feel much better. I told some of my friends about my Idea but they only laugh at me, and I get discouraged but when I look at my Little mother I run upstairs in my room and cry. I have Mr. Roosvelt's picture in my room and his name in big read and blue letters. And when I looked at his picture it gave me an Idea and my Idea was writing to you. Please Mrs. Roosvelt answer my letter, and please oh please say yes that you'll try your hardest. God will never forget you in the next world. And what you do for your father and mother will never be forgotten. My father is also a sickly man, he had two nervous breakdowns but never got over the second one. But I am a healthy child. I am fourteen years old, blue eyes, about sixty in. tall, weigh 105½ pds, hair is long and curly sort of natural the color is light brown my complexion is very white. I have big eyes. Please trust in me with all your heart and I will trust in you with all my heart. Please just for my Little mother (That's what I call her because she is so small.)

If you the Secretary should open this letter Before Mrs. Roosvelt please give it to her. Thank You. A Little Girl who is still Unkown and Just Became Your Friend

J. I. A. Luck Love and Hope

SCOUTS

■ [East Orange, N.J.]
March 20, 1935
Dear Mrs Roosvelt,

I have heard that you are the head of the Girl Scout troups. I have read about you in the "American Girl" magazine at our library. I thought it would be good to join the girl scouts and now I have finished my tenderfoot test, and received my pin. My father is out of work and cannot afford to buy me a uniform so I am asking for your help. I will appreciate anything you can do for me.

Sincerely yours,
M. C.

■ April 7, 1938
New York, N.Y.
Dear Madam,

I am a boy scout of first class standing, but I have no uniform. This fact keeps iritating my patrol, of which I am patrol leader, because for each scout in uniform the patrol get five points. Also, my district, the Stuyvesant district, is going to give a program for the parents of the scouts of the district. Each troop is to send two scouts to represent the troop in the program. In my troop, I was the first nominee, but fell out because of the fact that I had no uniform. This fact made my patrol angry. They had lost the honor of having one of their members representing the troop. This fact comes up at many incidents. The money I save goes to troop dues and for hikes in which I participate in order to help the scouts in my patrol pass their tests.

I have heard that you have helped many other scouts in this predicament. Therefore, I appeal to you to aid me.

Respectfully yours,

Scout J. G.

POST SCRIPTUM: I thank you for the aid you are giving me. My gratitude has no limit or boundry. I am 69" tall and weigh 153 pounds. I am 14 years and nine months old.

J. G.

Hat size 7"

Shirt " 14½

Pants " 36

Stockings " 10"

Shoes " 8

DOLLS

. . . .

■ [Chicago

acknowledged Nov. 13, 1935]

Dear Mrs. Roosevelt,

You have nieces and sons who were young and some still are wanted a thing very much but tried hard to get it and can't. I a girl from Chicago have tried so so hard to get five suscriptions to get a 22 inch Shirley Temple which the Daily Chicago Tribune is giving away. It is cheap for at 65 cents a month you get daily paper. You have millions of friends couldn't you please ask them to take for one year at 65 cents a month the Daily Chicago Tribune. I don't know how I'd ever thank you if you got them. I know one thing I'd pray with all my heart in Holy Mass and when receiving Holy Communion pray to God to bless you and all. Please please do help me. Here is a picture of the Shirley Temple. If you do get them send them as soon as you can.

Yours truly,

W. C.

[The writer includes a cut-out picture of the doll.]

■ Springfield [Ill.]

[acknowledged Mar. 7, 1936]

Dear Mrs Rosevelt

I am 6 years old this is my first year in school i am a little colored girl my name is B. J. R. I wish you wold please send me a Sherley temple Doll

Shirley Temple doll. When the *Chicago Tribune* in 1935 offered to give away this twenty-two-inch replica of the popular child film star in exchange for five subscriptions to the paper, a child from Chicago sent this picture of the doll to Mrs. Roosevelt, along with a plea that she ask a few of her "millions of friends" to subscribe.

(From the collection of the Franklin D. Roosevelt Library, Hyde Park, N.Y.)

because my doll got broke i will take good care of the doll if you sen me one please Answer. My daddy helped me to writ you yours with lots of kisses X X X X X X

B. J. R.

■ St Antonville Tenn
[acknowledged June 27, 1938]
Dear Mrs. President
I am a little girl 5 years old I have a little brother he calls me Sistie I call him Buzzie after your little grandchildren. I wish I had a Shirley Temple doll. Dady cant not buy one
I love you
P. A. C.

SPORTS

· ·

■ Blacksburg, S.C.
January [1934]
Dear Mrs. Roosevelt,
Mrs. Roosevelt will you send me and my sister a pair of ball bearing roller skates? Our friends have skates and we are not able to buy them. We sure will thank you if you will.
yours trully,
L. L.
P.S.—I am twleve years old and in sixth grade at Blacksburg Grammar school. My friends at school have skates and laugh because I don't have some.
yours truly,
L.

■ January 4, 1935
Baraboo, Wis.
Dear Mrs. Roosevelt,
I am a little boy 12 years old, live in Baraboo Wis. and my Daddie working on the relief and only getting $9.00 a week and there 9 of us in the family, six other boys besides myself. We never can have shoe skates and clothes like other boys, I sure would like to have a pair of shoe skates, so does my two brothers age 9 and 15, so we could go skating with the other boys. They

seem to such fun. I have never had a new suit of clothes just have to ware old clothes that others give me. It just breaks my Mother's heart to see us boys go without so many things we need and cannot have, but Daddy don't seem to care.

I also would like to live on a little farm and take care of little chickens, and sell them to bring school cloths.

Mrs. Roosevelt if you lend me enough money to buy shoe skates I sure would be happy and would pay you back when I get big and can earn money. I go to St. Joseph's School the sisters are very kind to me.

My Mother is kind to me too. I worry about her she is not very strong and trys so hard to keep us boys in school and have to do all the washing by hand, and suffers from the cold because she has no warm cloths to ware. Please write to me, for I'am interested in you and President Roosevelt, I read so much about you. I will say Good-bye.

Very truly Yours,

V. C.

This is a picture of my little brother, was taken last winter in school. Would love to have a pair of shoe skates, he cried yesterday when he saw others boys skating in front of our house in the fair grounds. He is now nine years old. If you should write would you please kindly return this.

V. C.

■ New York City

April 25, 1935

Dear Miss Roosevelt,

Please if you dont mind please try to send me five dollar. Because all my friends have everything they need for baseball and I will want the same things but my mother can not afford to give me the amount of money I need to buy these things. If you will do me this faver I will be very thangfull.

Sincerely Yours,

S. N.

■ Rushville, Missouri

June 20, 1935

Dear Mr. and Mrs Roosevelt,

We are writing to ask a favor of you. My smaller brother and I are interested in boxing and we wondered if you would please send us a pair of boxing gloves apiece.

Our father is on the relief and is unable to buy anything like that for us because there are five children in our family.

My smaller brother is 10 years old and I am 14.

If you would be so kind as to send them, we thank you.

F. and R. C.

■ Ladysmith, Wisconsin

Jan. 4, 1939

Dear Mrs. Roosevelt

I am writing a letter to ask you if you could help me out. I live in a neighbor hood which are many kids my age. They all have some ice skates except me. For I cant afford it. And almost every day I sit down on the river bank watching all the others skate. My feet just ache to be on skate. Once a girl let me use hers. And boy! Oh! Boy! was it fun!

My family all like Mr. Roosevelt for a president and hope he gets in for a nother term.

No body knows about this except me. And I think I shall keep it for a secret a long time.

And now I shall tell you something about myself. I am 12 years old and shall be 13 on Jan 13, 1940 and I am 5 ft 1 in. And also in the 7th grade.

We live right on the bank of the flamheaw river.

One of your many friend,

M. S.

I am a Negro girl. . . . I have a NYA job. . . . My work is to take dictation.
. . . I have received many compliments on my work. Some of the girls
have received government positions on this job but they have not
been able to place any of the Negro girls because they can't find
anyone who wants a colored secretary. I feel fully capable of handling
any secretarial position. . . . I take 96 words in shorthand,
type 50 words a min.
—M. C., a nineteen-year-old from Buffalo, New York,
to Eleanor Roosevelt, November 1940

African American teens employed by the National Youth Administration
working at the "colored" YWCA in Chicago, 1936.
(From the collection of the Franklin D. Roosevelt Library, Hyde Park, N.Y.)

chapter 4

Minorities

Despite the egalitarianism embedded in the Declaration of Independence—and Jefferson's lofty phrase "that all men are created equal"—more than a century and a half after that document was written America remained a nation riven by social inequality. Indeed, America entered and left the Depression decade an inequitable society, favoring whites over blacks, Native Americans, and all other people of color, Anglo-Protestants over ethnics as well as new immigrants, and men over women. Depression America was also a society that often shunned the disabled, treating them with scorn and disgust rather than respect or compassion—a tendency so pronounced that it led even the president to hide the physical disability that polio had visited upon him. These inequities must be borne in mind if we are to understand how Americans experienced the Great Depression; they caused the burdens of the economic crisis to fall unevenly on the American people. Those who entered the 1930s at or near the bottom of the American social order or faced discrimination in such critical areas as employment and education were especially vulnerable to the Depression's ravages and at the greatest disadvantage in struggling to overcome them, for they had to battle both a horrendous economic crisis and American prejudice, a double burden whose weight was especially oppressive. The letters in this chapter from African Americans, a Native American, feminist-minded teens, immigrants, and the disabled document both this oppression and the determination of minority youths to free themselves from it.

Most of the letters that Eleanor Roosevelt received from African American youths came from the South, where some three-fourths of blacks lived. Conditions were grim with regard to both civil rights and economic opportunity. Between 1933 and 1935 racist mobs lynched sixty-three black southerners. Blacks were denied the right to vote (and could not serve on juries) in most southern states, and so lacked the political power to insure equal treatment in the federal aid and relief programs administered by local white officials, who were often bigoted. The majority of southern blacks were landless or small farmers badly hurt by the collapse of the cotton economy and the plummeting demand for other staple crops. Nor was the situation notably better in southern cities, where in the early Depression years job discrimination helped to drive the black unemployment rate above 50 percent.[1]

The situation in the North was better politically, but economically conditions were still dire. Although northern blacks could vote and did not face the rigid segregation of the South, job discrimination was rampant, forcing four out of five blacks who could find work to labor in unskilled or semiskilled jobs. The combination of racial prejudice and low skill levels meant that blacks were literally the last hired and first fired. A study done in the wake of the Harlem riot of 1935—a riot fomented by discrimination and the economic downturn—found that blacks lost their jobs three to four times faster than whites did in the early Depression years and regained private employment half as quickly.[2] Income levels between whites and blacks were vastly unequal. A study of close to a million families in Chicago found that in 1935–36 the median income for native whites was $1,580, more than twice the median level for blacks, which was a meager $726. Studies by the American Youth Commission found a similar disparity in youth wages, which in 1936 was $15.17 for white teens working a forty-nine-hour week and only $8.71 for black teens.[3]

Whether from North or South, letters from black youth to the First Lady centered on economic and social issues rather than politics. These youths did not ask her to stop racial violence or to help blacks win the political rights of citizens. Instead, they usually asked for help in securing jobs and education. Their demands reflected their most immediate needs, and the bread-and-butter issues that they confronted in their daily lives. But by no means were the letters apolitical. A definite political sensibility informed many of these letters, a sense that vital facilities and services available for whites were not provided to the black community—including playgrounds, youth centers, and libraries—and that this was an unjust situation that Mrs. Roosevelt should ameliorate. Several of the letters, moreover, are also political in that the youths wished to do something about prejudice themselves. But rather than tackle prejudice head on by confronting white America, they sought instead to build institutions in the black community, as did one teen from Georgia who asked the First Lady's help in starting a black home for the aged.

That these young African Americans sent Eleanor Roosevelt such appeals was evidence of her popularity within the black community—which arose because no First Lady had ever been so supportive of black aspirations. Mrs. Roosevelt befriended civil rights leaders, spoke out against lynching, racism, and black disenfranchisement, promoted black appointments to New Deal agencies, championed federal aid to impoverished African Americans, and at one point even defied the segregation laws of Alabama.[4] It was with this role in mind that one black teen from Connecticut, whose letter appears in this chapter, confided to the First Lady in asking her for a job for her father, "I couldn't . . . ask just anybody to do this. I had to ask someone who is kind and good to *colored* people and does not *hate* them. . . . I know you have done a lot for my race and we appreciate it immensely."

Although there were far fewer letters related to gender discrimination than to race, these too were a testament to Eleanor Roosevelt's egalitarian tendencies. In 1933 she had convened a White House Conference on the Emergency Needs of Women to highlight the problem of female unemployment, at a time when most of the public's attention had been on male unemployment.[5] This and many other actions that the First Lady took on behalf of poor and working women led teens concerned about gender inequality to seek her out. Their letters are impressive because they came at a time when the feminist movement—having lost the battle for an Equal Rights Amendment—had almost disappeared from view. Somehow, without the help of an organized women's movement, these teens developed elements of a feminist ideology. Young as they were, they had nonetheless learned through their own life experience that gender discrimination existed and that it proved an unfair obstacle to them as girls and young women working to make their own way through a bleak economic landscape.

Gender inequality manifested itself in a variety of ways in Depression America. It was most blatant in annual pay levels. According to figures from the Social Security Administration, men in 1937 earned average wages of $1,027, almost twice the $525 earned by women. The female unemployment rate was slightly lower than the rate among males, but this was only because domestic-service, secretarial, and other jobs were considered "women's work," offering too little pay and status to be pursued by men. Several of the feminist-minded letters in this chapter express the frustration that bright and ambitious girls and young women felt about being relegated to this kind of work. Thus we read of a waitress and an out-of-work secretary—perhaps influenced by Amelia Earhart's example—longing to cast aside their low-skill vocations and take to the skies as aviators. At a time when many Americans were thankful for any type of job, these letters are a reminder that aspirations for more fulfilling and exciting kinds of work had not been extinguished by the economic crisis.[6]

The other form of gender inequity reflected in the letters concerned the New Deal itself. Despite Mrs. Roosevelt's best efforts, the New Deal's relief programs were marred by sexual discrimination. Most of the programs focused upon men, because of the assumption that family breadwinners were male, and created the kinds of jobs that men had historically held (especially in such areas as construction). Out of some four million jobs created by the Civil Works Administration, only about 300,000 went to women.[7] It is fitting, then, that the first letter in the feminist section of this chapter complains about the even more discriminatory Civilian Conservation Corps, which was one of the first federal programs to aid needy youths and was initially open only to males. While we have no way of knowing, it is unlikely that the authors of these letters would have called themselves feminist—since the term had virtually fallen out of popular discourse in the 1930s—but they are feminist in the sense that all express either implicitly or explicitly a belief that equal opportunity and equal rights ought not be constricted by gender discrimination.

Among the forms of discrimination that pervaded America none was uglier than that directed toward the disabled. Those who suffered from serious physical disabilities were rejected by public schools, denied admission to public transportation, and shunned not only by potential employers but even by their families. As Hugh Gregory Gallagher explains in his pioneering study of FDR's battle with polio, "to be handicapped in some visible way carried with it social opprobrium. The handicapped were kept at home, out of sight in back bedrooms, by families who felt a mixture of embarrassment and shame about their presence."[8]

As FDR learned how to deal with his own disability in the 1920s, he sought to help others by setting up a center for the treatment of polio victims at Warm Springs, Georgia. FDR designed Warm Springs to help polio patients deal both with their physical disabilities and with the depression and shame stemming from mistreatment by the public. Even many hospitals treated polio patients as if they were helpless invalids rather than people who through rehabilitation could become self-sufficient. FDR wanted Warm Springs to be as bright and cheerful as a resort. Gallagher argues convincingly that in his work at Warm Springs FDR was on the cutting edge of the effort to promote new ways of treating polio and more compassionate and humane ways to deal with the disabled—and that even if

Roosevelt had never become president he would still have been famed for his important disability work.[9] Yet Gallagher also shows that FDR did not directly challenge prejudice against the disabled. When healthy residents of a local hotel in Warm Springs complained that they found it distasteful to eat in the same dining room with polio patients, Roosevelt built a separate dining room rather than attack them for their prejudices. Similarly, in the political arena FDR sought to evade rather than challenge popular prejudice against the disabled by leaving the impression that he had been pretty much cured of his own disease. And as president, FDR, a paraplegic, did all that he could to keep from public view the extent of his physical disability, almost never allowing himself to be photographed in a wheelchair and keeping as hidden as possible his inability to walk without assistance. This was, as Gallagher puts it, "FDR's Splendid Deception."[10]

If even so powerful a politician as President Roosevelt dared not directly challenge prejudice against the disabled, it is not difficult to imagine how vulnerable ordinary disabled Americans were to such bigotry. For many of the disabled, in fact, directly challenging this prejudice was not even considered; they focused instead on overcoming their disabilities and obtaining the services that they had been denied—particularly education. By the standards of the twenty-first-century—an age in which there is an activist tradition among the disabled and federal legislation protecting their rights—FDR's unwillingness to tackle this form of prejudice head-on and his "splendid deception" might seem timid. But such a judgment would be anachronistic if applied to the 1930s, given the depth of popular prejudice then and the lack of an activist tradition or protective legislation. Indeed, FDR's disability work was in its time considered bold and courageous. His work at Warm Springs and his own example of returning to a successful political career after being stricken by polio were viewed by the disabled as an inspiration. As one teen from Chicago with polio explained in a letter to the First Lady published in this chapter, "I get so lonely and depressed some days—then I think of President Roosevelt and all the great things he has done and he has also suffered from this dreadful disease—I only hope some day I may get to Warm Springs." These words are a reminder that while Mrs. Roosevelt's work in behalf of the disabled (including her generosity in funding youth treatment at Warm Springs) inspired disabled youths to write to her, disability was one area where the key impetus for the letters was probably her connection to her husband, a pioneering and beloved figure among the disabled. In the areas of gender and race, by contrast, the First Lady was far more egalitarian than the president.

By far the largest minority represented in this chapter is first- and second-generation immigrants, who together represented roughly one out of four Americans during the Depression decade. Although the restrictive National Origins Act of 1924 kept the immigration rate low throughout the 1930s, popular fears of immigrants as possible competitors for jobs surged nonetheless along with nativism during the economic crisis. According to the White House Conference on Children in a Democracy, immigrants in Depression America were "often made the butt of attack . . . by the Klan, the Silver Shirts and shirts of every other hue, the Vindicators, and various so-called 'Christian Front' organizations. . . . Many anti-alien bills, under cover of ostensible attack on subversive activities, infringe on civil and political rights of foreign born citizens. . . . Such intimidation has a bearing on the extent to which minority groups can be effective in obtaining better services and conditions for their children."[11] This anti-immigrant impulse was so strong that it even led Congress to turn its back on the mostly Jewish children seeking to flee Nazi Germany. In 1939 the Wagner-Rogers bill, which would have allowed into the United States 20,000 refugee children and teens from Germany, was defeated—a defeat which public opinion polls indicate reflected the anti-immigration sentiments of an overwhelming majority of the American public.[12]

In the face of this kind of prejudice new immigrants tended to cluster into their own communities, building their own institutions—schools, churches, synagogues, and fraternal organizations—which buffered them from hostility. Perhaps this is why nativism and prejudice did not loom large as issues in the young immigrants' requests for material assistance to Mrs. Roosevelt. The letters focus instead on the economic and social aspirations and needs of the youths. This focus is even more understandable when one considers that income levels for immigrants were substantially lower than that of native whites. According to the U.S. Bureau of Labor Statistics, for example, 27.4 percent of native white families in Chicago had annual incomes below $1,000 in 1935, compared to 34 percent of the city's foreign-born.[13]

Revealing as these letters are about the economic crisis, they also touch on issues that transcend the Depression, raising perennial themes in the history of immigration, including the idealization of America as a land of opportunity and the difficulties that immigrants had as they adapted to a new culture. This adaptation process placed the young in a particularly awkward position: because of their schooling in America, children often adapted faster and more thoroughly to American culture than their parents did, sometimes undermining the deference of the young to their elders. This faster pace of adaptation is visible in the letter in this chapter from a young Polish immigrant living in Minnesota, written to the First Lady on behalf of her mother, who was illiterate in English. The problem of being caught between two cultures in Depression America is captured in excruciating detail in a letter from the immigrant daughter of sugar-beet farmers in Colorado. She wrote to Mrs. Roosevelt that she felt like an outsider among her American schoolmates but also an outsider in her own home, as she had transcended the culture of her immigrant parents and community. It is again a tribute to Mrs. Roosevelt, who as the 1930s progressed became increasingly active in the struggle for a more open and humane American immigration policy, that immigrant teens would confide in her so, sharing such deeply personal concerns.

As a result of her extensive international travels and her post–New Deal role in the United Nations, Eleanor Roosevelt would become one of the best-known Americans abroad. Several of the letters in the immigration section of this chapter attest that even in the early New Deal years, she was an international figure of great appeal. Here we encounter letters from overseas in which poor people aspiring to come to the United States were familiar with and fond of her work in behalf of those stuck in poverty; they were every bit as confident as their American counterparts that Mrs. Roosevelt would care about them and their problems. Even when the New Deal was new, Eleanor Roosevelt was already earning the global reputation that would later lead her to be dubbed the First Lady of the World.

The letters from abroad hold additional lessons about America and immigration. They remind us that as bleak as life might have seemed in Depression America, it was often grimmer still in poorer countries which had fewer resources to fall back upon when the capitalist crisis of the 1930s hit. Thus we read that even at the bottom of the Depression poor people in other countries still longed to emigrate to America. The letter in this chapter from Hungary, however, complicates this golden door vision of America, reminding us that some immigrants, such as the coal miner described in the letter, returned to their native lands after failing economically in the United States. We learn that the coal miner's daughter, born in West Virginia but living impoverished in Hungary, hoped desperately to return to America—evoking the international reach of the Depression and the endurance of the American dream, which in this case had faded for the father yet was resurrected by his daughter.

▪ Chicago. Ill.

April 12, 1934

Mrs. F.D. Roosevelt

Dear Madam I am writing Asking you for help. I am a colored girl. I am 17 years and 10 mo. old. I go the Wendell Phillis High School Branch. I am in my first year. I am behind but I would like to finish if it is possible.

I have a brother and two small cousins their mothers are dead. We all live with our grandmother but she is 66 years old.

We are on reflief. My brother is married he has been married two years I have two cousins their mothers are dead. We are all living with our grandmother two. The girl is 12 yrs and 11 mo and the boy is 11 years 11 months they both are in 6/8. I am very fat. I weigh 225 lbs. I wont to ask you to send me a winter coat no. 24 a pair of stocking out of size a dress no. 52 a pair of shoes 9EEE. I have one pair of shoes for every day and Sunday two. The small kids can do without. But I come in contack with so many school girls and boys of my own age. They all look so nice and I want to look nice too of course I dont wont luxury I would not ask you for that of course. I need underclothes too. . . . If I made many mistake please excuse me. I am so nervous I hope you will get this letter I will be so anxious to hear from you so please ans this letter. I am think you in return I will be patiently waiting.

Yours Truly,

G W

Please ans soon.

▪ Wachapreague, Va.

June 20, 1934

Dear Mrs. Roosevelt,

Please don't consider this a foolish idea but, I knew no other to call on for help than the one who has been a mother to the country, regardless of color or creed.

Mrs. Roosevelt, I am eager for an education. I have worked out since I was 11 yrs old. I missed four school terms out of school, and graduated from high school at the age of 19 yrs.

I want to enter college in September. I have'nt a dime, and I cannot find work. What shall I do? To whom shall I turn to for help if you fail me? Mrs. Roosevelt I feel that you can help me and I feel that you will.

I am willing to work for you night and day to pay you for all that you do for me. Help me if you can.

The school that I have made application for is West Virginia State Teachers College, Institute, W. Virginia.

I want to make a woman of my self. I want to be some body. Help me in any way that you can. I'll do any kind of honest work and I have had lots of experience.

I have a good reccomendation. Please, Mrs. Roosevelt, may I count on you to help me? I am sick at heart.

I graduated in "33" and I have been out of school all this winter.

I hope to hear from you at once please.

Sincerely yours

B. A. G.

Brunswick, Ga.,

Aug. 4, 1934

Dear Mrs Roosevelt,

Having the very highest respect for you as "First Lady" of the Land" and feeling that you have much interest in and deepest sympathy for suffering humanity, I am appealing to you on the behalf of the aged people of my race and community who are in need of care and attention.

I am a colored girl nineteen (19) years of age and a high school graduate. My main source of pleasure lies in caring for helpless people and especially the aged.

There are unfortunately in my community many people who are old and unable to care for themselves properly, and it is for these people I am seeking aid.

I am quite sure those in charge of this work are doing their duties yet the physical conditions of these people will not allow them to care for themselves properly.

My one hope is to have an institution established for the purpose of caring for the aged, one in which they might be able to enjoy real comfort, well-prepared meals which are so essential to health, happiness and peace, as well as are comfortable surroundings.

I feel as though they deserve consideration along this line in as much as their lives have been for the most part, lives of hard work and sacrifice; and perhaps most of them have never actually known real pleasure, and being deeply indebted to them for their many sacrifices, I feel it my duty to appeal for aid on their behalf.

I am totally unable financially to carry out the plans I have in mind, as are other interested members of my race, however I shall be very happy to contribute my time and self in whatever way I might be of assistance.

I am not asking you for a personal donation, but am humbly begging that you consider my plans and aid me in securing funds for carrying them out.

Believing in you as I do, I am sure you won't refuse me your aid, and though I shall never be able to repay you and they can never hope to do so, I know that you will find supreme joy in the knowledge that you have aided a deserving and needy group, moreover Our Heavenly Father will reward you for this kindness even as he has blessed you with the honor of being the nation's First Lady.

Please help me, I beg of you in my effort to aid these unfortunates. And may I, please expect a reply?

Sincerely Yours,

H. E. G.

Huntsville, Ala.

Feb 27, 1936

Dear Madam,

After listening to you over the radio and reading of your interesting topics in different magazines I ve become greatly interested in you.

I know you must be very busy these days. I am one who like to be busy too. I am seeking some advise from you. I am interested in a library for my people (Negroes) in the city we have none I am asking what steps should I take toward establishing one I am willing to work hard. I am greatly interested in social service work would like to do something to help conditions of our underprivledged group.

I've worked hard have my brother in school he finishes in June I am unable to obtain funds to help him finish at present I am $120.86 in arrears with his bill please help me I'll return it when I begin teaching a rural school in the fall I know you dont know me but I can furnish references my statements are true. I am sure if you knew my heart my desires my intentions you would be willing to help me Now help me and see how much I'll appreciate it and how quickly I'll repay.

Please may I ask may this letter be strictly confidential between you and me. Should you desire references I can furnish some gladly.

I am sure you dont know me at all, but it seems that I know you. I've never had privelege to write one so honored please excuse me for gathering the courage

Please may I expect a reply I shall not mention one thing you do for me Therefore you will not be flooded with letters of this nature.

I pray that you open your heart and help me I can furnish you will all information that you may require if you desire.

I hope for a reply

Thanks Very Truly

My brother is at Knoxville College, Knoxville Tenn.

McGehee, Arkansas

January 22, 1937

Dear Madame

I just read in our local paper that you are to be in Little Rock which is only one hundred miles from here. If you go by way of New Orleans by way of the Missouri Pacific Lines, you will pass through here. How I wish I could glimpse the First Lady of the Land.

For a long time I have been reading your articles in the paper, and I find them to be be very interesting and inspiring.

I am a Negro, 22 years old; and I have not quite finished my work on my A.B. degree. This is my third year to teach here in my home town for forty dollars a month. I haven't been able to save anything because I have been trying to free our home of debt. A loan of Five hundred dollars would put me over the top. Could or would you feel justified in lending me the money on just a promise to pay within three years? From the time of receiving the loan while I'm in school I could make a small monthly payment of two dollars, and after I begin work naturally the payments will increase. I have no securities to offer except true woman-hood, and honesty.

If I could receive the loan from you I would like to receive a leave of absence from my work. By doing so I would leave here about the last of February in order to complete my work in the summer session. I attended Dillard University last summer, and I would like very much to go back there.

My real interest in life is to help others; that's why I'm so anxious to reach a definite goal. The conditions of young Negroes in my hometown are deplorable. We have no recreational center, and we don't even have any playground facilities at school. Something should be done about these conditions, and I'm going to do what I can as soon as I return, if I am fortunate enough to go.

I am a believer in Christ; and I am a member of Scott's Chapel Methodist Episcopal Church. At present I am superintendent of our Church School Department.

Please give me some kind of relief at the earliest moment possible in your column, and if you do think this cause is worthy enough for you to respond to at once, I'll prove myself worthy of your trust and assistance.

A part of this money will be used to clear up old debts, and the other for school expenses, food, and clothing.

And if by chance I'm in New Orleans when you arrive, I hope you will find time to slip off from the group and come out to Dillard University where I'll probably have the honor of meeting you.

Thanking you in advance I am

Yours sincerely,

F. M. S.

■ Old Saybrook, Conn.

July 27, 1938

Dear Mrs. Roosevelt:

I am a poor colored girl who thinks quite a lot of you and your family, and I know you have done a lot for my race and we appreciate it immensely.

Now I am going to ask you two personal favors which I hope you can do. The first is *will you find my daddy* a job as caretaker and gardner on an estate or as a janitor of a club or theatre. He can't find one and we can't afford to put an advertisement in the papers. He has sixteen years experience.

The second thing I want to ask you to do for me is a *big* favor but I do hope and pray you will do it. My situation is as follows: I am a girl who lives in this small town called Old Saybrook. I was born here and have lived here all of my life. In June of 1935, I was graduated from the Old Saybrook High School and in June of 1936, I was post graduated from the same high school. Now I desire to continue my education by studing "theology" at the "Moody Theological College" in Chicago. Upon graduation from Moody College I would like to become a foreign missionary or professional quoir singer or teacher.

I am ambitious and determined to succeed, and because I am determined to succeed and ambitious, I am writing to ask you if you *will* and *could* please finance my expenses for me. You don't know what it would mean to me if you would do it for me. You see I couldn't bring my self to ask just anybody to do this. I had to ask someone who has money and some one who is good and kind to *colored* people and does not *hate* them. You know as well as I do that a lot of the white people hate the colored people, so I couldn't ask just anybody like a white girl could. Therefore I was doomed until I thought of you. I hope you won't think I am bold in asking you to do this for me.

I would try to complete my course in about 2½ years. There is no charge for tuition. But I must pay for my room and board which would be about seven (7) dollars a week. Then I must pay for incidentals etc. I figure that if you would allow me ten (10) dollars a week I could make my ends meet. We go to school from setember to the first week in August. Negros are not allowed to stay at the dormitories so I would have to room and boad outside. The superintendent said that she would find me a suitable place to stay. Then I would need about eight dollars ($8) extra to have four of my teeth fixed before I can get my doctors certificate in and checked by Moody College.

I would like to go this fall in September so I wish you would let me hear from you right away. I have been out of school 2 years already and I would not like to keep waiting. I tried to get a job but none of the people wanted me because I have no experience in house work. Now it is too late for me to get a job because August is here and it will soon be September. I don't feel smart enough to work my way through and keep up my studies at the same time. Therefore, now that it's so late I am asking you for help. I want you to understand that I would be willing to pay you back after I had been graduated and received a position. I would like to pay you so much at a time until I had it all paid up.

I beg and implore you please do not give my name to the newspapermen and please do not give them this letter to print. I woud be very hurt and embarrassed; this is a personal matter between you and me. I do not want my name in the papers because I live in a small town and everyone knows me and they would make fun of me, I know. So, once again I beg you do not let the newspapermen hear of this. *Thank you very much.*

Hoping you will get my daddy a job so that he can pay his bills and hoping that you will lend me the money for my schooling so that I may go in September, I am

Yours affectionately,

P.S. I have tried to get a loaning concern to lend me the money, but they don't want to wait, until I have been graduated, for their money. I have been trying to get work or some means to get to Moody ever since I was graduated and because *my future looked black* I have come to you in desperation. I hope you will lend a hand to a *poor colored* girl who would appreciate it and I will endeavor to make myself worthy of your extented hand and kindness.

You understand that I would like to pay it back and would like about ten (10) dollars a week and eight dollars *extra* in advance. I want to go in September. Once more I will beg you not to give my name and this letter to the newspapermen or any officials. Thanking you for what you will do for me, I remain

Yours respectfully,

■ Birmingham, Alabama
January 31, 1940
Dear Mrs. Roosevelt,
I am a negro boy who sang for you when you visited our school a few years ago in Birmingham.

I have attended College one year, and one month. Due to the lack of money, I had to quit school and try to find work so that I could continue my education. I have looked everywhere, but Cannot find anything to do. I am very eager to finish my schooling, but I cannot find work at all. Some days I walks over twenty miles trying to find work, but all in vain. All of my efforts have been a complete failure. So Mrs. Roosevelt I appeal to you for help.

The course that I was taking requires two years of college training then one is eligible to teach for a limited time of six years. I need only six more months of training then I will be able to help myself. Please Mrs. Roosevelt, send me a donation so as to help me in this dilemma. I do not have relatives that is in a position to give me any financial support, so you see Mrs. Roosevelt, my future is very dark and discouraging. You are the only one that I know to come to for relief, please look at my condition, and consider this matter noteworthy because I am striving to be somebody, and I am trying in my young days.

Please let me hear from you. I can get the other six months of College training for $160. It wouldn't be that much but when I left, I wasn't able to pay my back loand and before I re enter I must pay it before I can get my credits.

Please don't think hard of me Mrs. Roosevelt, but I didn't have any one else to call on but you.

Yours Truly,
A. L.

■ Buffalo, New York

November 11, 1940

Dear Mrs. Roosevelt:

I am a Negro girl 19 years of age who saw your article in the paper relative to what you do with the money you make from writing.

I have been looking for someone to help me out in my problem of higher education. I see, from reading your article, that you have helped some boys and girls go to school through your scholarship fund. I wonder would you consider me as eligible for the next scholarship you give.

My family consists of three children myself included, and also my mother. My mother is a widow and it takes all she can make to feed and cloth us. I have a NYA Job, but do to the fact that my mother is not able to help me I can not go to school. On this NYA job I get $18.48 a mo, the place is located at 243 Washington, Buffalo N.Y. My work is to take dictation from the head Supervisor and the counselors. I have received many compliments on my work. Some of the girls have received government positions on this job but they have not been able to place any of the Negro girls because they can't find anyone who wants a colored secretary. I feel fully capable of handling any secretarial position. I have had 2½ yrs, of experience in this line of work under the NYA. First two years was while I was in high school the next was at the Personnel Office of the NYA.

Mrs. Roosevelt I have been very despondent over the fact that I have been trying any and every means to go to college, but to no avail. I have competed in oratorical contests in which they offered as first prize a scholarship. The first time I tried I received first place in the state of New York, second time 2nd in New York, 3rd time 2nd place again at which time I graduated from high school which automatically eliminated me because after you graduate you can no longer compete. I wrote stories, poems, songs, & titles, but only received small prizes, but however I saved this.

What I would like to do Mrs Roosevelt is go to some school to take business administration to study higher in my secretarial work. I would like to go to Howard Uni., or the University of Buffalo because these schools offer the complete course. If you help me go to college Mrs. Roosevelt, I will work and pay you back.

When I saw your article I thought maybe you would aid me, that is if you consider me worthy, which I hope you will. If you can not help me in my school problem please help me get a job, I am willing to leave the city. I am also willing to work while I go to school. I take 96 words in shorthand, type 50 words a min.

I hope that you will see fit to aid me, I await your speedy answer.
Sincerely
Miss M. C.

■ Louisville, Miss.
Oct. 7, 1941
My Dear Mrs. Roosevelt,

I hardly know how to begin this letter, but I have made up in my mind to write you and believe me I am talking from the bottom of my heart.

This may be a strange request but I do feel that you will help me if it is possible, Our school has a band and I was in it until a short while ago I played alto saxophone and my father partly lost his job and I have had to give it up and it has almost broken my heart to do so but I havent lost hope yet.

I saw in the paper where you were behind the movement to help the negro fireman hold their jobs Well, my father was one of those unfortunate men whose job was taken and he has not been able to do by his family as he has done in the past. His name is E. T. he is the one that put the suit in against the brotherhood and we are hoping and praying that something will happen soon. My mother has also been forced to go to work which hurts me very much I am a junior in high school and I hope to continue my studies but without money some other means will have to be provided.

So if you could find a second hand alto E-flat saxophone some where cheap will you please do this for me and I shall make it my aim to make good.

To prove to you I am not pretending my first horn was purchased from the George E. Diver Music Co. in Chicago my fathers name may still be on file, but due to this condition it was taken.

So please try to do some thing for me if you can't please answer this letter and let me know you got because I will be worried until I hear from you.

I guess by now you know I am a Negro. I am also a girl.

My father's name is E. T. and he is a member of the N.A.A.C.P. They are also behind his case.

I am yours truly,
H. T.

Eleanor Roosevelt with a student at the Haskell Institute Indian School, Lawrence, Kan., 1938. (Photo courtesy of United Press International)

NATIVE AMERICANS

· ·

■ St. John's U.
Collegeville, Minnesota
March 8, 1934
Dear Mrs. Roosevelt:

I have just finished reading "Man of Action" . . . and I find that it is honestly the best book that I have ever read. It has made my liking for both you and the president more strong.

As many others have, I too have troubles to tell you. I am attending this high school, and I am a Junior. This school is a private boarding school, and also one of the Benedictine Abbeys.

I am an Indian by birth. American Indian, Chippewa tribe. As everyone knows I am an Indian, they do not associate with me very much. This, of course, makes me most lonesome, and last week I wrote to my mother telling her that I wished to come home. She told me to stay, of course, and I am, although it is hard for me. My grandfather is putting me through school, and while he is not rich, we have enough to be comfortable. I always have money, and many of the other students do not. When they see I have money, they are friendly, and I treat them and I have a good time. I know I am a fool to do this, but it does give me a little fun.

I am sixteen years old, (my birthday was March 7, so it is a treat to be 16) and I think I am quite smart. I take English III, Religion III, Latin, Modern History, typing, piano, and pipe-organ. I just started pipe organ last month.

I expect of be a dentist or a Catholic priest when I grow up. I most likely will be a dentist!

I am writing this in order to ask you what I should do, when the other boys shun me. They make fun of me, and imitate Indians and other such things, that hurt me very much.

I would like to hear from you ever so much. It would make me ever so happy to know that you're interested in me. Would you have the president sign your letter too, so that my pleasure will be still more great? I'm sure you will.

As I look up from this letter, I see a picture of your husband and a crucifix hanging close together, and I'm positive that our Dear God is pleased with his actions.

I remain trustworthy and happy

L. E. C.

Since L. E. C.'s letter is one of the few in this book which elicited personal advice from Mrs. Roosevelt or her staff, the response to this letter is included below.

■ March 15, 1934

My dear Mr. C.,

Mrs. Roosevelt has received your letter and asked me to say that she feels you are probably supersensitive, and that your companions knowing that probably tease you more than they would ordinarily. I am sure there is no reason for your feeling in any way different from any of the other boys because of the fact that you are an Indian. They have always been greatly admired and certainly you can claim to be a true American. If you will accept the teasing of the other boys in the spirit in which it is done, I am sure they will soon learn to admire your good sportsmanship.

Very sincerely yours,

Secretary to Mrs. Roosevelt

IMMIGRANTS

. . . .

■ Utuado, Puerto Rico

Jan. 5, [1934]

My dear Mrs. Roosevelt,

I think you will pardon my boldness. My desires were to write you, so as to be in contact with our new well prepared president and wife.

We the portoricans are very happy to have such a president at the head of the White House. We think, to see President Rooselvelt very proud of you, that is giving such a help, with the benefits to all kind of people.

As we are with him, because of the progress he has made with his recovery plans; giving shelter and food to the poor people, saving farms and homes and giving work to millions of people.

My dear you had gained a good place in my heart. From the first moment I saw your picture I loved you, because I noticed the kindness that the whole world cant see in your face. For that reason I take such confidence.

I am a student of 19 years old. My parents are very poor and they cant not give me the education I want. Here in ours schools, the poor children are nothing; the riches earns the high marks, the teacher's affections, the ones that later could have a title.

I have eight sisters and brothers; I am always thinking of my future, because if my parents died, I will take their place, and want to have a title sow I could educated them.

Will you lend me a passage to go to the United States? My purposes are, to go to New York to work and with earn money study in the Franklin Institute, & then I will pay you the passage.

My dear Mrs. Roosevelt, I will never paid this favor to you. Will you help me? Oh! I will kiss your feet if you do so. If you do so, write some words to my dear mother advising her to let me go. This should be for the *last days* of *January.* So as to beging immediately my new life because I have a very poor one here. Think if you do it with me, God will do many great things with you—your husband.

John J. Heenan, the president of the Institute wrote me this wolds. "Commence today. . . . Delay often means Failure. The successfull man or woman decides on the spot; the other says 'Oh! Wait Until Tomorrow,' and then forgets until it is too late. Shake off that tomorrow habit, say 'I will; nothing will Prevent My Getting Steady Work in a U.S. Gov. Life Position.' . . . That spirit will always win for you."

I remember: Of all sad words of tongue or pen,

The saddest are these "It might have been."

I wish to all your family happiness and many good things in the new year. Waiting for your affirmative answer,

The one that love you very much

(Miss) C. L. C.

■ Szommasszeg, [Hungary]

July 3, 1934

Dear Mrs. Rossevelt.

I will have to apologize in the beginning of my letter to you. I am a american citizen by birth. I was born in the year (1916) March the twenty seventh, state of West Virginia Grant Town. My mother died in the year 1931 May the eleventh, leaving eight orphan children to face the world alone with their broken-hearted father, after suffering two years in America with eight orphan children neither of us able to earn our own living except My self, but I could not go out to earn my living because I had younger brothers & sisters to take care of, While my broken hearted father was working in the coal mines to try to earn a decent livening for his children and him self, the work got bad in the coal mines & my dear old father was not able by no means work day after day in the mines, so while working we saved enough money so we could come home to his country, Hungry, before we would become a burden to the United States, We thought that here we would be able to work out in the open fields, plow pol & other farm work which they do over in Hungry, He is not able to support us, he is so worried & down hearted that I am afraid he is going to end his life so that he will not see us suffer from cold & hungry,

He came over to protect his children from beging alone without a mother so he brought us to grandmother but she died in 8 months of time.

Mrs. Roosvelt I have read & heard of your kindness Our in Hungry, What feeling you have towards the poor & the needy, so I am going to ask A great favor from you, Please for a orphan sake take me out to my own country America.

My heart is turning home again there's where I long to be. I am wanting to go out & work in the world & help take care of my younger brothers & sisters.

No one will every no what we whent through with out A mother it hurts me to see them eat rye bread day after day.

They cry for America but what good does it do when I can not help them, for God's sake I ask you take me out of this Country I do not want to see my brothers and sisters died before the coming winter,

I will pay you back Only take me out of this Country I am willing to be a Maid or anthing Only help me.

What does a $150. dollors mean to you not anything. It means a fortune to me when I could help my brothers & sisters, please get me a steam ship ticket so that I may go out and work and help my dear old father & sisters & brothers.

I want to try and raise them as fine American citizens, only if you will help me,

Please do not thing hard of me for asking so much from my Country.

Please forgive for beying so brave as writing this letter to you is the only way I saw in to my terrible troubles.

Please answer my letter if you will be so kind. I do not now how I will be able to repay you if you will only help me out.

I remain as A True American Citizen

M. S.

■ Elgin Ill.

[acknowledged July 9, 1934]

Please read all my letter, and answer it I am waiting for an answer.

Dear Mrs. Roosevelt:

I am writing you this letter because I have to, or else I wouldn't trouble you about it, cause I know that you have enough on your mind without my bothering you. So if you will please excuse me, I am a poor girl I do not know how to explain it to you so well. The saying is, "Never give up hope." But it depends on what it is. As to start with I am a girl nineteen and a half years old. I am Italian my parnts come from Italy. I was born in the little city of Elgin Ill. We are six in the family, With mother and daddy. We have to pay $800.00 or $900.00 dollars to the Home and Loan Bank. And we have other big bills also. But I do so want to help the family so much.

What I wish to tell you is, that I want to have a nice & neat resterent not in town just on the state road. I do not want my parents or anyone in the family or my good friends to know. I want to srprise them all when everything is going on swell. I know that mother is suppose to know every thing that goes on in the family. But she has eonoph to think about.

Mrs Roosevelt I will repay you ever thing when I am on the smooth road. The only thing that I wish to sell is spaghetti and stuff pepers on toast. and of course if I may some beer. I do not want a ruff place, I want a nice & clean place. I will have a cop in the place without anyone knowing it. Oh please help me out that is my only dream. Please do not speak of this fore it is between you & I.

Yours,

■ Marinette, Arizona
[acknowledged Aug. 16, 1934]
My Dearest Mrs. Franklin Roosevelt,

I am just writing you this few lines to ask you a favor. Will you please help me to go through Hi school? You know I just love to study. I do not ask for any money, but please oh please send me a typewriter. I sure need one. All my wish is to be a stenographer and someday I may get a job & I will pay you. I hope you will not mind because I am a Mexican girl but being that I love to study. My parents are very poor our family is big mostly small kids and they cant afford to send me to Hi-school. of course I need a latin book and an algebra, but I can borrow them (although I wish to own them) but I can't borrow a typewriter they wont loan them and wouldnt I love to have one! So please Mrs. Roosevelt send me a typewriter probably sometimes you felt like me when you wanted something very badly and couldnt have it. And I think you just love to type too and study also. Its no fun to be poor when you want things very badly. I am 16 years of age and my favorite hobbies are Reading, typing and blue printing sewing and cooking. Please send it and other hobby is music. I just love it. I wish I could be in the orchestra and play the violin but I havent one and dont I wish I had one. Please send me a typewriter and god will reward you for your kindness. Maybe you like to help the poor. If you send me a typewriter please do send me the color of your bedroom and size of your bed and I will send you a gift made by me I am clever with my hands. I can do most every thing. Please dont show or publish this letter or people will say I am a beggar but I am not I need help and you are the one and only one who could help me. Please Mrs. R. send it to me I am very anxious send it as soon as you can. Please also send me your picture not taken out of papers but a real big one & I will send you a gift. please oh please send me a typewriter soon. I would like a violin but dont take the trouble as you will spend too much money. Here's hoping to get it and may god bless you. Your friend who admires you and don't know you.

Best wishes to dear Mrs. R.
Mrs. Roosevelt:

Please excuse me for not finishing in ink but I ran out of it. I tried to make my letter neat but its impossible. Please dont show it to anybody but you and if you want to show it to Mr. President otherwise I would be ashame if you show it to the rest. How I wish and I wish you had the money when you read this letter so that you could send me the typewriter. There are only three things in this world that if I own them I would feel rich. They are a typewriter a violin and a wrist watch. They are things any girl would like to own. I also would like to have heaps of magazines and books. I have two books. I read them many times. I am just about to memorize them they are Elsie Dinsmore and "A Dear Little Girl at School." I have only one magazine "Child Life"

Please send my required article my dear Mrs. R. Remember someday I will reward you also I will send you a gift.

Sincerely

■ [Eaton, Colo.]

October 19, 1934

My dear Mrs. Roosevelt;

I feel that you have an understanding heart, else, I should not be writing this. Just as The President seemed a sort of god to the American people, you must be someone with a super-understanding. I know you must receive many letters, mostly of problems. My own may seem trivial among the many, but; since I cannot pour out my heart to anyone face to face, this at least can be done to an understanding heart—on paper. I am the kind of person who cannot tell other people things that effect me most, I cannot speak of them, but sometimes I am able to pour out my repressions on paper.

I am nineteen years old, and a Senior in college. I am working my way through with the help of God and the N.R.A. In a few days, on November first, I will be twenty years old—and life should seem to be before me. So often I feel a bitterness that I myself cannot understand. I wonder sometimes why I go on living, I wonder what is the use of it all, why do I work so hard to get ahead of what I was born into? Perhaps some one knows the answer. I am sure I do not.

My father and mother are German-Russian immigrants who have spent their lives in toil. Even now they are sitting about the table of our shabby kitchen, in our three room house, having come in from the sugar-beet fields at dusk. I know that somehow, I can never become a woman such as my mother is—a woman who toils all day beside her husband and children;

who bakes, washes, cleans, on Sunday; who is the first one up in the morning, cooks three meals a day, and is the last to bed at night; a woman who has borne seven children and reared them to the healthy group they are; who has been blamed for everything, been talked almost to death by a grumbling husband, and yet is ever loyal to him. (My father is really a good man, but he grumbles too much, and I have inherited his extreme stubbornness; and my views being different, we clash often.) I can see the wind-roughened skin, the shabby clothes, and broken nails of my mother, — but again, I feel that—well, she's just beyond me. I can never hope to be as noble as she is. My father, to whom I know I am a unmannerly, insubordinate child, is good to me; they both sacrifice for me, but I feel that they can never understand me as I wish they could. I have found that telling them my problems, especially father, only makes it worse for me—they cannot understand my view point. But why should they be able to? Their background is so different from that of their American born children. During my years of high school, and so far, I have grown farther and farther away from my parents, even my two older brothers, who are married, cannot see my side of the question. In the last few months, I have become more tolerant of all of them; I try hard to see the other side.

My parents are very poor. It is a veritable war to keep body and soul together; can you wonder, that like Topsy, I just growed? Can you wonder that people consider me dreadfully spoiled—and queer? I am decidedly not one of the mob. I have never been one of a crowd of young people, though there is no reason, in a physical way, that I should not be. I am rather attractive, though small (5 ft 1) and weigh only about one hundred pounds. I have worked very hard all of my life, but have kept the small shapely hands and feet that are a heritage from my father's family. Somehow, I suppose it is my attitude; I have been outside the circle of sociality always I am merely an "odd number." I would rather stay at home and read poetry, travel, or biography, or make a scrapbook, than go to a party. I have always felt that I could not bear the vulgar ways, coarse language, and loud clothes of the children of our Russian-German type. How can I join them? They cannot understand what I talk about, and I? Their petty gossip and vulgar speech, disgusts me. I am a "high-hat," they think.

And do I belong to the group, I go to school with? No, not after they know how my parents earn a living! Of course more and more poorer children are working their way through college, but I, how could I be on a social level with them? I'm just a "Dutchman"; I live on the wrong side of the tracks. However, I am really treated rather well by everyone. Perhaps it is only my super-sensitiveness. I mingle with the group, I am one of the company, but do I feel entirely one of them?—Never. I am wondering what some of my class would think, if they knew that the gray suit I had on today was one that was made of a suit my brother once had. They could not begin to imagine that this man's suit had been turned inside out, the trousers had become a skirt, and the coat a modish jacket—add a (20 cent) scarf, and a broadcloth blouse, and the buttons my mother has had for years—thus I go clad to school—not much different than anyone else.—But even make-overs do not last forever, though I am never "hard" on clothes. I have used everything available and some things impossible to make wearable clothes. I have become an expert seamstress, especially in the art of "make-over." This winter my only sister and I will probably have no winter coats. (Here I stop and think of people who will probably have no food—when I get to that point, I can only pray to a God that I know exists—He must know the answer.) We shall be happy, as in the past, with beans, and potatoes. We are really much better off than many, (even though we have no winter coats), living in the shadow of the beautiful Colorado Rockies, having enough to eat, and being together, keeping the higher ideals of life! I feel that often it is shameful of me to be crying for things I do not have—because I have so much. And, when things are at their worst, I can look, of an evening at twilight, from our front porch, across the plains to the magnificent hills—hills; I would die without their presence.

After such an outpouring, most of which has not been put into this letter, I feel that I can face the world again. That I can face the world, and some-day, I shall earn the salary of a school-teacher; my parents shall live better than they do now. It will all work out for the best.—And since you have been kind enough to peruse my epistle so far, I shall have "intestinal fortitude" enough to ask for the granting of a strange request. To face the world one needs not merely the spirit, but something more. I shall ask you bluntly—Do you not know of a people who have closets overflowing with clothes they can no longer use; who would understand the gratitude I could not express to them, if they were, in their kindness, willing to send me such articles?—Perhaps, you will understand that, to me, it is a thing almost impossible to ask—even though I cannot see you face to face; but I must—many things can be done if one must. You can understand, why it is quiet impossible for me to ask this of people I know, (who themselves have not over much)—they cannot offer me things, because they feel that my fierce pride will deem such an act insulting. Most of them do not, and will never know that I really need help. I wish that even you shall not ask things for me, but of kind souls who, at least, can try to understand. Even should I have no answer to this letter, it has helped me much. — But should I have an answer, my twentieth birthday would be the happiest I have yet had. I cannot thank you enough.

Most sincerely,

M. F.

■ May 7, 1935
Minneapolis, Minn.

Dear Mrs. Roosevelt:

I am sending this letter asking you to please help me pay for my communion cloths. My father works at Pillsbury mill. He works three days a week and has to work plenty hard to get 8.36 cents a week. I am a girl at the age of twelve and can do nothing to help my father. We have five children and have a high mortgage please help me by sending me some money.

Thank you very much

A. B.

P.S. I am making my communion May 19, 1935. My mother came from Poland and does not know how to write English so I'm writting in her place.

■ Portage, Pa.
June 17, 1935

Dear Mrs. Roosevelt,

I have read a lot about you giving money to the poor. So, I decided to write you a letter and ask you to help my mother. She wants to go to Czechoslovakia to see her mother. She always say's, "I wish I could see my mother before she die's." and then begins to cry often I cry with her. My father is a coal miner and dose not make much. We have a mortage on our home for thirteen years. I can not help my mother or father because I am only going to be twelve years old on July the second. So please Mrs. Roosevelt try to help my mother.

Yours truly,

S. W. Jr.

. . . .

■ Tulsa, Okla.

Aug. 16, 1934

My dear Mrs. Roosevelt:

If this letter ever reaches your hand please, please read it.

I am a negro girl, 17 years old, just finished the Washington High School and am trying to go to college. Mrs. Roosevelt I have of how you are helping the white women and girls; and the president has opended C.C.C. Camps for both colored and white but we negro girls don't get a break.

I have a mother dependent upon me and I am working for S. E. A's of this address at $6.00 per week. I am trying to save out of this to go to college in mid-term. My letter prehaps has no significance to you; but I am asking you for assistance. Would you please Mrs. Roosevelt give me $25.00 before January 1st. By Dec. 25th I will have saved $50.00 with $25.00 more I would be able to pay room, board, tuition and books. Would have about $15.00 left over on the next term.

If you get this letter and would like to find out something about me, you may write to the school from which I finished or the people for whom I worked. Hoping to hear from you.

Respectfully yours

B. L.

■ Lawrence, Mass.

August 21, 1934

Dear Mrs. Roosevelt:

I realize that you are an extremely busy woman but I wonder if you could possibly find time to help a girl of nineteen who is anxious to fulfill her ambition.

My main thought in life is to become a stellar aviatrix. Nothing else interests me. My folks cannot assist me, and I really don't expect it for I am one of nine children. I could venture out into the world if I were a boy. Being a girl has too many handicaps in that respect.

I graduated from the high school with high honors, edited the school newspaper and helped run affairs in general. For some reason I expected life would be just as rosy. But no. I passed the clerical and stenographic examinations for the state. A position in that line does not seem forthcoming. I seem to be making no advance in any direction. At present I am doing waitress work in a tea room. Don't you think that's a far cry from aviation?

I am tall, healthy, athletic, average-looking and with enough intelligence to want very much to get ahead and make something of myself. Could you help or advise me?

Oftimes I attempted to see you personally when you were in the vicinity of Boston because I could convey more fully what I am trying to write to you.

Sincerely,

J. R. G.

The following letter, from the files of the Children's Bureau of the U.S. Department of Labor, is the only one in this book that was addressed to Franklin Roosevelt rather than to the First Lady or the Roosevelts together. It appears here because it illuminates the thinking of feminist teens in Depression America.

■ Homer, New York

[acknowledged Feb. 11, 1935]

Mr. Roosevelt,

In Homer a lot of us girls think that seeing there is a ccc camp for boys that there should be one for girls. In a book we read about a military camp for girls, it told how in the morning the girls have to attend school for so long and in the afternoon too. They had to learn how to sew and nurse the sick. they had to make clothes for the poor. "Mr. Roosevelt" if there was a place or camp like that for girls a lot of young girls wouldn't have to be sent down the "Hudson River." A camp like that would give young girls a place to go. We are not very old ourselves from 13 on up but we get in a lot of trouble just the same. And we think you might try to do something about it so that girls in our age could do something like we mentioned and not have to wait until they are 17–18 or 19 years of age. We no how to sew and cook we use to belong to "4-H and "Girl Scouts" and in school we take home making. But we don't like Homer Academy school there are a lot of cranky old teachers, and the children think themselves so high above us girls. If you should care to give us your answer you can broadcast it over the Radio at noon between 5:00–5:30 at station B.E.N. Buffalo if you don't ans. before the 28th of February we will no you aren't going to help us. Why we are writing is because we want to get away from home get a change in life. And we thought maybe you would help us.

Don't put this in the papers. If you do leave out where the Letter came from.
Signed, The Eight
Secret X's
XXX

■ Everett, Mass.
Sept. 1939
Dear Mrs Roosevelt:
I am writing to you because you seem to always help persons that need help & I am one who needs it. I would like more than anything else in the world an "aviation School" for girls to help them in the future days. I will explain what I mean: We should have a building containing 3 large room which I believe the mayor of Everett could give us. 1st room would be for Gym & sports, the 2nd room for modeling & working on aeroplanes & the 3rd for discussion & Meetings. We could have uniforms like the air stewardess wears & you could send them to us & tell us the price & each girl could pay weekly till the price is all paid because I know they can't pay cash & when we have the money we will send it to you & for a discount for me for the ones I sell I could get a free one & so would Marie my girlfriend. Just like the girl scouts. My girlfriend Marie & I would like to have control of these girls if you please. The Uniforms we would like to have is a blue kioke skirt with four pleats in front & 4 in back. The Jacket to match & a little hat to match. Just like the Air Hostess. I am 14, yr of age and I am a Freshman in High School & hope to be like Emily Arharmt [Amelia Earhart]. Please Mrs. Roosevelt if theres any way of helping us please I ask you with all my heart to help us. Please don't disappoint us, we have our hearts set on it. We want to show the boys that the girls can do just as good. I wish I was a boy I would join the Navy & go in for aviation—honest I would & so would the rest of us girls. You will write first & tell me what you think can be done & if its good news then send the uniforms but I will send the sizes first & the names of the girls & then you have them made & tell us the price & we will pay for them I give You my word of honor. Please have medal on the uniforms like this* & in mine have Commander in Cheif & Marie's Commander in General. Please help us to organize.
Please help us thats all I can say & don't forget us.

*For the writer's drawing of the medallion, see illustration.

Everett, Mass.
Sept, 1938

Dear Mrs. Roosevelt:—

I am writing to you because you seem to always help persons that need help & I am one who needs it. I would like more than anything else in the world an "aviation school" for girls to help them in the future day. I will explain what I mean: We should have a building containing 3 large rooms which I believe the mayor of Everett could give us. 1st room would be for Gym & sports, the 2nd room for modeling & working on aeroplanes & the 3rd for discussion & meetings. We could have uniforms like the air stewardess wear & you could send them to us & tell us the price & each girl could pay weekly till the price is all paid because I know they can't pay cash & when we have the money we will send it to you & for a discount for me for the ones I sell I could get a free one & so would Marie my girlfriend. Just like the girl scouts. My girlfriend Marie & I would like to have control of these girls if you please. The uniforms

REPRODUCED FROM THE HOLDINGS AT THE FRANKLIN D. ROOSEVELT LIBRARY

In requesting Mrs. Roosevelt's help in establishing an aviation school for girls, this fourteen-year-old girl from Massachusetts even designed the medallion for the aviators' uniforms.
(From the collection of the Franklin D. Roosevelt Library, Hyde Park, N.Y.)

we would like to have is a blue & khaki skirt with four pleat in front & 4 in back. The Jacket to match & a little hat to match. Just like the Air Hostess. I am 14 yr of age and I am a Freshman in High School & hope to be like Emily Arkason. Please Mrs. Roosevelt if there any way of helping us please I ask you with all my heart to help us. Please don't disappoint us, we love our hearts set on it. We want to show the boys the girls can do just as good. I wish I was a boy I would join the Navy & go in for aviation — honest I would. & so would the rest of us girls. You will write first & tell me what you think can be done & if its good news then send the uniforms but I will send the sizes first & the names of the girls & then you have them made & tell us the price & we will pay for them I give you my word of honor. Please have medal on the uniform like this ⊙ & in mine have

Junior Student ⊙ Please help, Commander in Chief
us to organize. & Marie
Commander in General.

REPRODUCED FROM HOLDINGS AT THE FRANKLIN D. ROOSEVELT LIBRARY

With Love

The Gang

& M. & M.

I never asked such a favor in my life—but this favor is real in heart. Please ans this letter even if its bad news.

■ Oakland, Calif.

April 23, 1941

My Dearest Mrs. Roosevelt,

I have heard, you have helped many people, in poverty, (etc.) That is why I'm appealing to you today.

Mine is not only for myself but for many other girls, and women of America.

You see, I'm one of the young women who has enlisted in the ambulance and aviation corps. But here's the situation. Now, I have no job, no money, and I join this corps. They want $12.95 for a uniform.

We who have no job, cannot afford to put out this money as we do not get any money for our service, which we are willing to render, for the United States Army. Please don't take me wrong, I am not complaining, but most of the girls think we should have a camp, and at least the Government give us the uniforms, as we do not expect any money for it, & cannot use them after.

I'd be willing to sign for 3 yrs. If I had a place to hang my hat.

I hear, Mrs Roosevelt, that you have started a girls camp in Washington, and it is quite the thing. I'm wondering if you couldn't get some girls in a camp as such.

You see, I am writing you this letter, because I am a young girl just 18 years old, and just don't seem to get along at home with my parents. I don't, maybe it's my fault, but it seems that the more I try, the more I don't seem to get along.

But, you see I love sports and Mother doesn't, and we always fight over softball because we can't seem to agree on it. I want to play, and she wont let me. She wont let me go with fellows (which I don't care to.) So I signed up for the Defense program, and as I have no money or job, I'm begging you to please try and do something on this situation, and I know there will be lots more girls volunteering. Please try and get some camps started. We girls of today are not the dainty women of yesterday. We are not afraid of grease, we want to help out as much as we can, and we *can* do it.

As it is we only go, 2 nights a week, and what can any one do in so little time?

We want plenty of practice, and there is never to much for us. We can take it, Honestly we can.

Your Humble an Obediant friend,

Miss J. D.

DISABLED

. . . .

■ Clinton, New York

April 12, 1934

Dear Mrs. Roosevelt,

I am very sorry to bother you at this time of trouble, but I know that you have to travel quite a lot, and I have not known where I could get in touch with you until now.

I know that you and President Roosevelt are interested in people who have had infantile paralysis. I am writing you in hopes that you will be able to help me concerning my college course.

Two years ago last October my sister and I had infantile. My sister is all right now, but I had paralysis to the chest, arms, and neck. My neck and chest are fine now. My left arm is all back but the deltoid and that gets stronger all the time. My right arm is improving, but as yet I have no use of it. It is still in an airplane brace. As my right arm is the bad one, it was necessary for me to learn how to do everything with my left hand. I hope that it won't be to long before I will be able to use my right arm again. My people are doing all that is within their power to help me. Mother exercises my arms every night. I go to the Y.W.C.A. for swimming during the school year. In the summer I go to Thousand Island Park on the St. Lawrence River. The extreme cold water seems to help my arm as nothing else will. Perhaps you remember Mr. Louis Brockway of New York City who saw President Roosevelt about Mr. Arthur Carpenter, who, I understand, is holding a very important position at Warm Springs. Mr. Brockway is a Clinton man and knows us.

When I was taken with infantile in the fall of 1931, I was a freshman in High School. Next September I hope to have enough units to be more than a senior.

I had hoped to go to Goucher College in Baltimore, Maryland. Could you

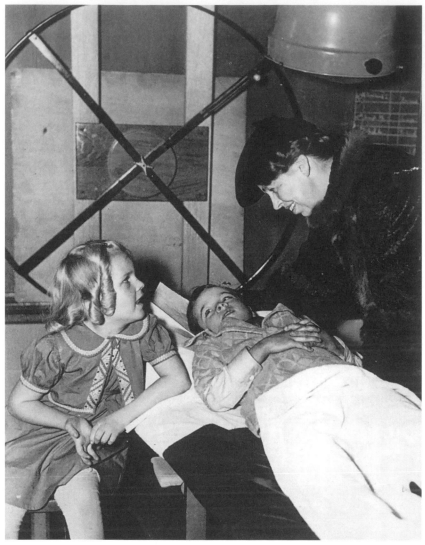

Eleanor Roosevelt visiting disabled students at the Langdon School,
Washington, 1938.
(United Press International)

tell me something about Goucher? Of course, our sickness has depleted
the finances of my people quite a bit, but I feel that I want to and must fit
myself for some work so that I may be able to take care of myself. I would
like to teach in a nursery school. I also think I would like welfare work if
I were able to do it. If you have any suggestions as to other types of work
which I would be able to do, I would be glad if you would tell them to me.

If we could arrange for a personal interview at your convience, when you are somewhere near Clinton or Utica, I would be very happy to do so.

Sincerely yours,

(Miss) D. J. K.

■ November 6, 1934

Pittsburgh, Pa.

Dear Mrs. Roosevelt:—

I read in the paper about the reward [Woman of the Year award] that you are going to get December 12th. And that you are going to help some poor unfortunate child. I am one one of the unfortunate girls. My name is B. L. and I have written to President Roosevelt twice already. And received an answer from President Roosevelts secretary it said that he had forward it to [Warm Springs] Georgia. And then I received a letter from Georgia and it said that they would love to have me but they are filled and that they wouldn't have any room for me for a long time if ever. And dear Mrs. Roosevelt I just hope and pray that I will be lucky enough someday to be sent to Georgia by a wonderful woman like you or by our dear beloved President Roosevelt. I'm 17 years old and I certainly do wish that I was well and able to go to school and learn like other girls. My parents would only be too happy to send me to Georgia if they could. My father is a poor working man and we just don't have the money. You know Mrs Roosevelt how a mother and a father is if there is a unwell child in the family, why they certainly would do anything in the world for them, but if you can't you know how bad they feel about it. But if they know if there is hope for some help and if I would ever get help how happy my father and mother would be. And of course I would be the happiest girl in the world. Mrs. Roosevelt I am writing this way to you because you are a mother too and you will understand. I will close this letter now hoping to get a happy answer from you. If you will take this into consideration I know that Our Lord will bless you and President Roosevelt for your kindness. I thank you from the bottom of my heart. May God be with you in all your undertakings.

Thanking you I remain

Miss B. L.

■ Salt Lake City
November 9, 1934
Dear Madam:

I recently read of the honor accorded you through having been chosen the most outstanding woman in the United States for 1934. The makers of the award surely express the feelings of all Americans. We are proud to have a First Lady of America who so nobly carries out the ideals of American womanhood.

We commoners are especially appreciative. You and your distinguished husband have lifted us from a position where we were regarded as not having the essential characteristics to lift ourselves from the bonds of dire want, to a position where we are regarded as a great people engaged in a mighty endeavor to conquer the evil of unemployment. However, we who suffer from another evil, that of physical impairment, are even more grateful. You and your husband have completely changed the not altogether kindly viewpoint of the public towards we who are crippled, through the consideration you have shown us.

My mention of physical handicaps reverts to the newspaper article expressing your wish to donate the money from you award to some child sufferer of infantile paralysis. I am not hardly a child, being twenty years of age, and I am not sure that I suffer from that particular kind of paralysis. I also do not want to take away the opportunity to be treated from a little child who is perhaps worse off than I am. But if you could make me the recipient of your gift, I would appreciate it as a favor I could never repay, regardless of my efforts to recompense you.

I will mention some facts which will help you to render a decision. I was given a sound mind and body with which to begin life. Until the summer of 1927 nothing retarded my natural progress. However, that summer I fell from a swinging horizontal bar and injured my spine. From that time I was was not exactly the same boy, although I did not realize it. Three weeks after the fall a severe pain developed across the lower portion of my back. After the pain had been there a few days paralysis of my legs took place, followed by a long period of intense suffering. About a year after being paralyzed, we put a full-length brace on my left leg and a brace on the lower portion of my right limb. The supports enabled me to walk a little with the aid of crutches. I soon grew out of the brace on the right leg, but I continued to wear the other brace for approximately six years. Now I wear no braces and am able to stand on my feet and take a few steps without any support. Outside, I still use crutches.

This misfortune has not deprived me of an education. I graduated from high school in 1932, attended the University of Utah during the during the following year, and shall graduate from the L.D.S. Business College of this city in a short time.

Should the information given not prove sufficient, you may be sure that I will gladly do anything I can to further assist you . . .

Very Truly Yours,

D. W. R.

■ Duncan, Okla.

Nov. 17, 1934

Dear Mrs. Roosevelt;

I read in the Current Event column about you being awarded a medal and $1,000, I also read what you have decided to use it for. You see I had a stroke of Infantile Paralysis four years ago last July the eleventh. I stayed in the state Hospital, at Oklahoma city, four months they just put braces on me. I've worn one for the last four years, they have told me they have done all they could, Aside, from keeping braces on me. I might possibly out-grow it. I am only fourteen years old. And I think if I had money enough to go to Warm Springs I might be well. My right leg is the only place paralysis affected me. If you havent already decided to give the money to some other child I would never be able to express my appreciation, if you would give it to me. I am a freshman in Highschool but I think I would have plenty of time to finish school after I had six months treatment. I think it was awfully kind of you to use the money that if it doesent help me it will do me good to know it helped some other child suffering from infantile paralysis Won't you write to me and tell me whether or not you'll give me the money? You probably don't know how it is to be crippled and how it would be to walk naturally after walking on a crutch four years I think you'll never regret the way you are going to use the money. At least, I hope you don't. My wish is that whoever gets the money becomes well and can walk. I would like to get an answer to my request.

Yours truly,

R. W.

■ Chicago, Ill.

Nov. 6, 1935

My dear Mrs. Roosevelt,

I am a little girl, fifteen years old. I was stricken with infantile paralysis last August 15 — My legs are paralyzed — I am heart broken. I was going
into my second year in High School — I am enclosing my picture, also the
clipping about you — I think you are the most wonderful woman, and also
our dear President to help so much in this sad world of ours. I get so lonely
and depressed some days — then I think of President Roosevelt & all the
great things he has done and he also suffered from this dreadful disease — I
only hope some day I may get to Warm Springs — I pray dear God will soon
help me walk again — Mrs. Roosevelt please write me a little letter, it would
make me so happy — My best wishes to you and yours.

Love

V. F.

■ Cleveland, Ohio

Jan. 22. 1936

Dear Mrs. Roosevelt:

Its a great pleasure to write to you. And I know quite well that you will be
glad to do what you could for us. I have written to President Roosevelt about
a few months ago, stating that we have a crippled sister, who is seventeen
yrs. old and who has never walked in all her seventeen yrs. We were asking our President to help us out by putting my sister R., in some home. My
mother and father aren't as strong as there were once upon a time. Papa has
been sick since 1928 with Diabetes and he is not himself anymore. Mama's
health isn't very good. So with a crippled daughter in our house is such a
burden to my parents. She has to be carried to bed at night and lifted up
from bed in the morning. She is a very heavy set girl Mrs. Roosevelt. Its
such a strain on my parents lifting her up always. She has never been to
school, she doesn't know how to read or write, she doesn't have any pleasures, all she does is sit in a chair all day long. I'm doing this because I have
pity on her leading such a life. We have received a letter from W.D.C. saying
that we should tell our visitor, at the Relef Office all about the letter and he
would know what to do. But they haven't even bothered Mrs. Roosevelt. I
knew they wouldn't because they dont even care to help us out now that
we need help badly. We have such a large family, there are nine of us and all
of the children are growing boys and girls. We are having such a hard time
at our home. We have a brother who is working at the Annit Bill Dept, and

what he gets Mrs. Roosevelt isnt enough to support such a large family. Pay rend, gas & electric bills, food & clothing and my father has a special diet, how could he ever keep well if he doesn't keep up with his diet. Thats why father isn't getting well he has too many worrys. He is always grouchy and scolding at us children. Please do something for us Mrs. Roosevelt, there is never peace and happiness in our home. I know just what Ive went through thats why I am asking for your help. I am nineteen yrs. old with no freedom at all I had to stop school at the age of sixteen because I was needed at home to help mother. I know if you will help us things will be so different for me and the rest of the family. So I am hoping and praying that you will be able to help us out. Im thanking you in advance I remain,

Respectfully

Your humble friend

Miss H. P.

Holland, Texas

Nov. 28. 1941

Dear Mrs. Roosevelt: —

I am a Boy 18 yrs of age. Who has been very unfortunate the past 3 years. I am the the Son of a tennant farmer and while helping my Father plant corn on March 22. 1937. I got my left leg caught in the wheel of the planter. and failed to stop the mules, and pulled my leg off at the knee joint except the blood vesels and some skin — they set my leg. against my parents protest to remove it. Ostheomylite's set in (Bone infection) and I have been in and out of the Crippled Childrens Hospital at Marlin, Tex all these 3½ years. My leg is stiff and Bone is still drainig. and I suppose it will continue to drain all my life. I cannot do any hard labor as my leg is stiff and sore. one nerve has been removed and my foot has dropped and I have to wear a brace — the state Hospital is treating me and will pay my tution in special training when I have finished High School. I am now in the 10th grade. Would have been through high school, had not I had this misfortune. my parents are not able to help me get through School since they have spent every thing they could get trying to keep me in the Hospital when I got hurt. Was in a Temple Texas Hospital 2 months before getting in the State Hospital. I have a great desire to finish school and college so that I can be self supporting. I can never do any farm work. I cannot ever take part in sports like most youths do. I have heard you talk to the youths of our great United Sates of wich I am one. I have been uplifted by your talks and that of your great Husband. the president of our United States. and I am not going to give up. I'm going to get an education and make my life worth-while to serve my home and my country. I would be so inlightened to get a contribution from the Gracious Lady of our President. It would be to pay for my schooling—I hope you will acknowledge my letter, and my desire to contribute a little to my present needs. am inclosing cards to back up my letter—from my Dr.

Sincerely, a true youth of our America

E. C.

Please read this. 5-10-36

If a Sec. opens this please give to the addressee

Hector, Ark.

May 9, 1936

Mr. and Mrs. F. D. Roosevelt
Washington D.C.
White House
Dear Friends:

I have written you two or three times before but you have not given me any satisfactory answer, so I am writing you again and sending you an invitation to my graduation exercise. I am asking that you send me a suit of clothes, and I will give you the honor of buying my first suit in my life. My measurements are as follows:

Size hat - - - - - - - - 6 7/8
"   shoe - - - - - - - - - 10
"   shirt - - - - - - - - - 15 1/2
"   undershirt - - - - - - 3 Y
Waist measure - - - - - - 31 inches
Inseam   "   - - - - - - 36 "
Chest   "   - - - - - - 36 "
Arm   "   - - - - - - 26 "
Hips   "   - - - - - - 34 "

Your friend

A high school senior disappointed that his prior requests for assistance have been turned down by the White House writes again asking the Roosevelts for graduation clothes.
(From the collection of the Franklin D. Roosevelt Library, Hyde Park, N.Y.)

Responses to the Letters

After poring through approximately two hundred pages of letters requesting help from Mrs. Roosevelt, readers will more than likely be curious about how the First Lady responded to them. Practical problems, above all time limitations, impeded her ability to respond personally to this correspondence. In the Depression decade Mrs. Roosevelt received so many letters—300,000 pieces of mail in 1933, 90,000 in 1937, 198,000 in 1939, and 110,000 in 1940—that she simply could not personally reply to or even read most of them.[1] She did take a strong interest in the correspondence, so that despite her hectic schedule and frequent travels she managed to read about fifty pieces of her general mail per day. But fifty letters constituted only a small proportion of the daily mail that poor people sent to her. The First Lady's immense amount of mail led her to rely heavily upon her staff members, who handled most of the correspondence, including the youth letters published here. The staff responses to these youth letters suggest that Mrs. Roosevelt read less than 5 percent of them.[2] Most of the responses were written and signed not by Mrs. Roosevelt herself but by her personal secretary Malvina T. ("Tommy") Scheider and her assistants. Thus the question of how well Mrs. Roosevelt responded to these letters is less about her own humanitarianism than about how able an administrator she was and how sensitive her staff was to the distress of those who wrote to her.

In most cases the First Lady's staff was unable to fulfill the requests that Depression youths made for material assistance. Less than 1 percent of the needy youths whose letters appeared in this book obtained the material aid they had requested of the First Lady. About 5 percent were told by the First Lady's staff that they should seek help from New Deal agencies, while 3 percent were directed toward charities, and another 3 percent to educational institutions. But these figures were dwarfed by the overall rejection rate. The remaining 88 percent of these young letter writers were simply turned down by the First Lady's office.[3]

These figures are disappointing on two counts. First and foremost they leave us with a sense of disappointment about the fate of the children. After reading of their travails, we all want a happy ending for these needy youths, much as movie audiences in the 1930s wanted a happy ending for the orphaned child played by Shirley Temple. But the figures suggest that unlike in those Hollywood films, in which a wealthy benefactor saves the day by lifting a Depression child out of poverty, the needy youths in real life found no such benefactor. The figures are also disappointing because of the way they seem to clash with Mrs. Roosevelt's reputation as a humanitarian. We almost expect her to work miracles for all who needed them. In this spirit Joseph P. Lash, in his Pulitzer Prize–winning book *Eleanor and Franklin*, made a special point of her compassion toward strangers who wrote to her asking for help. Lash told the story of Bertha Brodsky, an impoverished young woman with serious medical problems, whose letter requesting assistance from Mrs. Roosevelt led to immediate action. The First Lady arranged for Bertha's treatment in a local hospital, visited her there, and sent her gifts and flowers on holidays. When Bertha got out of the hospital Mrs. Roosevelt helped find jobs for Bertha and her brother, attended her wedding, and served as godmother to her child. Lash concluded that Eleanor Roosevelt's "relationship with Bertha was not untypical. She . . . responded to every appeal for help, indeed sought to anticipate them. To friends who felt that she ought to save her energies for more important things, Eleanor replied that 'whatever comes your way is yours to handle.'"[4]

Judging by the inability of the First Lady and her staff to comply with most of the requests for material assistance published in this book, Lash seems to have erred in claiming that Bertha's case "was not untypical." But there is no question that Eleanor Roosevelt's manner of interacting with the public was so ingratiating, especially to the poor, that cases like Bertha's did seem typical to many Americans. Soon after becoming First Lady Mrs. Roosevelt had written an article encouraging ordinary Americans to write to her.[5] In her newspaper columns there were repeated references to this correspondence and the ways in which it illuminated the problems of the poor.[6] The First Lady's sympathetic reference to the correspondence and her calls for expanded federal antipoverty work convinced needy youths that she cared about them and took their problems and their letters seriously. In other words, Mrs. Roosevelt's concern for the poor and her effort to be accessible to them were not figments of Lash's or the public's imagination. The way she spoke about her correspondence with those hurt by the Depression suggests a high degree of sensitivity. She explained:

> I think perhaps when people feel that they are not apt to see a person to whom they are writing, it may seem easier to open their hearts. In many cases I feel I have gained tremendous insight into the experiences and feelin[g]s of men and women, young girls and boys, even children in many places . . . [across] the length and breadth of this land and I hope that this mail has served to broaden my vision . . . deepened my understanding and [helped] on the whole to make me a better citizen.[7]

These remarks suggest that there is more than one way to assess Eleanor Roosevelt's response to the letters from poor youths published in this book. We can, of course, judge that response in its most literal sense by assessing whether she had the time and resources to meet the specific requests for material aid made by these needy correspondents—which in at least 88 percent of the cases she did not. Such cold statistics may, however, underestimate the meaning of the correspondence. Their significance lies not only in the rate at which Roosevelt and her staff complied (or failed to comply) with the needy letter writers' requests for assistance. It lies also in the impact that the letters had on Mrs. Roosevelt. As her remarks quoted above and similar comments in her newspaper columns imply, the letters helped her to understand, publicize, and seek a solution to the problems of poor youths. By keeping the First Lady informed about the hardships that the economic crisis imposed upon needy teens and children, these young letter writers facilitated her work in championing such initiatives as federal aid to low-income students through the NYA and other New Deal programs.[8] In this sense the letters had more impact, the poor letter writers more historical agency, and Eleanor Roosevelt a more meaningful response than statistics alone might suggest. Whatever her failures to meet requests for individual aid from poor youths, the First Lady could and did respond to them at the policy level by becoming the New Deal's most outspoken advocate of federal aid to needy youth. This is why letters from poor teens and children kept pouring in to Mrs. Roosevelt's mailbox throughout the Depression.

At the same time, the way that Roosevelt and her staff replied to the letters should not be immune from criticism. Mrs. Roosevelt herself did not shy away from criticizing the way that previous administrations had handled the White House mail. Aware that she was receiving far more correspondence than any previous First Lady, Mrs. Roosevelt prided herself on having modernized the system through which the White House responded. In an article that she wrote about the mail she received as First Lady, Mrs. Roosevelt pointed out that she had inherited a hopelessly outdated system, which consisted largely of sending out form letters, some dating all the way back to the Cleveland administration. Poking fun at the inadequacy of this system, Mrs. Roosevelt explained that if a woman asked the First Lady to provide an elephant for her child, the form letter system would generate a reply to the effect that the First Lady "has had so many similar requests she deeply regrets that she cannot comply with yours!" "The gravity of the questions that were coming in" by mail because of the economic crisis persuaded Mrs. Roosevelt to do "away with many of the old forms" and set up a new system in which letters were read and responded to by her staff individually rather than through form letters, with the most important letters flagged for Mrs. Roosevelt's personal attention.[9]

In assessing the way that Mrs. Roosevelt and her staff handled her mail, historians have taken her at her word and echoed her own account of how she personalized and improved the White House system.[10] But if the responses that the First Lady's staff sent to the letters from needy youths in this book are any guide, the improvements are virtually impossible to detect. Indeed, despite the abandonment of the old form letter system, most requests from youths were in fact turned down by form letter. With minor variations most were answered with notes of the following form:

> Mrs. Roosevelt asks me to acknowledge your letter and to express her regret that because of the great number of similar requests she receives, she has found it impossible to comply with them, much as she would like to assist all those who appeal to her. Assuring you of Mrs. Roosevelt's sympathy, I am
>
> Very sincerely yours,
> Secretary to Mrs. Roosevelt[11]

The problem with this form letter is similar to the one that the First Lady highlighted in criticizing the form letters used by her predecessors and recounting the anecdote about the request for an elephant: the letter was appropriate in some cases, but inappropriate and even insensitive in others. In light of the anecdote, it is ironic that Mrs. Roosevelt's staff responded to an impoverished Alabama boy's request for a mule by writing that the First Lady could not help him "because of the great number of similar requests she receives." While an impersonal brush-off letter might seem fitting for a young person making a casual request, for another who was despondent it seems quite the opposite. In numerous letters the writers mention that they are crying as they write, and a few are even contemplating suicide. Yet some of these letter writers received the same form letter as other youths, or a very similar one.[12]

This kind of insensitivity leads one to wonder whether all the letters were read closely or even read at all by the staff members who drafted responses on behalf of Mrs. Roosevelt. Of course, given the avalanche of mail that the First Lady received, it is not surprising that many of these letters were processed with more dispatch than care, in an operation almost resembling an assembly line. In addition to Tommy Scheider, some twenty clerks were involved in this work. As Scheider explained, "the file boys open the letters and glance at them, separating the routine letters from those which need individual answers . . . [those meriting individual answers generally consisted of] Mrs. R's regular correspondence and the people in whom she is interested. The next step would be to take formers [former letters on the same subject] out where they would help in answering new letters." During the summers and at other times when Roosevelt and Scheider were away from Washington, letters were answered by members of the social correspondence staff, who were another level removed from the First Lady. Under such circumstances it was difficult indeed for many letters to receive careful consideration by either Mrs. Roosevelt or staff members close to her.[13]

Even had Mrs. Roosevelt had the time to read each of these youth letters individually, she still would have been able to comply with the requests of only a small number of the needy young people who wrote to her. While on the West Coast in 1938 the First Lady commented in her column "My Day" on this problem with regard to her general correspondence:

All kinds of people are inspired to write me when they hear that I am somewhere near, and I only wish that it was possible to accede to all the requests that are made. I did a little mental arithmetic this morning and found that if I said "yes" to the requests that came to me just in this morning's mail, I would need $2,000* before night to send out to various people. I would like to help them all, but I think it will have to be done in some other way, for at this rate it would take a millionaire many times over to meet the demands.[14]

*More than $25,000 in 2001 dollars.

In addition to the cost, Mrs. Roosevelt also had two other concerns about serving as the kind of fairy godmother that so many letters writers were seeking. First, one had to be willing to invest time and take the trouble to verify the claims of the correspondents. This would mean contacting either local relief authorities or Mrs. Roosevelt's own friends, who could inquire whether the stated needs were genuine. Given the First Lady's heavy schedule and how overburdened local relief agencies were, it would have taken a very special case indeed to convince Mrs. Roosevelt that a request from her to those agencies was justified.[15] Second, Roosevelt worried that even the most generous gift to an impoverished person would only mask the problem of poverty while doing nothing to uproot it. This is what she had in mind when she wrote: "I think perhaps there are more constructive ways of doing things than simply sending people the money which they think they need today, but which undoubtedly, they will need over and over again in the near future."[16]

But even if one finds persuasive the reasons for turning down the requests made by the children and teens in this book, that does not justify the manner in which the replies were handled. Judging from her essay about the way her mail was handled, Mrs. Roosevelt seemed unaware that the form letters she so disliked were being employed frequently and at times insensitively by her staff. A more imaginative and personal mode of replying could have been used even to turn down requests for material assistance. Roosevelt had written advice columns and even a book for mothers on coping with the economic crisis, and she gave many speeches offering advice to Depression youth—about whom she cared deeply.[17] It would have been a relatively simple matter, and potentially very helpful, if someone on the First Lady's staff had been assigned to do the same for these needy young letter writers. There were many things that the staff could have offered: a kind word, a note of encouragement, a few sympathetic lines critical of those mentioned in the letters who had mocked poor youths for lacking material goods. All would have given at least sorely needed moral support in place of the material assistance that the letter writers were being denied.[18]

There is a risk of reading too much into the replies by Mrs. Roosevelt and her staff. The letters and responses are historical evidence, but like many other historical sources they cannot be completely contextualized. Only Roosevelt and her staff saved large quantities of the correspondence, which were deposited in her files of requests for material assistance, and therefore in compiling this book I had to rely heavily on Eleanor Roosevelt's files at Hyde Park. The problem is that in many cases we cannot follow the trail of the letters that left the First Lady's files because she forwarded them to New Deal agencies for help. It is possible that she forwarded many such letters. As for the agencies themselves, such as the National Youth Administration and the Federal Emergency Relief Administration (FERA), they saved mostly correspondence relating to administrative and policy matters rather than letters from individuals requesting personal assistance. It is evident from Mrs. Roosevelt's correspondence with Ellen S. Woodward, the director of women's work at the FERA, that she referred a number of requests for material assistance to the agency, and yet those letters have not survived.[19]

This means that although the letters in this book capture the realities of Depression life for needy youth, there is much that we cannot know. The letters in Eleanor Roosevelt's files may represent a high proportion of all the requests for material assistance that she received, or only a small one. It is even possible that the files hold only letters that the First Lady's staff viewed as coming from the less needy, with those from the more serious cases sent to other agencies. In short, while it seems fair to criticize the First Lady's staff for its handling of the youth letters published here, it would be arguing beyond the available evidence to suggest that they dealt similarly with all other letters requesting material assistance.

Any criticism of the response by the First Lady's office to the letters in this book must therefore be tempered by an awareness that there were likely many other needy youths for whom Mrs. Roosevelt and her staff did provide individual assistance. But the letters of the poor youths who received such assistance have not survived. The most extensive record of the involvement of Mrs. Roosevelt and her staff in helping needy young correspondents is found in their relationship with charitable organizations and New Deal agencies regarding Christmas letters. Press accounts make it evident that the First Lady received many more Christmas appeals than have survived in her files. It seems that these Christmas letters left the files because the First Lady's staff sent them to the heads of community funds across the country and local relief administrators for the FERA and WPA (who were apparently expected to play Santa Claus). But again the youth letters appealing for assistance have not been preserved, so it is not possible to compare the number of requests from needy youths who were helped in this way by the First Lady and her staff with the number of Christmas appeals still remaining in Roosevelt's files that were turned down (and some of which appear in chapter 3).[20]

There is also evidence in Roosevelt's correspondence with Clarence E.

Pickett of the American Friends Service Committee (AFSC) that the First Lady either personally provided funds or enlisted others to give assistance to some poor young people who wrote to her seeking scholarships and jobs. In addition, as noted in the Introduction, Roosevelt made generous donations through Pickett and the AFSC to the education of poor children in Arthurdale, West Virginia. The First Lady also intervened to help a variety of financially strapped private institutions that aided the young by trying to secure federal aid for them.[21] Correspondence between Roosevelt, her staff, and local social work and public welfare leaders further suggests that the First Lady did assist a significant number of needy youths.[22] By any normal standard, then, Mrs. Roosevelt was deeply involved in aiding poor youths. But of course the Depression was not a normal time, and it is an open question whether Roosevelt should be judged by normal standards after having raised expectations so. The youths who wrote her the letters published in these pages were looking for an angel to help them through hard times, and most did not find one.

Depressing as it seems, it may not be inappropriate for this book to end on this note of disappointment. For the needy youth turned down by the First Lady's staff were certainly disappointed.[23] And this disappointment can be seen as symbolic of the way many others in need felt about the New Deal's limitations.[24] It reminds us that although the liberal reform movement to which Eleanor Roosevelt belonged (and that her husband led) provided employment and aid to millions of poor people, it was not large, ambitious, or radical enough to reach millions of others. The New Deal helped and inspired many, yet it could neither end the Depression nor provide federal aid for all of those that the crisis left impoverished. The letters published here—and the inability of the First Lady's staff to meet their requests—underscore that for millions of poor people neither Eleanor Roosevelt nor her husband nor the New Deal could provide a Hollywood ending or any ending at all to their suffering. They attest to how overwhelming the Depression was; it hurt so many people that even Eleanor Roosevelt, who ranks among the most warm-hearted humanitarians in American history, could not come close to meeting their needs or fulfilling their dreams. The grim realities of life facing millions of Americans stuck in hard times would change for the better only when the American economy picked up steam, as the nation prepared for a different type of crisis: the Second World War.

Notes and Sources

All of the youth letters to Eleanor Roosevelt (ER) published in this book and cited in the endnotes are from the Eleanor Roosevelt papers in the Franklin D. Roosevelt Library (FDRL), Hyde Park, New York. In 1934 Mrs. Roosevelt's staff officially began filing in her Material Assistance Requested files (listed as the 150.1 files in the ER papers) the letters that needy youths (and adults) had sent to her asking for help; the 1934 files also contain letters from 1933. For the Depression era there are eighteen containers of letters from 1934, sixteen containers from 1935, ten for 1936, eight for 1937, ten for 1938, nine for 1939, and twelve for 1940. See ER papers inventory, FDRL.

The FDR Library is in the process of reorganizing Mrs. Roosevelt's papers, and since this will involve changing the container numbers in the collection I am not listing the old numbers for the containers from which the letters in this book were drawn. But readers interested in examining the originals of the letters to Mrs. Roosevelt published here will find most of them in her Material Assistance Requested files (150.1), with the remainder drawn from her Donations Requested files (150.2). Note that though this second file (150.2) was supposed to house letters requesting donations to organizations, the First Lady's staff misfiled in it some individual material assistance requests. Both files are arranged chronologically and alphabetically, so that even with new container numbers readers will be easily able to locate the letters from their year and initials.

Rather than merely sample the teens' and children's letters in Eleanor Roosevelt's Material Assistance Requested (and Donations Requested) files, I read them all. The letters which appear in this book were selected from the much larger group of youth letters in those files. They were selected on the basis of how well they conveyed the situation of the letter writer: those with extensive autobiographical data were the most revealing about Depression conditions and thus the best candidates for publication. But in terms of the kinds of requests made and the political orientation of the letter writers, there was no difference between the letters chosen and the many more which could not fit into this book.

INTRODUCTION

1. Ernestine Guerrero to Franklin D. Roosevelt, San Antonio, Oct. 17, 1937, Franklin D. Roosevelt papers, FDRL. In carving the clock case Ms. Guerrero worked from a pattern that was part of a kit for fret work "coping saw" sculpture. She was too poor to place a clock mechanism in the clock case that she made for FDR. For these and other details concerning the sculpture, I am grateful to Tex Parks, the FDR Library's Exhibition Specialist, who shared with me his knowledge of the sculpture along with the notes of an interview (on July 5, 1978) with Ms. Guerrero's brother Nicholas by Margerite Hubbard, the former curator of the FDR Library and Museum. For the president's response to Guerrero's letter and gift—which he termed

an "especially beautiful carving," see Franklin D. Roosevelt to Ernestine Guerrero, Nov. 6, 1937, Franklin D. Roosevelt papers, FDRL.

2. Historians have published very little on the ways in which children and teens experienced the Depression. The only book-length scholarly study of this subject appeared over a quarter-century ago and was not written by a historian, but by the sociologist Glen H. Elder Jr., whose *Children of the Great Depression* (Chicago: University of Chicago Press, 1974) is a pioneering work that has generated curiously little response from historians. There is some useful data about the educational system of the 1930s in David Tyack, Robert Lowe, and Elisabeth Hansot, *Public Schools in Hard Times: The Great Depression and Recent Years* (Cambridge: Harvard University Press, 1984), but this work is mostly adult-centered and concerned with school administration, finance, and pedagogy; it gives little attention to the students' views of the Depression experience. My own work on Depression-era college student protest, *When the Old Left Was Young: Student Radicals and America's First Mass Student Protest Movement* (New York: Oxford University Press, 1993), has not inspired anyone to look at student protest at the high school level in Depression America. There are, however, two informative chapters on high school student life in Grace Palladino, *Teenagers: An American History* (New York: Basic Books, 1996), 16–47. Also helpful on postadolescent social life in the Depression era is the chapter in John Modell, *Into One's Own: From Youth to Adulthood in the United States* (Berkeley: University of California Press, 1989), 121–61. On government policy toward children and teens during the 1930s, see Richard A. Reiman, *The New Deal and American Youth: Ideas and Ideals in a Depression Decade* (Athens: University of Georgia Press, 1993); Kriste Lindenmeyer *"A Right to Childhood": The U.S. Children's Bureau and Child Welfare, 1912–1946* (Urbana: University of Illinois Press, 1997), 163–202. Also see the book of photographs, Kathleen Thompson and Hilary MacAustin, eds., *Children of the Depression* (Bloomington: University of Indiana Press, 2001).

3. At least 90 percent of the Material Assistance request letters to Eleanor Roosevelt are from adults. Consequently, the historians who have worked most extensively with these letters, Robert S. McElvaine and Leila Sussmann, have focused primarily on the adult response to the Depression and the New Deal. Nonetheless, their work has been of great value in showing the rich potential of these sources to illuminate the ways in which those near the bottom of American society experienced the Depression. See Robert McElvaine, ed., *Down and Out in the Great Depression: Letters from the Forgotten Man* (Chapel Hill: University of North Carolina Press, 1983), 113–20, especially his suggestive chapter on "the forgotten children"; also see Leila A. Sussmann, *Dear FDR: A Study of Political Letter-Writing* (Totowa, N.J.: Bedminster, 1963).

4. Joseph P. Lash, *Eleanor and Franklin: The Story of Their Relationship Based on Eleanor Roosevelt's Private Papers* (New York: New American Library, 1971), 493; Sussmann, *Dear FDR*, 11, 60, 72, 87, 139–41. On the ways in which Eleanor Roosevelt encouraged ordinary Americans to write to her, see the epilogue to this book.

5. Note that during the 1930s, the terms "teenager" and "teen" were not yet popularly used. The term "youth" was used primarily to refer to teens, but also to children. For clarity's sake, I prefer to use "children" and "teens" rather than lump all together as "youth," though on occasion I am drawn back to use "youth" as

well (since at times it does make sense to generalize about both groups). The vast majority of youths who wrote to Mrs. Roosevelt were teens, though a significant minority of children (five- to twelve-year-olds) also wrote to her.

6. Robert S. McElvaine, *The Great Depression: America, 1929–1941* (New York: Times Books, 1993), 75.

7. John Gabriel Hunt, ed., *The Essential Franklin Delano Roosevelt* (Avenel, N.J.: Portland House, 1995), 131.

8. Homer Rainey, *How Fare American Youth?* (New York: D. Appleton, 1938), 34–36.

9. Dixon Wecter, *The Age of the Great Depression, 1929–1941* (New York: New Viewpoints, 1975), 181; Steven Mintz and Susan Kellogg, *Domestic Revolutions: A Social History of American Family Life* (New York: Free Press, 1988), 140; Rainey, *How Fare American Youth?*, 68; Howard M. Bell, *Youth Tell Their Story* (Washington: American Youth Council, 1938), 29.

10. Tyack, Lowe, and Hansot, *Public Schools in Hard Times: The Great Depression and Recent Years*, 32; Robert Cohen, ed., "Public Schools in Hard Times: Letters from Georgia Teachers and Students to Franklin and Eleanor Roosevelt," *Georgia Historical Quarterly* 82, no. 1 (Spring 1998): 121–49.

11. Cohen, *When the Old Left Was Young*, 15–16. Note that this dip in school and college enrollments wrought by the onset of the economic crisis ended long before the Depression did. For a discussion of the recovery and growth of these enrollments, see the introduction to Chapter 2 of this book.

12. Reiman, *The New Deal and Youth.*

13. Maxine Davis, *The Lost Generation: A Portrait of American Youth Today* (New York: Macmillan, 1936); Bruce L. Melvin, *Youth—Millions Too Many?* (New York: Association Press, 1940); Homer Rainey, "Problems of Unemployment among Youth," American Youth Commission Report (unpublished, 1936), 1, in Charles Taussig Papers, FDRL.

14. Kathy M. Jackson, *Images of Children in American Film: A Socio-cultural Analysis* (Metuchen, N.J.: Scarecrow, 1986), 59.

15. Irving Bernstein, *A Caring Society: The New Deal, the Worker, and the Great Depression* (Boston: Houghton Mifflin, 1985), 160–64; Tyack, Lowe, and Hansot, *Public Schools in Hard Times*, 105.

16. Betty and Ernest K. Lindley, *A New Deal for Youth: The Story of the National Youth Administration* (New York: Viking, 1938), 211, 215.

17. E.B. to ER, Double Springs, Ala., Dec. 27, 1934.

18. On the ways in which lack of funds pushed youths out of school, see J.B.J. to ER, Keegan, Me., Dec. 23, 1933; L.B. to ER, Chicago, Feb. 14, 1934; E.M. to ER, Fallsville, Ark., Jan. 3, 1934; E.S. to ER, Amarillo, Tex., Jan. 4, 1934; M.A. to ER, Jan. 31, 1934; L.H. to ER, Granette, Ark., Nov. 6, 1936; L.N. to ER, Firebaugh, Colo., Dec. 20, 1933; I.E. to ER, Bedford, Ohio; L.J. to ER, Cincinnati, June 6, 1936; G.O. to ER, Taylor, Ark., Sept. 3, 1934; H.L. to ER, Sabraton, W.Va., Jan. 17, 1936.

19. See, for example, W.B. to ER, Old Saybrook, Conn., July 27, 1938.

20. M.S. to ER, Meadowview, Va., Apr. 17, 1934.

21. D.C. to ER, Dallas City, Ill., July 22, 1939.

22. F.H. to ER, Pittsburgh, Dec. 1, 1937.

23. E.H. to ER, Ironton, Ohio, Nov. 21, 1940; C.B. to ER, Rushylvania, Ohio, Mar. 29, 1935; E.A. to ER, Little Rock, Sept. 26, 1936.

24. E.B. to ER, Milwaukee, Mar. 12, 1934.

25. *New York Times*, Mar. 14, 1933; Allida M. Black, *Casting Her Own Shadow: Eleanor Roosevelt and the Shaping of Postwar Liberalism* (New York: Columbia University Press, 1996), 23–50; Lash, *Eleanor and Franklin*, 477–570.

26. The *New Yorker* cartoon appeared on June 3, 1933, and the hobo cartoon on Jan. 10, 1940; both are reprinted in Jess Flemion and Colleen M. O'Connor, eds., *Eleanor Roosevelt: An American Journey* (San Diego: San Diego State University Press, 1987), 197–98.

27. Rochelle Chadakoff, ed., *Eleanor Roosevelt's "My Day": Her Acclaimed Columns, 1936–1945* (New York: Pharos, 1989), 94; Eleanor Roosevelt, "My Day: First Lady Visits Projects in Louisville," *Atlanta Constitution*, Oct. 6, 1938; Eleanor Roosevelt, "My Day: First Lady Visits Various Federal Projects," *Atlanta Constitution*, Oct. 20, 1938.

28. M.E.B. to ER, Crisfield, Md., Aug. 21, 1935; E.H. to ER, Ironton, Ohio, Nov. 21, 1940; M.J.F. to ER, Bessemer, Ala., July 8, 1938.

29. On Eleanor Roosevelt's work at the Henry Street settlement house, where she served as a volunteer teacher, see Blanche Wiesen Cook, *Eleanor Roosevelt*, vol. 1, *1884–1933* (New York: Viking, 1992), 134–35; on her role as a teacher at Todhunter School, see Eunice Fuller Barnard, "Mrs. Roosevelt in the Classroom," *New York Times Magazine*, Dec. 4, 1932, 1–2, 14, and Cook, *Eleanor Roosevelt*, 1:397–408. On Eleanor Roosevelt's youth work, see Winifred D. Wandersee, "ER and American Youth: Politics and Personality in a Bureaucratic Age," in Joan Hoff Wilson and Marjorie Lightman, eds., *Without Precedent: The Life and Career of Eleanor Roosevelt* (Bloomington: University of Indiana Press, 1984), 63–87.

30. Ruby A. Black, *Eleanor Roosevelt: A Biography* (New York: Duell, Sloan, and Pearce, 1940), 210–21; Ruby A. Black to Malvina (Tommy) Thompson, July 5, 1940, ER papers, FDRL.

31. *New York Times*, May 7, 1934; Eleanor Roosevelt, foreword to Melvin, *Youth—Millions Too Many?*, 6.

32. Lash, *Eleanor and Franklin*, 698–721, 774–91; Cohen, *When the Old Left Was Young*, 188–94, 301–4.

33. E.C. to ER, Holland, Tex., Nov. 28, 1940; V.A. to ER, Philadelphia, Jan. 18, 1934.

34. *New York Times*, Dec. 13, 1934, Dec. 14, 1934, Feb. 26, 1933, Aug. 4, 1933, Dec. 22, 1933; Report of E.R. Transit Funds of American Friends Service Committee, May 14, 1934, to Dec. 31, 1934, ER papers, FDRL; Report of E.R. Transit Funds of American Friends Service Committee Year Ended Dec. 31, 1935; ER to Clarence Pickett, Mar. 4, 1937, ER papers, FDRL. There was a kind of spiraling effect which followed Eleanor Roosevelt's more public charitable activities. When some donation of hers hit the press, the news would prod other needy young people to write to the First Lady for help. For examples of this, see D.W. to ER, Lena, Ill., Jan. 4, 1934; M.P. to ER, Union City, N.J., Jan. 1, 1935; V.F. to ER, Chicago, Nov. 6, 1934. Her aid to the schools of Arthurdale represented private charity, but it was also linked to the federal public relief efforts, as Arthurdale itself was a New Deal resettlement com-

munity aimed at aiding unemployed miners and their surrounding community in West Virginia. On Arthurdale, see Lash, *Eleanor and Franklin*, 520–50.

35. *New York Times*, Dec. 13, 1934, Dec. 14, 1934; M.H. to ER, Darlington, S.C., Aug. 12, 1934.

36. H.S. to ER, Mar. 26, 1934, Moorhead, Minn.; M.C. to ER, Buffalo, N.Y., Nov. 11, 1940.

37. W.H. to ER, Wolfe City, Tex., Sept. 13, 1934; R.R. to ER, Niles, Mich., May 17, 1938; A.P. to ER, Wallingford, Conn., Dec. 8, 1937.

38. H.M. to ER, Harrodsburg, Ky., Dec. 18, 1933; C.B. to ER, Park Rapids, Minn., Jan. 16, 1935.

39. E.F. to ER, Iron Mountain, Mich., May 12, 1938; E.C.N. to ER, Aurora, Ill., Aug. 18, 1934. There were, however, a few instances when the class resentment directed against the First Lady was so bitter as to imply that she was selfish or insensitive. Thus a "lonely and blue girl" of sixteen wrote from Oklahoma: "I read where you have so many fine clothes. I would like to know how you feel to buy them and know you do not take it away from others mouths. Do you get a thrill or not," J.P. to ER, Sapula, Okla., Apr. 8, 1935.

40. This lack of a right wing sets the needy young apart from some of the more affluent members of their generation. Among college students, for example, a group that was generally middle to upper class, a leftist-led student movement dominated student politics but often encountered vocal and even violent opposition from anti–New Deal conservatives on campus. See Cohen, *When the Old Left Was Young*, 56–57, 62–64, 121–22.

41. D.B. to ER, Greensboro, N.C., Feb. 12, 1938. Note that it was not just youths who were conflicted and inconsistent in advocating greater government aid to the poor, while also personally regarding it as shameful to go on relief. A study of Chicago families in 1938 reported on a family that refused relief or charity even though the parents were socialists—"their pride prevented them from accepting any aid from the government," Ruth Shonle Cavan and Katherine Howland Ranck, *The Family and the Depression: A Study of One Hundred Chicago Families* (Chicago: University of Chicago Press, 1938), 56.

42. For the best summary of the history of American youth during the Depression, see Leroy Ashby, "Partial Promises and Semi-Visible Youths: The Depression and World War II," in Joseph M. Hawes and N. Ray Hiner, eds., *American Childhood: A Research Guide and Historical Handbook* (Westport, Conn.: Greenwood, 1985), 489–531.

43. For an example of a youth who did exaggerate his plight to obtain aid and was caught in his lie, see L.B. to ER, Grove Spring, Mo., Feb. 14, 1934, and the investigation of this letter writer discussed in Deloss F. Teed to Lucile Bruner, Jefferson City, Mo., Mar. 27, 1935; Malvina Thompson to Lucile Burner, Apr. 5, 1935, ER papers, FDRL.

44. Mira Komarovsky, *The Unemployed Man and His Family: The Effect of Unemployment upon the Status of the Man in Fifty-nine Families* (New York: Dryden, 1949), 74–77; Lizabeth Cohen, *Making a New Deal: Industrial Workers in Chicago, 1919–1939* (New York: Cambridge University Press, 1990), 246–49.

45. J.A.G. to ER, Barboursville, W.Va., Aug. 23, 1934; M.M. to ER, Springfield, Mo., Dec. 5, 1937; C.J. to ER, Calument, Ala., Dec. 28, 1933.

46. J.H. to ER, Cleveland, Jan. 17, 1935; F.C. to ER, Brooklyn, June 25, 1941. Also see S.W. to ER, Maplewood, N.J., Oct. 16, 1934.

47. S.J.S. to ER, Clairton, Pa. [n.d. but acknowledged by ER's staff Mar. 1, 1934]; M.N.C. to ER, Stillmore, Ga., Oct. 14, 1936.

48. This adult-centered quality to the historiography continues to this day. Historians who cover youth in the 1930s do everything except ask how the young viewed their situation. Thus one finds a book on the history of toys, whose chapter on the Depression offers not a single quote from children on how they viewed them, and a book on the New Deal and youth that looks at how New Deal adult policymakers viewed the young but not at how the young viewed their poverty and the New Deal. See Gary Cross, *Kid's Stuff: Toys and the Changing World of American Imagination* (Cambridge: Harvard University Press, 1997), 103–20; Reiman, *The New Deal and American Youth*.

49. B.T. to ER, Le Moure, N.D., Oct. 12, 1936. I do not mean to imply that these letters prove paternal authority to have gone unscathed during the Depression—only that damage to parent-child relations was far from universal and seems to have been less widespread than some social scientists and historians have indicated. Actually the best studies of the family during the Depression acknowledge a wide range of family responses to the economic crisis, with some economically deprived families disorganized by indigence while others became more unified as family members worked together to weather hard times. There is some disagreement as to why these differences occurred. Some have stressed that in families bound by cultural patterns and traditions which legitimated strong paternal authority, such authority had greater resilience during the Depression than in families that lacked these traditions. Others have stressed that economic know-how or experience with crisis management left some families better prepared than others for the shocks of the Depression. See Cavan and Ranck, *The Family and the Depression*, 76–149; Elder, *Children of the Great Depression*, 83–118; E. Wight Bakke, *Citizens without Work: A Study of the Effects of Unemployment upon the Worker's Social Relations and Practices* (New Haven: Yale University Press, 1940), 109–52; Louis Adamic, *My America, 1928–1938* (New York: Harper and Brothers, 1938), 283–93; Robert Cooley Angell, *The Family Encounters the Depression* (New York: Scribner's, 1936), 55–231.

50. M.B. to ER, Methuen, Mass., Mar. 31, 1935; A.L.C. to ER, Sikeston, Mo., Jan. 20, 1938.

51. M.B. to ER, Chicago, Nov. 4, 1936.

52. M.K. to ER, Boston, Apr. 25, 1938. Also see S.L. to ER, Kansas City, Kan., Feb. 15, 1934.

53. A.K. to ER, Norfolk, Va., Apr. 7, 1939. This concern about their parents' morale and welfare was expressed with particular eloquence and emotion in the many appeals that the young wrote to secure loans for their fathers and mothers. See, for example, S.W. to ER, Maplewood, N.J., Oct. 16, 1934; M.M. to ER, Richmond, Utah, Mar. 25, 1939.

54. V.T. to ER, Brooklyn, N.Y., Nov. 18, 1937; E.J. to ER, West Warwick, R.I., Jan. 30,

1936; S.J. to ER, Westbrook, Minn., Jan. 30, 1938; August B. Hollingshead, Elm-town's Youth: The Impact of Social Classes on Adolescents (New York: John Wiley & Sons, 1949), 204–42.

55. M.M.H. and E.A.B. to ER, Lackawanna, N.Y., June 15, 1939; L.B. to ER, Dows, Iowa, Mar. 24, 1934; E.B. to ER, Bangor, Mich., Apr. 27, 1935.

56. Palladino, Teenagers, 9–11. One of the more memorable letters suggesting the influ-ence of relatively affluent youths in the school peer culture came from a fourteen-year-old, lower-middle-class girl, worried because she could not pay the bill on $30 worth of clothes that she had charged. This girl had bought the clothes because she wanted to be part of "a certain group of [well-heeled] kids in town who are called the society," S.T. to ER, Newton, Iowa, Mar. 15, 1940.

57. Hollingshead, Elmtown's Youth, 183–92; Tyack, Lowe, and Hansot, Public Schools in Hard Times, 172.

58. McElvaine, The Great Depression, 198–202.

59. D.A.H. to ER, St. Louis, Jan. 6, 1934; B.J.V. to ER, Garfield, Ark., Jan. 14, 1934.

60. A.S. to ER, High Point, N.C., Jan. 1937; Harry Crews, A Childhood: The Biography of a Place (Athens: University of Georgia Press, 1995), 58.

61. A.C. to ER, Port Morris, N.J., Mar. 20, 1934.

62. M.C. to ER, Epps, La., Nov. 18, 1939.

63. For some typical requests for used clothing, see L.B. to ER, Chicago, Feb. 1934; B.M. to ER, Minneapolis, Oct. 31, 1936; M.C. to ER, Sasakwa, Okla., Feb. 27, 1939; L.B. to ER, Reading, Pa., June 16, 1938; L.K. to ER, Fingal, N.D., Aug. 8, 1936; A.M. to ER, Menomee Falls, Wis., Jan. 1, 1935. On this egalitarian sensibility regarding educational opportunity, see M.H. to ER, Scotland, Ark., Aug. 25, 1941; M.M. to ER, Ocean Springs, Miss., May 29, 1934; M.A. to ER, Independence, Mo., Aug. 22, 1934.

64. R.C.T. to ER, Big Rock, Tenn., Aug. 1934.

65. Studs Terkel, Hard Times: An Oral History of the Great Depression (New York: Pantheon, 1970), 47.

66. This is especially striking with regard to graduations and proms, as a strong ma-jority of requests were prefaced by sad or indignant statements about needy stu-dents not having the money for these events while everyone else did. See the "Grad-uations" section of Chapter 2.

67. Philip Levine, The Bread of Time: Towards an Autobiography (New York: Alfred A. Knopf, 1995), 37–38. Note that Elder's Oakland case study confirms the perception of these youths that the Depression did not hurt all socioeconomic classes equally. As Elder puts it:

> The degree of economic loss among families in the Oakland sample disputes a popular assumption that economic hardship in the Depression was a pervasive experience which placed American families in a common situation of shared misfortune. While most of the Oakland families were placed in a deprivational situation, some did not experience the additional burden of unemployment, and there were enough families in the "well-off" category to increase feelings of deprivation among the less fortunate. . . . The likelihood of income and job

loss was lowest among the professionals in the Depression and greatest among the unskilled, with self-employed men tending to lose their money, but not their employment.

Elder, *Children of the Great Depression*, 47–48.

68. Lorena Hickok to Harry L. Hopkins, San Antonio, Apr. 17, 1934, reprinted in Richard Lowitt and Maurine Beasley, eds., *One Third of a Nation: Lorena Hickok Reports on the Great Depression* (Urbana: University of Illinois Press, 1981), 229.

69. S.J.S. to ER, Clairton, Pa. [acknowledged by Mrs. Roosevelt's staff Mar. 1, 1934].

70. H.L.M. to ER, Harrodsburg, Ky., Dec. 18, 1933; F.M. to ER, Graniteville, Mass., Mar. 18 [no year] and Apr. 16, 1935; P.S. to ER, Hector, Ark., May 9, 1936.

71. A random sample in 1934 consisting of 244 youth letters to Mrs. Roosevelt revealed that more than two-thirds came from females, raising questions about how representative the writers were of needy youth as a whole. We cannot, of course, know for certain how or whether our letters would be different if more of their authors had been male. It may be useful in this regard to refer to Elder's Oakland case study, since it offers some of the best data on Depression children and teens of both genders. Elder suggests that girls may have been more sensitive than boys to the outward signs of deprivation (especially with regard to clothing) and to their lack of status in the peer culture of youth. This he attributes to the tendency of girls' socialization, unlike that of boys, to favor "interpersonal sensitivities, which are in keeping with traditional concepts of feminine behavior." He also finds that "in particular girls from deprived families were highly critical of elitist behavior on the part of their classmates." Elder is contradictory with regard to the relevance of gender to family conflict. He asserts that "in the family experience of boys and girls, conflicted relations generally increased by economic deprivation . . . but deprivational effects were significant only among girls," and that he was struck by "the prominence of social distance and conflict between father and daughter in deprived households." But on the same page Elder asserts to the contrary that "boys were just as likely to experience conflict in deprived families as girls."

Judging by Elder's work, then, one might expect our female-heavy corpus of letters to be more peer conscious, more critical of social elitism within peer culture, and possibly more critical of paternal and family relations than documents written by a more male group of youths would be. It is true that those who wrote the most eloquent indictments of the youth peer culture and the most anguished cries about diminished status within that culture (especially over problems related to clothing) tended to be female. But it is impossible to say whether this is because of differences in gender socialization, as Elder might suggest, or simply because my sample of female letters is so much larger than the male, increasing the odds of finding more eloquent female letters. However, as noted earlier, the letters tend to be strikingly uncritical of paternal or family relationships, so that the supposedly more critical female edge suggested by Elder is largely absent. While this issue merits further study, my reading of the great bulk of youth letters does not leave me convinced that Elder's Oakland findings regarding gender differences among impoverished youth hold up with regard to a larger national sample. Most of the gender-based attitudinal differences that Elder stresses are not pronounced in the letters. In most respects differences in the authors' gender do not make for significant differences in either personal or political attitudes in the letters to Mrs. Roosevelt. If one disregards the phrases in which the authors identify themselves as boys or girls explicitly (or implicitly, for example by asking for boys' or girls' clothing), it is almost impossible to distinguish the males' from females' letters based on the attitudes or ideology expressed in them.

The one area where differences might have played a role is work. Elder's data suggest that young males were more than twice as likely as their female counterparts to work outside the home. So if more young males had written to the First Lady there probably would have been more discussion of work in the letters (unless, of course, the males who wrote could not have found work because of the Depression). It is also possible that this greater access to paid work was an important reason why boys were less likely than girls to write letters to Mrs. Roosevelt requesting material assistance (as they may have had more ways to get the money they needed). See Elder, *Children of the Great Depression*, 58–59, 65–66, 93–94, 134–35.

72. On *Babies—Just Babies*, see *New York Times*, Sept. 20, 1932; on *It's Up to the Women*, see *New York Times Book Review*, Nov. 2, 1933.

73. On Eleanor Roosevelt's work in getting educational camps set up for girls and women as a kind of female answer to the CCC, see *New York Times*, June 2, 19, 20, Aug. 8, Oct. 24, 1933; Joyce L. Kornbluh, *A New Deal for Worker's Education: The Worker's Service Program, 1933–1942* (Urbana: University of Illinois Press, 1987), 81–95. On her leadership in the establishment of rest areas for poor girls and young women seeking jobs, see *New York Times*, Jan. 7, May 10, 12, 14, 1933. These rest areas came to be known as the Eleanor Roosevelt Clubs for Unemployed Girls and were located at 22 East 38th Street and 247 Lexington Avenue in Manhattan. See *New York Times*, May 14, 1933, Apr. 3, 1935. On Mrs. Roosevelt's role in prodding the Civil Works Administration to fund female relief projects, such as sewing rooms, so that not all New Deal relief work would go to men in large-scale construction projects, see *New York Times*, Oct. 26, 1933. For examples of how needy young girls saw the First Lady as having a special concern with female suffering and opportunity, see V.C. to ER, Sacramento, Nov. 25, 1935; A.A. to ER, Camden, N.J., Dec. 3, 1934; K.B. to ER, New York City, June 6, 1934; W.R. to ER, Happy, Tex., Aug. 1, 1936.

74. B.L. to ER, Tulsa, Aug. 16, 1934.

75. F.W. to ER, La Mesa, Tex., Dec. 18, 1933; A.E. to ER, Brownsville, Mo., May 25, 1934; A.S. to ER, Kansas City, Mo., Jan. 23, 1936.

76. There is some discussion of these more affluent youths and youth magazines in Palladino, *Teenagers*, 3–33. Also see Cohen, *When the Old Left Was Young*, 3–20.

CHAPTER I

1. John Gabriel Hunt, ed., *The Essential FDR* (Avenel, N.J.: Portland House, 1995), 131; *The Public Papers and Addresses of Franklin Delano Roosevelt*, 1940 vol. (New York: Macmillan, 1941), 56.

2. White House Conference on Children in a Democracy, "Preliminary Statement on

Economic Resources of Families and Communities" (Washington, Jan. 18–20, 1940), 10–11, U.S. Children's Bureau Papers, National Archives, College Park, Md.

3. Ibid.

4. Ibid., 3, 7.

5. Ibid., 7, 11.

6. *Children in a Democracy: General Report Adopted by the White House Conference on Children in a Democracy* (Washington, 1940), 11, 12, 14.

7. "Preliminary Statement on Economic Resources of Families and Communities," 10.

8. *Children in a Democracy*, 26.

9. Richard Polenberg, *One Nation Divisible: Class, Race, and Ethnicity in America since 1938* (New York: Penguin, 1980), 19.

10. Ibid.

11. A.V. to ER, Chicago, Aug. 3, 1938. Note that although most of the letters that I have selected are by youths five to nineteen years old, I did include a few letters from men and women in their early twenties (like this one from A.V.) because they were particularly illuminating about the aspirations and problems of youth.

12. A.S. to ER, High Point, N.C., Jan. 1937; B.D.S. to ER, New Bedford, Mass. [acknowledged Mar. 12, 1940].

13. *Dorothea Lange: Photographs of a Lifetime* (Oakland: Aperture Foundation, 1982), 76; Lawrence Halprin, *The Franklin Delano Roosevelt Memorial* (San Francisco: Chronicle, 1997), 70–73.

14. Louis Adamic, *My America, 1928–1938* (New York: Harper and Brothers, 1938), 279.

15. *New York Times*, Dec. 18, 1932; Grace Abbot, "Child Health Needs Close Watching during These Times," *Nation's Schools*, Apr. 1934, 29–30; "The Proposed National Conference on Child Health Recovery," *School and Society*, Sept. 23, 1933, 401.

16. Harvey Levenstein, *Paradox of Plenty: A Social History of Eating in Modern America* (New York: Oxford University Press, 1993), 53–60.

17. James T. Patterson, *America's Struggle against Poverty, 1900–1980* (New York: Oxford University Press, 1981), 57.

18. Levenstein, *Paradox of Plenty*, 60–61.

19. Edgar Sydenstricker, "Health and the Depression," *Milbank Memorial Fund Quarterly*, Oct. 1933, 278; Polenberg, *One Nation Divisible*, 20.

CHAPTER 2

1. Research Division, NEA, "Current Conditions in the Nation's Schools," *Research Bulletin*, Nov. 1933, 102, 104; Advisory Committee on Education, Report of the Committee (Washington: U.S. Government Printing Office, 1938), 22; Doxey A. Wilkerson, *Special Problems of Negro Education* (Washington: U.S. Government Printing Office, 1939), 50.

2. U.S. Office of Education, *Biennial Survey of Education in the United States, 1936–1938* (Washington: U.S. Government Printing Office, 1943), 7.

3. Edward A. Krug, *The Shaping of the American High School* (Madison: University of Wisconsin Press, 1972), 2:218; Robert Cohen, *When the Old Left Was Young: Student Radicals*

and *America's First Mass Student Protest Movement* (New York: Oxford University Press, 1993), 10; David O. Levine, *The American College and the Culture of Aspiration* (Ithaca, N.Y.: Cornell University Press, 1986), 191.

4. Grace Palladino, *Teenagers: An American History* (New York: Basic Books, 1996), 5, 7–8, 14–15.

5. "The School Crisis," *School and Society*, Feb. 25, 1933, 243; Belmont Farley, "The Citizens Conference on the Crisis in Education," *School and Society*, Jan. 21, 1933, 79–81; Milton S. Mayer, "When Teachers Strike: Chicago Learns Another Lesson," *Forum and Century* 90 (1933): 122; Eunice Langdon, "The Teacher Faces the Depression," *Nation* 137 (1933): 181–82.

6. M. Gaibeau to Charlotte Berkman, Oct. 13, 1935, ER papers, FDRL.

7. M.T. to ER, Sweet, Idaho, Aug. 5, 1934.

8. Frank Allen, "Trends in Textbook Placement," *Nation's Schools*, May 1936, 33–34. Even states that had a tradition of providing free textbooks had difficulty continuing to do so as the Depression deepened. Nationally, school spending on textbooks declined by 30 percent between 1930 and 1934. An urban school survey in the mid-1930s found that the average history textbook was more than ten years old. See W. S. Deffenbaugh, *Effects of the Depression upon Public Elementary and Secondary Education and upon Colleges and Universities* (Washington: U.S. Office of Education, 1938), 29.

9. David Tyack, Robert Lowe, and Elisabeth Hansot, *Public Schools in Hard Times: The Great Depression and Recent Years* (Cambridge: Harvard University Press, 1984), 172–76.

10. Carl M. Hulbert and Harl R. Douglass, "Commencement Activities and Practices in Wisconsin High Schools," *School Review*, May 1934, 347.

11. Gertrude Jones, *Commencement* (New York: A. S. Barnes, 1929), 75.

12. M. E. Bruce, "Suitable Promotion Exercises for the Junior High School," *Junior-Senior High School Clearing House*, May 1931, 554–58; James Allen Schultz, "A New Deal in Commencement Programs," *School Board Journal*, Apr. 1934, 16, 73; Harold Steele, "Experimenting with High School Commencements," *Nation's Schools*, May 1935, 25 27; George A. Dawson, "The Evolution of a Commencement," *Progressive Education*, Apr. 1937, 274–77; "Planning the 1938 Commencement," *Nation's Schools*, Mar. 1938, 83; Educational Research Service, *Vitalized Commencement Manual 1938* (Washington: National Education Association, 1938), 4–59; G. W. Kirn, "Pupils and Parents Liked This Commencement," *Nation's Schools*, May 1934, 37–39; William Leroy Fink, *Evaluation of Commencement Practices in American Public Secondary Schools* (Philadelphia: University of Pennsylvania Press, 1940).

13. Hulbert and Douglass, "Commencement Activities," 348. Apparently quite unaware of the way his opposition to caps and gowns penalized low-income students, one Iowa school superintendent in the midst of the Depression argued that in his school system "caps and gowns have never been used since this custom tends to destroy individuality and to make the pupil merely a unit in a group. The boys wear their customary dark suits. The girls wear inexpensive white dresses and carry bouquets of roses," G. W. Kirn, "Pupils and Parents Liked This Commencement," *Nation's Schools*, May 1934, 38. I have found only one instance in which a school

official promoted cap-and-gown ceremonies on egalitarian grounds. This was in 1939, when the principal of a New York high school argued that "the cap and gown is a formal attire but it is a most democratic tool. Uniformity is an advantage. All the members of the class are dressed alike and no one feels any embarrassment because his clothes suffer by comparison with those worn by the pupils next to him," O. Wendell Hogue, "Shall We Use Caps and Gowns?" *Nation's Schools*, June 1939, 26.

14. Tyack, Lowe, and Hansot, *Public Schools in Hard Times*, 108–9.

15. *Athens Banner-Herald*, May 16, 1998; Robert Cohen, *When the Old Left Was Young: Student Radicals and America's First Mass Student Protest Movement* (New York: Oxford University Press, 1993), 12, 17.

16. Student radicals during the 1930s criticized the NYA for hiring too few students and paying them too little; they lobbied unsuccessfully for a much larger-scale federal jobs program for both low-income students and drop-outs. See Cohen, *When the Old Left Was Young*, 188, 190–95.

CHAPTER 3

1. William Leuchtenburg, *FDR and the New Deal* (New York: Harper and Row, 1963), 120–21, 123–25.

2. *New York Times*, Dec. 25, 1934.

3. Ibid.

4. Ibid., Dec. 20, 1936.

5. Ibid., Dec. 31, 1935.

6. John Modell, *Into One's Own: From Youth to Adulthood in the United States, 1920–1975* (Berkeley: University of California Press, 1989), 134; Elaine Tyler May, *Homeward Bound: American Families in the Cold War Era* (New York: Basic Books, 1988), 40.

7. T. H. Watkins, *The Great Depression: America in the 1930s* (Boston: Little, Brown, 1993), 305–6.

CHAPTER 4

1. Richard Polenberg, *One Nation Divisible: Class, Race, and Ethnicity in America since 1938* (New York: Penguin, 1980), 25–32; Harvard Sitkoff, *A New Deal for Blacks: The Emergence of Civil Rights as a National Issue: the Depression Decade* (New York: Oxford University Press, 1978), 35–36.

2. Cheryl Lynn Greenberg, *Or Does It Explode?: Black Harlem in the Great Depression* (New York: Oxford University Press,, 1991), 44.

3. White House Conference on Children in a Democracy, "Preliminary Statement on Economic Resources of Families and Communities" (Washington, Jan. 18–20, 1940), 4, U.S. Children's Bureau Papers, National Archives, College Park, Md.; Ira De Augustine Reid, *In a Minor Key: Negro Youth in Story and Fact* (Washington: American Youth Council, 1940), 56.

4. Harvard Sitkoff, *A New Deal for Blacks: The Emergence of Civil Rights as a National Issue: the Depression Decade* (New York: Oxford University Press, 1978), 50–62.

5. Susan Ware, "Women and the New Deal," in Maurine H. Beasley, Holly Schul-

man, and Henry R. Beasley, eds., *The Eleanor Roosevelt Encyclopedia* (Westport, Conn.: Greenwood, 2001), 574.

6. Susan Ware, *Holding Their Own: American Women in the 1930s* (Boston: Twayne, 1982), 21–27, 32; Alice Kessler-Harris, *Out to Work: A History of Wage Earning Women in the United States* (New York: Oxford University Press, 1982), 250–73.

7. Ware, *Holding Their Own*, 37–41.

8. Hugh Gregory Gallagher, *FDR's Splendid Deception* (Arlington, Va.: Vandamere, 1994), 29. Just how isolated and marginalized the physically disabled were in the 1930s is suggested by the very term that was used to describe them: "shut-ins." See Rose Barrow to ER, Feb. 26, 1935, ER papers, FDRL.

9. FDR's activism in behalf of the disabled also included his work in founding the March of Dimes, an organization that raised funds to combat polio. See Gallagher, *FDR's Splendid Deception*, 145–52.

10. Gallagher, *FDR's Splendid Deception*, 20–105.

11. White House Conference on Children in a Democracy, "Preliminary Statement on Children in Minority Groups" (Washington, Jan. 1940), U.S. Children's Bureau Papers, 6.

12. Pollenberg, *One Nation Divisible*, 41–42.

13. "Preliminary Statement on Children in Minority Groups," 6.

EPILOGUE

1. Eleanor Roosevelt "My Mail," and "Mail of a President's Wife" [1940], Speech and Article File, 1940, ER papers, FDRL.

2. This response rate—and all the other statistics used in this epilogue to discuss the way in which the First Lady's office handled the letters to her published in this book—is based upon a sample of 142 responses to those letters.

3. Ibid. Sometimes persistence overcame the odds and caught the attention of the First Lady's staff. In the case of a New Jersey teen with vision problems whose father, a WPA worker, could not afford to buy her glasses, three letters to the First Lady over three years finally yielded a reference and the possibility of help. See Malvina T. Scheider to H.W., Lawnside, N.J., Jan. 28, 1938; H.W. to ER, Jan. 24, 1938, ER papers, FDRL. For an example of help coming more quickly, see Ellen S. Woodward to ER, Dec. 21, 1934; Malvina T. Scheider to Woodward, Oct. 10, 1934; Mary Ward to Malvina T. Scheider, May 2, 1936; Scheider to James. M. Hepbron, Dec. 17, 1934, ER papers, FDRL.

4. Joseph P. Lash, *Eleanor and Franklin: The Story of Their Relationship Based on Eleanor Roosevelt's Private Papers* (New York: New American Library, 1971), 518–19.

5. Eleanor Roosevelt, "I Want You to Write Me," *Women's Home Companion*, Aug. 1933, reprinted in Allida M. Black, ed., *Courage in a Dangerous World: The Political Writings of Eleanor Roosevelt* (New York: Columbia University Press, 1999), 18–20. Note that the typescript version of this article indicates that it was written in May 1933. See ER Speech and Article File, 1932–33, ER papers, FDRL.

6. Eleanor Roosevelt, "My Day" columns, Oct. 25 and Dec. 8, 1936; Aug. 8 and Dec. 10, 1937, Feb. 16, Aug. 20, and Sept. 12, 1938, Feb. 17, Feb. 25, and June 20, 1939;

Eleanor Roosevelt, "The Kind of Mail the Governor's Wife Receives," Feb. 17, 1933, Radio Speech #11, ER Speech and Article File, 1932–33.

7. Eleanor Roosevelt, "The Kind of Mail the Governor's Wife Receives."

8. For an example of the way in which Eleanor Roosevelt's mail from the poor raised her awareness of their problems, see ER to Ellen S. Woodward, Jan. 11, 1935 (File 70, ER correspondence to governmental organizations), ER papers, FDRL. Also see Eleanor Roosevelt, "My Day" columns, Oct. 25 and Dec. 8, 1936, Aug. 8 and Dec. 10, 1937, Feb. 16, Aug. 20, and Sept. 12, 1938, Feb. 17, Feb. 25, and June 20, 1939.

9. Eleanor Roosevelt, "My Mail."

10. See Lash, *Eleanor and Franklin*, 493–94; Frances Seeber, "Correspondence," in Beasley et al., *The Eleanor Roosevelt Encyclopedia*, 111.

11. Malvina (Tommy Thompson) Scheider to M.J.F., Oct. 25, 1934, ER papers, FDRL.

12. The "mule" letter is C.D. to ER, Daleville Ala., Feb. 12, 1934; its response is secretary to Mrs. Roosevelt to C.D., Feb. 27, 1934. For the case of a young letter writer who wrote to the First Lady saying, "I cry and sometimes think I'll kill myself" and received a form letter from her staff, see N.C. to ER, Joplin, Mo., Oct. 27, 1939; Administrative Officer, Social Correspondence to N.C., Nov. 4, 1939.

13. Molly Somerville, *Eleanor Roosevelt as I Knew Her* (Mclean, Va.: EPM, 1996), 60–61; Administrative Officer, Social Correspondence, to J.M.H., Statesville, N.C., July 12, 1935.

14. Eleanor Roosevelt "My Day," *Atlanta Constitution*, Nov. 8, 1938.

15. On the need for such verification, see the correspondence of one teen whom the First Lady's staff was planning to help until local relief agencies revealed that the writer had exaggerated her plight to the First Lady in her letter: Lucile Bruner to Malvina T. Scheider, Apr. 1, 1935; Douglas F. Teed to Lucile Bruner, Mar. 27, 1935, Material Assistance Requested files, ER papers, FDRL.

16. Eleanor Roosevelt, "My Day," *Atlanta Constitution*, Nov. 8, 1938.

17. Eleanor Roosevelt, *It's Up to the Women* (1933); Eleanor Roosevelt, "Conserving Our Greatest Resource—Youth"; "Youth Today Is Tomorrow's Nation," Commencement Address at Chapel Hill, N.C., ER Speech and Article File, 1935.

18. There were only a few such expressions of advice and moral support in the responses to the letters. But even these few suggest the possibility of a more humane approach to these passionate pleas for help. See Malvina T. Scheider to M.A., Feb. 16, 1934. Also see secretary to Mrs. Roosevelt to L.E.C., Mar. 15, 1934, which is in the "Native Americans" section of Chapter 4.

19. In Eleanor Roosevelt's files are a series of letters from Woodward attesting that the First Lady and her staff did refer some material assistance requests from youths to her at the FERA. But such requests were surprisingly few. See Ellen S. Woodward to Malvina T. Scheider, May 4, 1934, Sept. 10, 1934, Dec. 15, 1934; Ellen S. Woodward to ER, Dec. 21, 1934, File 70, ER papers, FDRL. Note that in each instance the letter from the needy young person which originally led to this FERA referral has not survived. Faced with a heavy volume of mail in the days before photocopying, the First Lady's staff apparently found it too time-consuming to keep a copy of material assistance letters referred to other agencies. Note that the Works Progress

Administration, the massive public works project that replaced the FERA, was another agency to which Mrs. Roosevelt referred some material assistance requests—and again her contact person there on such matters was Woodward, who became a WPA administrator.

Although the youth letters that the First Lady and her staff sent to Woodward have not survived, Mrs. Roosevelt's files of her letters to government agencies (File 70) do contain some correspondence between Eleanor Roosevelt, her staff, and Woodward referring to the youth letters (and in some cases briefly summarizing the nature of the request from the needy letter writer). And since Woodward was the government relief official with whom Roosevelt and her staff had the most extensive correspondence about individual hardship cases, I took an entire year of their correspondence with her, 1936, to see how many of these youths cases they referred to her. In that year the First Lady and her staff enlisted Woodward's aid in helping 104 needy Americans, but of these no more than 22 were youths. Even less impressive were the number of needy youth letters sent annually to such other key relief officials as Aubrey Williams and Harry Hopkins, which—at least as reflected in Eleanor Roosevelt's files—were barely a handful.

Note that according to correspondence from Woodward, by the spring of 1936 the Women's Division of the WPA was answering some of Mrs. Roosevelt's mail along with quite a bit of other White House mail related to the WPA (about 400 letters a month, but apparently most were complaints about the WPA and requests for WPA jobs rather than requests for material assistance). See Ellen S. Woodward to Harry L. Hopkins, Apr. 6, 1936; Ellen S. Woodward to ER, Apr. 6, 1936, File 70, ER papers, FDRL.

20. Malvina T. Scheider to James P. Hepbron, Dec. 17, 1934; Gay B. Shepperson to Malvina T. Scheider, Dec. 23, 1935; John Jennings to Malvina Thompson, Dec. 19, 1938; John J. McDonough to Malvina Thompson, Dec. 19, 1938; Clarence Triggs to Malvina T. Scheider, Dec. 26, 1940, ER papers, FDRL.

21. Clarence Pickett to ER, Feb. 26, 1935, and Dec. 4, 1940; Malvina T. Scheider to Clarence E. Pickett, Aug. 7, 1937, Aug. 10 and 13, 1940; June Hamilton Rhodes to Malvina T. Scheider, June 17, 1934, ER papers, FDRL.

22. Secretary to Mrs. Roosevelt to Elizabeth Conkey, Oct. 8, 1934; secretary to Mrs. Roosevelt to Alice Cooper, Apr. 30, 1934; secretary to Mrs. Roosevelt to Richard Conant, June 20, 1934, ER papers, FDRL.

23. On the sense of disappointment which needy youth experienced over the First Lady's inability to meet their requests for aid, see the letter displayed in the illustration on page 235.

24. Langston Hughes articulated the disappointment over the failure of the Roosevelt administration to aid all the poor in his powerful poem "Ballad of Roosevelt," which opened with the lines:

The pot was empty,
The cupboard was bare,
I said, Papa,
What's the matter here?

I'm waitin' on Roosevelt son,
Roosevelt, Roosevelt,
Waitin' on Roosevelt, son

The Rent was due
And the lights was out.
I said Mama,
What's it all about?
We're waitin' on Roosevelt son,
Roosevelt, Roosevelt,
Just waitin' on Roosevelt . . .

Arnold Rampersad, ed., *The Collected Works of Langston Hughes*, vol. 1, *The Poems*, 1921–1940 (Columbia: University of Missouri Press, 2001), 239.

Index

tion, 94–95, 108–19; requests for related to Christmas, 147, 152–55, 157; requests for related to Scouts, 150, 187–88; request for related to communion, 220

College Humor, 23

Colleges: enrollment in during Depression, 7, 92, 247 (n. 11); NYA aids students attending, 8, 92, 97, 121, 123, 127; Hoover administration and students in, 9; requests for aid in attending, 97, 119–29; FERA aids students attending, 145; student politics at, 249 (n. 40)

Colorado: letters from, 61, 87, 217

Connecticut: letters from, 86, 158, 206

Consumer culture: and youth peer culture, 22–24, 149–50, 151; and graduation activities, 94–95; and Christmas celebrations, 147–48; and automobiles, 151

Crews, Harry, 23

Davis, Maxine: *The Lost Generation*, 7

Dayton, Ohio, 6

Debts, requests related to, 74–80

Denver, Colo., 6

Detroit, Mich., 6

Disabled: New Deal aid for, 8; ER's work for, 14, 199; and poverty, 42; FDR as, 195, 198, 199; unequal treatment of in Depression America, 195, 198, 257 (n. 8); FDR's work for, 198–99, 257 (n. 9); and education, 199; requests from, 227–34

Dolls, requests for, 150, 188–90

Earhart, Amelia, 197, 223

Earl, Steve, 86

Easter, requests for clothing for, 23, 113–15, 148, 162–66

Education: effects of Depression on, 7, 8, 91–93, 247 (n. 11); New Deal support for, 8–9; ER's work for, 13–14; and class consciousness/interaction, 22, 24–26, 95–96; and youth peer culture, 23; requests for assistance with, 23, 24, 93, 97–107, 202–3, 205, 206–9, 216–17, 227–28, 234; and African Americans, 91, 196; and disabled, 199; and immigrants, 200–201. *See also* Art and music education, requests for assistance with; Colleges; Graduation; Vocational education, requests for assistance with

Elder, Glen H., 246 (n. 2), 251–52 (n. 67), 252–53 (n. 71)

Eleanor Roosevelt Clubs for Unemployed Girls, 253 (n. 73)

Ethnics. *See* Immigrants

Evictions, requests related to, 71–74

Family: effect of Depression on, 18–20, 21, 250 (n. 49), 252 (n. 71); size of as contributor to level of distress, 37. *See also* Parents

Farmers, 5, 145, 196

Fathers: write to ER out of concern for children, 6; effect of Depression on authority of, 18–19, 250 (n. 49), 252 (n. 71); LWs' positive views of, 18–20, 252 (n. 71); Depression's psychological burden for, 21. *See also* Parents

Federal Emergency Relief Administration (FERA), 9, 26, 145; LW makes mention of, 112; ER's staff forwards requests to, 243, 258 (n. 19)

Federal Music Project, 146

Feminists: oppression of in Depression America, 195; LWs as, 197–98; requests for assistance from, 221–27

Franklin D. Roosevelt Library and Museum (Hyde Park, N.Y.), 3, 5, 245

Gallagher, Hugh Gregory, 198–99

Gender: of LWs, 27–28, 252–53 (n. 71); discrimination based on, 195, 197–98

Georgia, 91; letters from, 67, 203

health care, 7, 42; and youth peer culture, 22; effects of fall from, 23. *See also* Class consciousness/interaction

Minnesota: letters from, 50, 131, 134, 157, 211, 220

Minorities. *See* African Americans; Disabled; Feminists; Immigrants; Native American(s)

Mississippi, 91; letter from, 210

Missouri: letters from, 54, 56–57, 79, 172–73, 176, 180, 183–84, 191

Mothers: write to ER out of concern for children, 6; LWs' positive views of, 18–20. *See also* Parents

Music education. *See* Art and music education, requests for assistance with

National Association for the Advancement of Colored People (NAACP): LW makes mention of, 210

National Education Association, 91

National Origins Act of 1924, 200

National Recovery Administration: LWs make mention of, 47, 86, 217

National Youth Administration (NYA): work relief programs of, 8, 10, 91–92, 96, 127; LWs' appreciation of, 10, 158; ER and, 12–13, 239; LWs make mention of, 59, 121, 123, 125, 127, 157, 209; college students aided by, 91–92, 97, 121, 123, 127; ER's staff refers LW to, 125; ER's staff forwards requests to, 243; criticism of, 256 (n. 16)

Native American(s): unequal treatment of in Depression America, 195; letter from, 211–12; response to, 212

Nebraska: letter from, 50

Newark, N.J., 6

New Deal: LWs' gratitude for assistance provided by, 3, 16, 17, 29; and expansion of federal aid, 4, 16; and unemployment, 6; and "youth crisis" of 1930s, 8–9; work relief programs of, 8–9, 10, 18; and aid to education, 8–9, 96, 97; inability of to aid more than a minority of needy youth, 9, 30, 146, 244; ER and, 11, 27–28, 239; and alleviation of hunger, 41–42; opposition to, 96, 249 (n. 40); idealism of, 146; appointment of African Americans to agencies of, 197; gender discrimination in programs of, 198; ER's staff forwards requests to agencies of, 243; resettlement community of Arthurdale, W.Va., established by, 248–49 (n. 34). *See also specific agencies and programs*

New Jersey: letters from, 64, 70, 118, 151, 162, 187

New York, 7, 28, 91; letters from, 52, 73, 119, 121, 125, 132, 160, 164, 167, 169–70, 174, 176, 184–85, 187, 191, 209, 222, 227

New York, N.Y., 6, 40, 41

North Carolina: letters from, 52, 66, 77, 140, 181

North Dakota: letter from, 132

New Yorker, 11

Oakland, Calif., 251–52 (n. 67), 252–53 (n. 71)

Ohio, 7; letters from, 48, 51, 72, 75–76, 80, 83, 101, 130, 136, 139, 177, 232

Oklahoma: letters from, 104, 110, 115, 183, 221, 231

Parents: dependence of children on, 7; children's concern for and desire to help, 10, 21, 150, 151, 250 (n. 49); LWs' positive views of, 18–20; Depression's psychological burden for, 21; and family income/circumstances, 37, 43; and health concerns, 42; requests for aid with burial of, 43

Parents Magazine, 29

Patterson, James, 41

Pennsylvania, 6, 7, 41; letters from, 45, 47, 97, 106, 129, 133, 157, 163, 175, 220, 229

Perkins, Frances, 41

Pickett, Clarence E., 243–44

Pittsburgh, Pa., 7

Polenberg, Richard, 37

Poor: letters to ER from, 5; and health care, 7; New Deal relief efforts for, 8–9, 10, 16, 249 (n. 41); ER's perceived concern for, 11–14, 238–39; and youth peer culture, 23, 25–26, 149–50. See also Class consciousness/interaction; Poverty

Poverty: scope of in Depression, 7, 35; and educational opportunity, 7, 92–93, 95–96; and youth peer culture, 21–22, 24–26; study and understanding of, 29; definition of in Depression, 36; in rural areas, 36, 37, 91; in urban areas, 36–37; and family size, 37; and hunger, 40, 42; and health, 42; and burials, 43; and celebration of Christmas, 145–48. See also Poor

Proms. See Graduation

Puerto Rico: letter from, 213

Radios: in American culture, 149; requests for, 149, 182–84

Reconstruction Finance Corporation (RFC): LW makes mention of, 120

Recreational activities, requests for items related to, 149–50, 187–92

Relief Census of 1933, 7

Rhode Island: letter from, 185

Roosevelt, Eleanor: volume of mail received by, 5, 6, 146, 237, 241; perceived concern for poor youth on part of, 5, 9–13, 16, 30, 238–39; papers of, in FDR Library, 5, 242–43, 245; LWs express trust in and love of, 9–12, 201; relationship of with FDR, 10–11; radio broadcasts of, 11, 12, 13, 14; "My Day" newspaper column of, 11, 12, 14, 238, 239, 241; and role of First Lady, 11, 16; and work of New Deal agencies/programs, 11, 27–28, 30, 198, 239; travels of, 11, 201; work of on behalf of poor, 11–12, 16, 239; and NYA, 12–13, 239; work of on behalf of young people, 12–14, 29, 30, 239, 243–44; charitable work/contributions of, 13–14, 30, 243–44, 248–49 (n. 34); work of on behalf of disabled, 14, 199; LWs express resentment of privileges enjoyed by, 14–16, 23, 249 (n. 39); as editor of Babies—Just Babies, 27; publishes It's Up to Women, 27; work of on behalf of needy girls/young women, 27–28, 197, 198, 199; historians' view of, 38; clothing of, 38–39; staff of forwards requests to New Deal agencies, 146, 243, 258–59 (n. 19); and African Americans, 196–97, 199; international reputation of, 201; and response to LWs, 237–44; impact of LWs on, 238–39

Roosevelt, Franklin Delano: LWs express trust in and gratitude to, 3, 9–11, 17; volume of mail received by, 5, 6; on scope of poverty in Depression, 6, 35, 41; on limits of New Deal's ability to aid needy youth, 9; perceived concern for poor on part of, 9–11; relationship of with ER, 10–11; and Warm Springs infantile paralysis treatment center, 14, 198–99; and White House Conference on Children in a Democracy, 35–36; Washington, D.C., memorial to, 40; and disabled, 198–99

Scheider, Malvina T. ("Tommy"), 124, 237, 241

Scouts, requests for uniforms for, 150, 187–88

Sears Catalogue, 23

Segal, George, 40

Skates, requests for, 150, 161, 190–91, 192
Social conservatism, 16, 249 (n. 40)
Social inequity: LWs complain of, 15–16; in Depression America, 195. *See also* African Americans; Class consciousness/interaction; Disabled; Feminists; Immigrants; Native American(s)
Social Security program, 8–9, 197; LW makes mention of, 61
South Carolina, 91; letters from, 55, 76, 121, 190
South Dakota: letter from, 60
Sports equipment, requests for, 160, 161, 190–92
Springfield, Ohio, 6
Sussman, Leila, 5

Temple, Shirley, 8, 238; doll with likeness of, 188–90
Tennessee: letters from, 102, 122, 190
Terkel, Studs: *Hard Times*, 25
Texas: letters from, 48, 98, 107–8, 124–25, 182, 233

Unemployment: rates of during Depression, 6; social effects of, 6, 7, 18–19; and health care, 7, 42; and youth peer culture, 22; among urban blacks, 196; among women, 197; among various social classes, 251–52 (n. 67)
United Nations, 201
Utah: letters from, 161, 230

Virginia: letters from, 74, 111, 166, 202
Vocational education, requests for assistance with, 93, 137–41

Wagner-Rogers bill (1939), 200
Warm Springs, Ga., infantile paralysis treatment center in, 14, 198–99; LWs make mention of, 227, 229, 232

Washington: letter from, 65
Washington, D.C.: letters from, 159, 164
Watkins, T. H., 149
West Virginia, 7, 248–49 (n.34); letters from, 43, 47, 133, 165
White House Conference on Children in a Democracy, 35, 36–37, 200
White House Conference on the Emergency Needs of Women, 197
Williams, Aubrey, 259 (n. 19)
Wisconsin, 94; letters from, 156, 182, 190, 192
Women: unequal treatment of in Depression America, 195, 197–98; unemployment among, 197. *See also* Feminists; Gender; Girls/young women
Woodward, Ellen S., 243, 258–59 (n. 19)
Working class: letters to ER from, 5; and health care, 7; and youth peer culture, 22, 25. *See also* Class consciousness/interaction
Working poor: letters to ER from, 5; and health care, 7; and youth peer culture, 22. *See also* Poor; Poverty
Works Progress Administration (WPA), 9, 146; LWs make mention of, 56, 59, 62, 132, 134, 157, 159, 160, 172, 173
Wyoming: letter from, 154

"Youth crisis" of 1930s, 7–9, 21
Youth peer culture: LWs' concern over position within, 21–23, 24; and clothes, 22, 23, 25–26, 94–95, 251 (n. 56); and class consciousness/interaction, 22, 24, 95–96, 149–51, 251 (nn. 56, 66); and acquisitive individualism, 22–24, 149–50; and education, 23; and graduation, 94–95, 251 (n. 66); and recreational activities, 149–50; and automobiles, 151; gender differences within, 252–53 (n. 71)

E
807.1
.R48
D43